D0856736

Tally-Ho!

Tally-Ho!

From the Battle of Britain to the Defence of Darwin

Wing Commander R W Foster DFC AE

with

Norman Franks

GRUB STREET · LONDON and SYDNEY

Published by
Grub Street
4 Rainham Close
London
SW11 6SS

Copyright © 2008 Grub Street
Copyright text © 2008 Norman Franks and
Wing Commander Bob Foster DFC AE

A CIP catalogue record for this book is available from the British Library

ISBN 978 1 906502 26 3

All rights reserved. No part of this publication may be reproduced,
stored in a retrieval system, or transmitted in any form or by any
means, electronic, mechanical, photocopying, recording, or otherwise,
without the prior permission of the copyright owner.

Cover design by Lizzie B Design

Formatted by Pearl Graphics, Hemel Hempstead

Printed and bound by MPG Ltd, Bodmin, Cornwall

Grub Street only uses FSC
(Forest Stewardship Council) paper for its books.

Contents

Acknowledgements

Help with this book has come from several kind people who have given time, photographs and assistance with the project. Many thanks therefore go to: Paul Baillie, John Larder (BoB Historical Society), Andy Saunders, Chris Shores, Andy Thomas, Barry Weekley, Mrs K Wright and her daughter Sarah, and the late Fred Woodgate.

Prologue

In a grey October sky we had scrambled once again, our second time up, but at least we had had time for something to eat. The controller was warning us of Messerschmitts in our vicinity and all eyes were straining to get sight of them. It was imperative that we saw them before they saw us.

Suddenly there they were. Fifteen grey-blue 109s came into view someway below us. Hooray, I don't think they have seen us. This was a luxury. I should have guessed it was too good to be true. Our leader gave us the order to attack and we began to dive. Already I was making a target selection. But what we hadn't seen were the 40 or more 109s above and behind us. Our leader didn't generally get into this predicament and it went through my head later that he must known what he was doing but we'd been caught out. Then someone behind me spotted the danger and yelled a warning over the radio. Some of the 109s were coming down on us.

When we initially heard the 'break, break, break!' we did just that. You never argued when you heard this instruction, or asked questions. If you take a moment to ask what or where, you are dead. So we turned – scattered – in all directions, the adrenalin pumping. Charles English, my No.2, must have been too slow in breaking as his Hurricane was hit badly. He tried to get out but apparently, as he did so, his parachute got caught on the Hurricane's tail-plane and he went down with his machine.

Meantime, I went curving away as fast as I could, my head turning in all directions, expecting at any moment to feel the impact of gunfire upon my aircraft, but nothing happened.

Then I pulled out, and looked around and there right ahead of me, for some unearthly reason, was a 109 peacefully going home quite happily, straight and level. After checking the sky all around me, I closed in and sat behind him, lined his silhouette in my gun-sight and shot him down. It was quite extraordinary. I don't know what the pilot was doing. I think it must have been one of the bunch that attacked us, had taken a shot and figured he was done. Or perhaps he was one of the bomb-carriers, and having dropped his bomb, was going home for his tea. His mind could not have been on the job, he just wasn't looking around. Inexperience, perhaps. Anyway, he thought he was going south towards home and he didn't make it. You can never relax when you are in action. This chap had and he paid the price.

Chapter One

Just a Lad from London

I was born into what might be called a military family. My paternal grandfather, William Foster, himself the son of a soldier, had at the age of 13 years and ten months, enlisted in the 36th Regiment of Foot at Peshawar, India, now Pakistan, in 1869 and spent altogether 26 years in the service. In 1885, whilst stationed in Jersey, he married my grandmother Frances Boyd Fasson, and when he retired from the army, they set up home in England, initially living in Broad Street, Holborn, London. They had three sons; William Thomas – my father [pictured overleaf], Robert Henry and Albert George. William and Robert both joined the army, while Albert went into the Metropolitan Police Force. Some time later, my grandparents moved to Sangora Road, Battersea, off St John's Hill, where my grandfather died in 1916.

Somewhere along the way, Robert met a young lady named Violet, who came from a farming family in Crowborough, Sussex, and just prior to the start of the 1914-18 war they became engaged to be married. Robert, a regular soldier, went to France with the British Expeditionary Force, as a lance-corporal with the 2nd Worcestershire Regiment, as soon as the war began in August 1914. He saw a good deal of action in those first weeks, but his luck ran out on 20 October, during what was later called the First Battle of Ypres, and he was reported missing, believed killed. He is remembered on the Le Touret Memorial, some five miles north-east of Béthune. Presumably Violet had also met my father when she was engaged to Robert, and subsequently, following Robert's death, their relationship blossomed after his eventual return from France.

My father, William Thomas Foster, had been a regular army man from 1901, having joined as a boy soldier with the Royal Engineers, did his twelve years, and came out in 1913. He too joined the police force, but was called back into the army with the advent of World War One on 14 August 1914.

He went to France with the REs but was wounded in 1915 whilst laying wire between front line trenches and 'no-man's-land', also somewhere near the Belgian town of Ypres – or Wipers as he and other WW1 soldiers would have called it. Due to the ferocity of the action at the time, he was forced to lay out on the edge of no-man's-land for some 48 hours before his mates could bring him back in, and as a result of his injury he had to have his right leg amputated. This had to be taken off very high which made it then impossible to fit a prosthetic – artificial leg – so this necessitated him having to get around on a pair of crutches for the rest of his life. He did however receive the Distinguished Service Medal for his bravery, of which he was very and rightly proud, although I personally have no doubt he would have preferred the leg to his medal.

He married my mother Violet (Vi) in 1919 and they lived in Mysore Road, Battersea, which for those who do not know the area, runs from Lavender Hill to Clapham Common, North Side, adjacent to Elspeth Road. When the time came for me to make my entrance, my mother went into a nursing home situated in nearby Lavender Gardens, just the other side of Elspeth Road, and she was delivered of me on 14 May 1920. I was to be their only child and was given the name of Robert in memory of my father's late brother. Battersea, of course, was a very different place then, than it is today.

Oddly enough we later moved to Lavender Gardens so remained near to two of London's famous landmarks, Clapham Junction railway station and Battersea Power Station with its four huge chimneys. In my early youth there were two great play areas very conveniently placed for me, Clapham

Common and Wandsworth Common, while London itself was just minutes away by train or just a little longer by bus.

Being educated in London in the 1920s and 1930s was a straightforward affair. Although the London County Council, which controlled schools was strongly Labour, pupil selection was the order of the day. At 11 years of age all children in council schools took an examination. Those who failed stayed on in the elementary school system till the age of 14, at which time they were sent out into the wide world. It sounds strange, but in those days there were plenty of jobs to be had in shops, offices and factories for these youngsters. Those who did slightly better in the exams went to a central school till they were 15, and were then sent out to make a living for themselves. The rest who had obviously achieved far better results were sent on to secondary grammar schools.

I was lucky enough to attend one such school, the Henry Thornton Grammar School, a newly built establishment on the south side of Clapham Common, and better still, it was within walking distance of home.

The name of the school came from the grounds of the house on which it was built, the former home of Sir Henry Thornton, who in the early 1800s, was one of the so-called Clapham Sect, a body of philanthropists and leaders of the anti-slavery movement. Men such as Cavendish, Cook, McCauley, Pepys, Stephens, Wilberforce, were all part of this sect.

The school was good enough to provide me with a wonderful education. I like to think I did fairly well, if not academically, then certainly as far as sport was concerned. I became captain of games, played lacrosse for the school, and the south of England against the north, enjoyed football and I was also quite a good runner. In 1936 I won both the 220 and 440 yards championships, also setting up a school record. In tennis I won in the doubles, the school fives and the Victor Ludorum.

This idyllic situation continued until 1937 by which time, having passed my matriculation and so on, I decided against further education and at the tender age of 17, left to become employed by the Shell-Mex company, at their offices in Shell-Mex House in the Strand, London, as a very junior office boy. Not that it was my own idea. In fact I had no comprehension of what sort of life lay ahead of me nor of what I wanted to do in it, so it was a comfort when someone else decided for me.

My father's brother Albert had by this time progressed with the police and was number two in Special Branch at Scotland Yard, and with that sort of job and an influential circle of friends and associates, he knew just the right people to ask about a job for his young nephew. One of these was Sir Robert Waley Cohen, the managing director of Shell, and I remember being instructed to put on my best bib and tucker and go with my uncle to lunch at the National Liberal Club in Whitehall, where an informal meeting was to take place. The lunch and casual interview must have gone well for a few days later I received an application form and was told to attend Shell-Mex House for a formal interview. From this I was taken on as an employee.

In those days one came into Shell, certainly at my level, as a very junior boy, starting off by taking messages around, going out and doing all manner of tasks for the company directors and board members. All very basic but to someone of my tender years, not totally unexciting and with a bit of freedom thrown in to discover London's west end. This went on for a while and I had obviously kept my nose clean and not been found particularly wanting, so I was sent along to what was then called the buying department and given a job which I found quite interesting. I was lucky in that the boss of the department, Mr Anderson, who in the Great War had been in the Royal Flying Corps as an engineer, was very keen on young people joining the military or territorial services, no doubt alive to the worsening situation in Europe in the late 1930s.

In the same department I had made friends with Dick Morley, and in early 1939, following on from the time of Munich and Neville Chamberlain's 'peace in our time' display after his talks with Herr Hitler in Germany, Dick and I made a decision. We thought that if there was indeed going to be a war, which despite Chamberlain, seemed almost inevitable, neither of us wanted to await being conscripted into something where we might have no choice but to accept. Dick had decided it would be a good idea to be an officer, so off he went and volunteered for service with the HAC – Honourable Artillery Company. This seemed to me to be far too noisy an outfit with guns going bang all over the place and in any event I had no desire to become some second-lieutenant in the army, feeling that this was the worst job anyone could have. So I took myself off to Adastral House, in Kingsway, which was within a short walk from Shell House, and applied to join the Royal Air Force Volunteer Reserve.

It wasn't long before I had the usual short, sharp medical, had my chest tapped, ears looked into, and after the obligatory trouser-dropping and cough, was moved onto the next stage. This consisted of some rudimentary tests, one of which was being swung round in a chair to see if I would become giddy and fall over. Having got over that hurdle without falling down, I suddenly found myself accepted into the RAFVR.

As can be imagined, Mr Anderson was very pleased at my acceptance and managed to get the Shell bosses to allow me two months paid leave of absence in order to have some *ab initio* flying training, which consisted of a short course which was run by the short service commission people. This led me to doing 50 hours of pre-war flying which became the start of my flying career. I had always been keen on aviation as many young lads in the 1930s had been, reading stories of air battles over France in WW1, and of men and women pioneers who had started to open up the Empire by flying to all parts of the compass in small, light aeroplanes, and being thrust into the forefront of the news with little less than hero status. However, equally like those many youngsters, I had never been anywhere near an aeroplane in my 19 years.

On 1 May 1939, just a couple of weeks away from my 19th birthday, I duly reported to Anstey, situated just outside Coventry, and to 9 E&FTS, where the *ab initio* courses were being held, and run by a civilian company called Air Service Training. The chief flying instructor (CFI) was Flight Lieutenant J B Veal RAFO. Their job was to train short service commission types and they had also agreed to take in a certain number of VR types on their courses.

So I reported to Anstey, where I found there was a mix of about 50/50 of VR and SSC people on the two-month course. We joined the VR as AC2s but we were then made sergeants two days after our arrival. This must have annoyed the poor old regular NCOs in the RAF who had struggled for years of peacetime service at home and abroad, the lucky ones having dragged themselves up to corporals, sergeants or even flight sergeants, to find all these 'wet behind the ears' novices, suddenly on a par with them, or for the corporals to be out-ranked by us. Still, there was little they could do about it, and

as the old saying goes, if you can't take a joke you shouldn't have joined!

I remember vividly my first flying day. We had been issued with flying clothing and there we were, all togged up and raring to go. With some anticipation we awaited the arrival of our flying instructors who were about to take us into the blue and make airmen of us all. Suddenly this chap came into the crew room and called for Sergeant Foster. I held up my hand and walked towards him. This was, I later discovered, Pilot Officer B R Tribe RAFO (Reserve of Air Force Officers) – pictured above in the front cockpit with me behind.

'Ah, Sergeant,' he began, and noting that I was an NCO continued, 'you've probably done a bit of flying, yes?' I told him that I had never been in an aeroplane in my life. He was visibly deflated.

'Oh, Christ,' was his response, then with a wave of his hand merely said, 'Come on,' and turned for the door.

The aeroplane in which I was about to ascend into the late spring day was an Avro Tutor, a single-engined biplane used by the RAF as an elementary trainer. It had an Armstrong Siddeley Lynx IVC engine, of around 220-240 horse-power and had been the replacement trainer after the old WW1 design, the Avro 504N, since 1932. Its maximum speed was 122 mph, it could cruise at 105 at 1,000 feet, was able to reach the dizzy height of 16,200 feet and stay aloft for nearly three hours. Of course, all this was lost on us and me in particular. All I saw as I manfully strode towards it, dutifully a couple of paces behind Pilot Officer Tribe, was a silvery looking machine with two wings looking like something from the films *Dawn Patrol* or *Hell's Angels* and aware that this man who was going to show me how it worked, was far from impressed at having this complete novice in his care.

However, I survived my first flight, which I enjoyed immensely, and knew that so long as I didn't break anything (me included) I was going to like this flying game. Pilot Officer Tribe did his job well and got me solo in about nine hours, but it wasn't a happy relationship. We just didn't get on and it seemed that everything I did was wrong, and as soon as I soloed, he very quickly handed me over to someone else. It was no doubt the system that newly soloed pupils went onto another stage with another sort of instructor, but there was certainly no love lost and we were both happy to divest ourselves of each other.

It had not helped when I blotted my copy-book with him after he sent me off on my third or fourth solo, for some local flying. I was so happy and absorbed flying around on my own that after about half an hour I looked down and about, only to discover I hadn't got the slightest idea where I was. There were no recognisable landmarks, nothing that looked even remotely familiar. In short, I was lost.

There was only one option for me, and that was to find a nice big, flat field where I could put down without smashing anything, and ask someone where the heck I was. This I proceeded to do, although it was then impossible for me to re-start my engine, so although I soon found where I was, I had then to telephone the aerodrome for help.

Tribe and the CFI, Flight Lieutenant Veal, both flew over, landed in my field, started up the aeroplane, and while one of them flew my machine home, I was taken back in the rescue 'plane. It was a rather frosty return to Anstey, although I thought that even though I had got myself well and truly lost, I had acted responsibly, had not bent the aeroplane and reported my location to my superiors at base in what I imagined to be good aviation practise.

It was long after the war, somewhere around 1960, that I bumped into Tribe again. It was at Farnborough during one of those annual air shows and I was in the Shell marquee when we suddenly came face to face. We both recognised each other instantly, but his only comment was, 'You're still alive then!'

Towards the end of the course we had to take examinations on all aspects of flight and flying, but one thing we were not very happy about was one exam that tested our knowledge of armaments. We were not happy because none of us had ever been given or shown any form of armament training. No lectures, no books to read, absolutely nothing, and it didn't seem to matter that we hadn't done anything, an exam on the subject was still to be taken.

Luck was with us, however, for there was an armament instructor at Anstey, an ex-army man, now a flight sergeant armourer, and when we voiced our misgivings to him, he told us not to worry. A couple of days before this particular examination was due, he turned up with what he said was a sample paper on the stuff we might expect to be asked in the exam. So we quickly studied this paper, and then he went through it all with us telling us what the answers to the various questions were.

Forty-eight hours later we all trooped into the examination room, sat down and our exam papers were dished out to us as we sat there with some trepidation. We could not believe our eyes. The exam paper was exactly the same as we had been shown in what he had said was a 'sample'. So we all passed with flying colours and the flight-sergeant's reputation as a great instructor was substantially enhanced. He was a real old soldier and did not want any of us to fail.

I continued to add flying hours to my log-book total and reached my 50 without any trouble, finishing up with an 'Average' pilot rating. It was now the end of June 1939, and having acquired the knowledge and ability to pilot an aeroplane, I returned home to Battersea, and back to the office, to await information and details of where I would be requested to continue weekend training. I fully expected to be asked to go to Redhill Flying Club which was about the nearest civilian airfield to me that also catered for VR pilots but of course, nothing happened. July came and went, then August, until Sunday 3 September 1939, the same Neville Chamberlain was talking on the radio in the late morning, informing the country that for the second time in 20-odd years Britain and her Empire were once again at war with Germany.

On Friday, 1 September I had received my call-up papers, so I said goodbye to everyone in the office, went home, packed my bags and, having been told to report to the VR centre in Coventry, probably because my records were still in the system at Anstey, started my journey north.

I duly caught the train to Coventry, reported to the centre, where I was asked who I was. Giving my name to the chap at the desk he promptly said he had never heard of me, and to return home! So, having left home in the morning, very much the young lion going off to a fate unknown now that Germany had invaded Poland, I was back home on leave that same night. This was a real anti-climax for me but I have to say it gave much relief to my parents.

The following day, Sunday morning, just after Neville Chamberlain announced that war had been declared, I was out in the street along with everyone else when the first air-raid siren went off. With thoughts of that Raymond Massey film, *The Shape of Things to Come*, buzzing through my mind, nothing happened and then the 'all clear' sounded. There were no hordes of enemy bombers overhead, no bombs blasting London into rubble; yet another anti-climax. The cause of the panic was a lost aeroplane over the Channel.

The only really warlike thing to happen at this time was that I received my RAF uniform with its three sergeant stripes up, and I was soon to be seen strutting around, amazing everyone that Foster R W, was all ready for action, even though nobody in authority was eagerly awaiting my participation in Hitler's downfall. This state of affairs went on till the middle of November, at which time my paperwork appeared to have been sorted out and I was ordered to report to No.1 Initial Training Wing (ITW) at Cambridge. The RAF, I discovered, had taken over parts of the colleges there so I can truthfully say on my CV that I have been to Pembroke College, Cambridge. I have to say, however, that its accommodation in those days left much to be desired.

Over the next few weeks the RAF did the usual things such as marching us hither and thither, along roads and back again, but it was an easy existence. We attended lectures and so on, and life was really quite pleasant. At Christmas we went home again on leave, but this time I knew that after the festivities I was going to Grantham and to No.12 Flying Training School (FTS, later renamed SFTS [Service Flying Training School] when WW2 broke out).

People now began to arrive and we discovered that in fact

we were the first VR course they had had so they were taken
aback at a sudden influx of around 60 sergeants arriving. The
sergeant's mess couldn't cope with such a large number so it
was decided that some of us would go into there, while others
would be housed in the officer's mess. These latter trainees had
to wear a white flash behind their cap badges. The story went
round that the station commander was an ex-public schoolboy
so that if you'd been to public school too you went into the
officer's mess, if not you went into the sergeant's mess. There
are no prizes if you guess which one I went into.

However, the sergeant's mess was all right as far as I was
concerned, although the regular sergeants, considering their
long service, were a bit sniffy about all these 19-20 year-olds
arriving with three stripes up. But they took it in their stride
and there was no animosity shown towards us. One thing I do
remember vividly was the station warrant officer (SWO), a
typical old grizzled long timer, who ran the mess with a rod of
iron. The drill was that when you went in for dinner at night,
he would be found standing by the bar. The form was to go up
to him and not only say good evening to him, but also ask if
he would care for a beer. He never refused and continued to
stand there all evening and he never had to buy a beer himself.
If anyone tried to sneak in without him seeing you, that lad
would quickly be in trouble.

Anyway, we settled in and the flying started. We had been
asked if we wanted to fly bombers, fighters or go into army co-
op. There have always been stories about chaps who asked for
fighters and got bombers but this didn't happen to us. I opted
for fighters and generally everyone got what they had asked
for. Opting for fighters meant I moved on to Hawker Harts
which was a wonderful aeroplane and a great flying
experience.

Although the Hart was a two-seat day bomber, its days as
such were over, and it became ideal as a training machine. It
was one of a long line of Hawker biplanes and hopefully our
next stage would be to fly the single-seat Hawker Fury. All
went fairly well and straightforward. I soon went solo on the
Hart and enjoyed flying it. Then, just as we had got into our
stride towards the end of January, it started to snow. It snowed
and it snowed and it snowed. This resulted in a complete shut-
down of the base as far as flying was concerned and I
personally didn't fly again until 28 February. We had a grass

airfield that obviously could not be cleared without great difficulty, no concrete runways, so everything was abandoned and, yes you've guessed it, we were all sent home on leave.

After something like a month out of our training schedule it was good finally to get back into the air on a regular basis as March began, and we moved on to Hawker Audax machines, another two-seater, but one that had earlier been used for army co-operation. Both the Hart and the Audax were powered by a Rolls-Royce Kestrel engine, which gave more or less the same speed of about 160-180 mph and the same ceiling – 21,000 feet. With the Audax we began to do some dive-bombing. Sometimes too, we carried someone in the rear cockpit. This was great fun, screaming down to a target, the wind whistling through the wires as we huddled behind the windscreen, the only protection against the cold air-stream. The trouble was that the bomb-release system with the Audax was not terribly efficient. It had a wire toggle which one pulled and of course the more you pulled the more you moved the stick backwards and forwards, so our practice bombs that we carried, were generally scattered all over the countryside and anyone who got a bomb anywhere near the target area was jolly lucky. As most of us agreed, it was a good job we didn't have to go to war in those things!

This thought was uppermost in our minds at this time, for on 10 May 1940 the Germans finally began offensive operations on the continent by invading France and Belgium. News from the front was not encouraging and it seemed that each day the British and French armies were being pushed back towards the Channel with hardly a pause. Stories of refugees clogging roads across France, of German aircraft strafing and bombing these defenceless people made everyone anxious about the future. It seemed obvious that if the Germans did reach the Channel coast and even defeated our troops, there would be no question about Britain capitulating. We would fight on and I must say, that however anxious and upsetting the news was, I and most of my colleagues never thought for a moment that we would lose the war. I remember, with all our collective wisdom, that we in the mess all assumed that just as in WW1, the armies would quickly retreat into trenches and by the time we got into the fighting, it might all be over. It was certainly never envisaged that the Germans would in fact be on the Channel coast in less than three weeks or that France would fall.

Eventually we finished the course at Grantham and it was then time for us to fly something a little more modern. Up till now I had never been in anything with an enclosed cockpit, or a retractable undercarriage. So, on 24 May we were sent off on a two-day course to RAF Kidlington, in Oxfordshire, to fly North American Harvards.

The North American Aviation company, based at Inglewood, California, had produced this excellent training aeroplane in the 1930s and the RAF took delivery of the first of many to see service in the UK, in December 1938. There are still a number of these machines flying today, generally owned by flying enthusiasts, and the Pratt and Whitney Wasp R engine still gives off that distinctive sound I remember so well. Many have described it as like a sewing-machine. It was a superb advanced trainer although its ceiling was no greater than the earlier biplanes I'd flown but its speed of over 200 mph and a longer endurance made it feel something more like a modern aircraft.

Although the flying took place at Kidlington, we were housed at Little Rissington and driven over by bus each morning. The airfields and both places suffered with snow and bad weather, but fortunately Kidlington's resident training unit, 6 SFTS, was able to cope a little better, hence our daily bus journey.

On the Harvard course we each managed about five hours in the air but after the weeks of open-cockpit flying, this was our first machine in which you could sit comfortably in the warm. After our two days, postings came through to return to Grantham, pack our things and go to RAF Sutton Bridge, just south of The Wash, just west of King's Lynn, which was the home of 6 OTU (Operational Training Unit).

I arrived there on 6 June. The evacuation of British and French soldiers from Dunkirk had by now ended so the feeling that momentous things were soon to begin over England was never far from our thoughts. Germany was rapidly mopping up the rest of France, with Belgium and Holland already overrun, and Norway more or less occupied, so western Europe would soon be under total control of Nazi Germany, leaving only Britain hostile but alone. The British bulldog still barked defiantly if somewhat encouraged by the fact that there was a lot of water between them and us. However, since Louis

Blériot had flown the Channel way back in 1908, this 'no longer an island' thinking was even more prevalent now.

Sutton Bridge was a strange place to have an OTU (it had previously been Fighter Command's 11 Group Fighter Pilot Pool). Pre-war it had become the Armament Training Camp and later in the war it became the Central Gunnery School. It only had one short airstrip along the side of the A17 road. It was really little more than a backwater in the fen country and, uniquely, part of the landing ground was in Norfolk, with the domestic site in Lincolnshire. I believe too that some bits of the camp even jutted into Cambridgeshire.

The place seemed awash with Hawker Hurricane fighters, plus a number of Harvards and Miles Masters. I think I read somewhere that its complement of Hurricanes was over 50. It was yet another grass airfield and to help the accommodation of so many embryo pilots, some huts had been erected in the centre of a small village on the other side of the road bridge. It was this bridge from which the airfield got its name.

I had a flying instructor who was to show me how to fly the Hurricane, a chap by the name of Pilot Officer Denis Smallwood, whom everyone called 'Splinters'. A pre-war short service commission entrant, he had been adjutant and instructor with 605 Squadron, Royal Auxiliary Air Force, and while experienced on Hurricanes, had yet to see operational service. He would soon remedy that, flying Hurricanes and Spitfires in the UK, winning the DFC and then a DSO. He later rose to become Air Chief Marshal Sir Denis GBE, KCB.

Unlike my other training aircraft, flying the Hurricane for the first time was something one did alone. There were no two-seat Hurricanes, so all Denis could do was to sit me in the cockpit, point out to me all the knobs and tits, push this, pull that, etc, and then say to me: 'Off you go, and don't break anything.' So that was my introduction to the Hurricane.

Well, I didn't break anything and found the Hurricane a delight. Big, rugged and powerful, the reader should bear in mind that in 1940, this aircraft, along with the Spitfire, were Britain's most modern and up-to-date fighters. They were what one calls today, state of the art. While there can be no comparison to the jet fighters of today, these machines in 1940, to us, were the *crème de la crème*.

After several more flights, we started to do a bit of air firing, not that I remember much about it, but it is recorded in my log-book so I must have done some. We did mock attacks as well and at one point I was designated the safety pilot, so I must also have done a bit of drogue towing work.

Being told not to break anything by Denis came back to haunt me on 24 June. He and I had taken off and were just settling in to flying next to each other when my machine developed a glycol leak. Suddenly the whole windscreen became misted up with muck and I quickly called him to report that I had a problem. He immediately told me that he could see all my glycol pouring out and to get back to the airfield and land as quickly as I could. I knew enough to realise that the Rolls-Royce Merlin engine didn't like running without coolant, and it wouldn't be too long before it seized and stopped.

Anyway, I found my way back to the airfield but came in too fast, overshot the landing strip and finished up through the hedge at the end, and finally crunching into a beet field. With the sudden end of forward motion the Hurricane went up onto its nose but luckily it didn't complete the loop and turn over. It was all a bit un-nerving but I got away with it. Nobody said anything untoward about the incident, so life went on.

I had previously met a chap named Dougie Hone who lived near Croydon and we had palled up at Grantham. He was a couple of years older than me and had been a bank clerk when he joined the VR. When our postings came through at Sutton Bridge, he was sent to 615 Squadron at RAF Kenley.

Dougie owned a motor-bike which we used to get around on quite a bit, such as trips into King's Lynn to have a few beers. We had used it to get from Grantham to Sutton Bridge too. Despite fuel rationing, Dougie managed to scrounge enough from a chap in the MT section, so we did OK. Then one day, over the tannoy system, came the call that Sergeants Foster and Hone were to report to the station commander immediately. On the face of it this didn't seem to bode too well. Had the MT chap been caught out, or had our seemingly inexhaustible supply of petrol become an item of scrutiny and question?

We met up and with some foreboding presented ourselves to Station HQ, trying desperately to think up something in our defence if challenged. We reported to the adjutant, but he gave nothing away and simply said that the station commander would see us at once. With that we both marched smartly into his office, bravely but full of apprehension.

'Hello,' he said, 'come in and sit down.' Well, that didn't sound too bad. He looked us over and then, with a smile we had not expected, continued, 'I'm very pleased to tell you that you have both been recommended for, and been granted, commissions.' Well, as can be imagined, you could have knocked us over with the proverbial feather. It had never entered our minds that anything like this would happen. How they had selected people from Grantham I have absolutely no idea, or how many others of our people had got them, but not very many I think. Then he said to us, 'I hear you've got a motor-bike!' We both thought, oh-oh, now we're for it. Are we to lose our commissions just as we had got them? Dougie nodded.

'Good,' he said, 'shoot down to London and get kitted out with officers' uniforms etc. See the adjutant and he'll give you a chit to draw petrol from the MT.' Well, that would be a first and I hope the station commander didn't think we smiled too broadly!

We were told to be back within 48 hours so off we raced. With a hastily packed bag, petrol in the tank, off we went to London. There was a company called Allkit just at the top of Charing Cross Road, which did instant uniforms, nothing bespoke, just off the peg. We rapidly got ourselves sorted out, had some time to ourselves in London, then it was back to Sutton Bridge, where we moved ourselves from the sergeant's mess to the officer's mess. Life went on, but in an even pleasanter way.

Coming to the end of our OTU course, by which time I'd done about 140 hours of flying, of which 40-odd had been on Hurricanes over the last month, we began to await our posting to operational squadrons. When they were finally pinned to the notice board, I was told to report to 605 Squadron, Dougie to 615. One chap I remember, lived in Edinburgh and his posting was to Kenley, like Dougie, while I, who lived in Battersea, was being sent to Drem, in Scotland, which is just outside Edinburgh.

We both went into see the CO and asked if we could swap postings but he gave us a firm 'no', so they had to stand. So, this chap went south to Kenley and was soon killed in action in the Battle of Britain, while I headed north to 605. It is

interesting to speculate about what might have happened had
we been able to swap postings. Would I have not survived
long, or would we have both survived. Who knows? What I
did come to realise was that by going north rather than into
11 Group, which was about to take on the might of the
Luftwaffe, I was given more time to gain valuable experience
with the Hurricane before being sent down to the main battle
area.

I was soon on my way to Drem. I was to travel up with
Sergeant E W Wright, a Cambridgeshire lad just a few months
older than me. He had joined the VR in mid-1939 and arrived
at Sutton Bridge the same time as Dougie and me. However,
although we travelled north in the same train, I went first
class, as befitted my new rank, while he, as a sergeant pilot,
had to put up with third class. Over the next few months I was
to get to know Ricky, as he was known, quite well. I am glad
to report that he eventually became an air commodore with
the DFC and DFM, and was later made a CBE.

Chapter Two

605 Squadron

So, ten months after the outbreak of war, and following seven months of intense flying training, I had at last reached my goal and become a fairly well trained fighter pilot. And what a great feeling it was; at the age of just 20 to be at the controls of one of the world's greatest fighter aircraft was a lot for a youngster just out of his teens to take in.

Sometimes there is this pointless controversy about the relative merits between the Hurricane and the Spitfire. In 1940 the Hurricane was probably the better known of the two partly because it had been well publicised. In February 1938, the CO of the first Hurricane squadron, 111, eager for a chance to put his squadron squarely on the map, had flown a Hurricane up to Turnhouse, in Scotland, and then, noting that there would be a strong tail-wind back to Northolt, took off for the return journey as flat-out as he could. Squadron Leader John Gillan's average speed south was recorded as 408.75 mph, thereby covering the 327-mile journey in just 48 minutes.

Hilariously, some of Gillan's pilots had achieved similar speeds the previous day while testing the route. Gillan, of course, in anticipation of a good result of his flight had immediately telephoned Air Ministry after he'd landed and was then on his way to meet the press in London, which he had previously arranged.

Meantime, James Sanders, one of 111's pilots who had been part of the earlier flight, told the story about Flight Lieutenant J W 'Baldy' Donaldson, who was in charge of the station flight at Northolt. Baldy had telephoned the newspapers too and arranged a press conference at Northolt, using Gillan's office and putting on one of Gillan's spare squadron leader tunics. Therefore, all the stuff that appeared in the newspapers actually came from Donaldson. Understandably, Donaldson, who was quite a character, and one of three famous brothers in the RAF, was reprimanded by the AOC for his actions.

Baldy, having won the DSO with 263 Squadron in Norway, died on 8 June with the sinking of the carrier HMS *Glorious*.

It had been the Hurricane that had taken the brunt of the air fighting over France both before the Blitzkrieg and afterwards, had also seen action in Norway, where frozen lakes were used as airfields, and had been very active over the Dunkirk evacuation. The Spitfire had, of course, been the first RAF fighter to shoot down German aircraft over Britain – Ju88s and He111s over Scotland and the North of England but the Hurricane, for the moment, held pole position in the public's eye.

Therefore, whatever fate took me along the route of either the Hurricane or Spitfire was of no account. Both were great fighter aircraft and capable of standing up to anything the Germans might throw at us. It was no let-down, therefore, for me to be posted to a Hurricane squadron. I mention this because I have recently read a comment by some historian writing about the Battle of Britain, quoting that some pilots came into the Battle with only a few hours of solo flying. If this is an accurate quote then it is absolute nonsense. It may be true that they had only a few hours on either Hurricane or Spitfire but flying solo – never.

This is how history is sometimes misinterpreted. This same historian also wrote that a lot of us were not very good at shooting, ie: air to air firing, and that may very well be true, but we all had to start sometime. Whatever experience one might have had firing at a drogue, being towed behind an aircraft, this does not compare in any way with trying to stay with a jinking, turning, twisting enemy aircraft, whose pilot is far from eager to be your next victory. One also must not forget that while thus engaged, there is more than a good chance that one of his pals is trying to line you up too.

With shooting, in common with the other "S's" – ski-ing, snooker, soccer, swimming and even sex – the more you practice, the better you get. When you go into action you have so many things to think about, things to do, that you are lucky to get in anything more than a few shots at a fleeting and fast moving target. My old friend Frank Carey, a particularly good exponent with a Hurricane in combat, once recorded that while training new fighter pilots, from his experience during a tour of some 300 operational hours a pilot might expect only to be in contact with enemy aircraft for about 30 of those hours. Approach and attack might occupy only a few minutes of that time, so that in consequence one must take the fullest advantage of those minutes to hit an opponent.

If you survive your first encounters and as time goes on, it all begins to fall into place automatically. You have more time to concentrate on your shooting; judge the size and type of aircraft in front of you; the amount of deflection you need to allow, and so on. In other words, practice makes perfect. In the Battle of Britain we all had to learn that the hard way, and fast.

When my posting came through, I had no idea what 605 Squadron was all about other than it had Hurricanes, and that it was stationed at Drem. Drem is not a particularly attractive name, something rather like Doom or Gloom, so it was with some mixed feelings that I travelled north to Edinburgh at the beginning of July.

Ricky Wright and I were picked up at Edinburgh railway station by RAF transport and as we left the city and travelled east along the coast road towards North Berwick, my spirits lifted somewhat. It was a beautiful sunny summer day and to the south were some lovely rolling hills, while to the north was the sparkling Firth of Forth. It was as if my foreboding about Drem was quite unfounded; and so it proved. We turned off the main road at the small village of Gullane, and within a few minutes driving inland we arrived at our destination.

Drem, in fact, was yet another large grass field, turned into an airfield with some semi-permanent and temporary accommodation. Although it was all grass, two airstrips had been cut and flattened out to make runways, one running north to south, the other east to west. I sorted out my accommodation and settled down for the night.

My new home was about two miles south of another village, called Dirleton. The field had been a home defence landing ground as far back as 1916-17 when it was known as West Fenton. In the last year of WW1 it had become the home of No.2 Training Depot Station (TDS) and after that it was re-named Gullane. It remained unused till 1933, at which time it was employed by 602 and 603 Squadron's Hawker Harts as a re-fuelling point during exercises. Then shortly before WW2 it became a training base once more and the home of 13 FTS.

Once war was declared, Drem was an ideal spot for the

fighter defence of the Scottish Lowlands, being on the approach to Edinburgh and for shipping in the Firth of Forth, and another auxiliary squadron – 609 – brought its Spitfires up from Acklington and the FTS was disbanded in October 1939, the airfield being taken over by Fighter Command. 602 Squadron were operating from Drem on 16 October and intercepted bombers attacking ships near the Forth Bridge. 602, and 603 from Turnhouse, each claimed one German bomber in the sea off Dunbar.

Several alerts, patrols and scrambles occurred over the next several weeks and further engagements took place in the first months of 1940. Not much had happened since, except pilots flying convoy patrols out over the sea and there was always the chance that raiders would again try to bomb shipping in the Firth of Forth, or even go for Edinburgh.

As I was soon to discover, 605 was named County of Warwick Squadron, and formed part of the important Royal Auxiliary Air Force. It had come into existence in late 1926, at Castle Bromwich and had originally been a bomber outfit. Its first aircraft were Avro 504s for training and WW1 vintage DH9A bombers. Over the next few years it had maintained its role as a training squadron for weekend airmen, keen to fly while holding down civilian jobs during the weekdays. It went on to fly Westland Wapiti IIs, Hawker Harts, the Hind and then Gloster Gladiator fighters as the squadron became a fighter unit at the beginning of 1939.

While I was finishing my training at Grantham, 605 were having their first encounters with enemy aircraft, while based at Wick. On 28 March the squadron shared the honours of bringing down a Heinkel 111, then on 10 April Pilot Officer I J Muirhead attacked a German recce aircraft but it went into cloud before he could see any results of his attack. However, Flying Officer P G Leeson was more successful and his attack on another raider brought results, with two of the crew baling out as the aircraft went down.

The day before the Germans began their move on France, Flying Officers G R Edge, G W B Austin and R Hope shot down a Dornier 17 off Dunnett Head. With things going badly in France and with an evacuation already on the cards, 605 were moved south to Hawkinge, near Folkestone on 21 May and began patrols over France. Graham Austin and Pat Leeson were two pilots the squadron lost in these skirmishes across the Channel. Leeson ended up a prisoner of war, but Austin, although wounded, was evacuated via Dunkirk. The squadron also lost Sergeant Moffatt and Flying Officer G F M Wright, both killed.

Further fighting took place during the Dunkirk show and more claims were made against the enemy. Ian Muirhead was shot down but landed safely despite being fired on by Belgian soldiers. Boarding a ship at Ostende, his journey was interrupted by a torpedo, but he was rescued from the sea and finally got home OK. In its final actions, the squadron lost is commander, Squadron Leader G V Perry and two other pilots, following which it returned to Scotland and to Drem.

Once at Drem 605's new CO arrived, Squadron Leader Walter Churchill, who was 32 years of age and had been in the AAF since 1931, and actually with 605 Squadron for a while. He had become a reserve officer in 1937 but was recalled once the war started and sent to France as a flight commander with 3 Squadron, flying Hurricanes. Despite failing eyesight and his age, Churchill did remarkably well. It was not long before he was commanding the squadron, and in three or four days he had shot down four German aircraft, had shared three more and claimed two others as probables. His actions resulted in awards of the DFC and then the DSO.

This was the chap I met on my first morning with the squadron. He was an impressive looking man, and those two medal ribbons beneath his wings attracted my attention. Here was a man who had faced the enemy, done well, survived and was now my boss. I had gone down to the squadron dispersal area and although when I met Churchill he was welcoming, I have to say that for some reason or other there was no great empathy between him and myself. There was no animosity at all, it was just one of those cases, and we never seemed to be on the same wavelength.

I was told I was to be in A Flight, and Gerry Edge was the flight commander. Gerry was a completely different type of man to Churchill, very easy to get on with and a great chap. He was several years older than me and had joined the RAuxAF in 1936, flying with 605 Squadron, and was called for full-time service just prior to war being declared. He had seen considerable action over France and Dunkirk and already had a creditable score of victories, including four Ju87 Stuka dive-bombers in one action east of Calais on 25 May. He was something of a perfectionist and got into the habit of wearing two wrist-watches. When asked why, he would confess: 'If you are 200 miles out over the North Sea, doing, say, 250 miles per hour and your watch fails when you are trying to rendezvous with other aircraft, you are going to end up very lost or very dead, or both.' Gerry I discovered, came from Staffordshire, had attended Oundle School before going into the family metal business in Wolverhampton, flying with 605 at weekends.

The other flight commander was Archie McKeller. Born in Paisley, outside Glasgow, he was 28 years old, and the son of a stockbroker. Not wanting to follow in his father's profession he became a plasterer's apprentice, and because his father disapproved of his desire to fly, took lessons in secret at the Scottish Flying Club at Abbotsinch. Once he received his A Licence, he was invited to join 602 (City of Glasgow) Squadron in 1936 and was commissioned that November. By the time the war came he was a flying officer, but he hadn't improved on his diminutive height of 5′ 3″; however, in those early skirmishes over Scotland in October 1939, he had shared in the destruction of two German raiders. It must have been quite a change for him to swap Spitfires for 605's Hurricanes, when posted in June 1940. He and Walter Churchill hit it off well together, the CO no doubt appreciating Archie's very press-on nature.

Among the other experienced pilots we had was C R 'Bunny' Currant. He was 28 and came from Luton, having received a direct entry into the RAF in 1936. As a sergeant pilot he had flown with 46 and 151 Squadrons but upon being commissioned, moved to 605 in April 1940. In one of those patrols over France pre-Dunkirk, Chris had been shot down south of Arras, force-landed, but not before he had actually got out onto the wing prior to taking to his parachute. Once there he thought it was possible to make a force-landing so he climbed back into the cockpit. Unfortunately he did not have time to put his straps back on, so when he crunched in, he smashed his face on the gun-sight, resulting in two black eyes and a broken nose. Having a 'Hurricane Nose' was something easily achieved by a number of pilots during these extreme ways of landing. His number two had circled and was able to report back that Bunny had survived the crash but it was uncertain if he would ever be seen again, such was the chaos in northern France.

Sorting himself out Bunny decided to walk to Calais and being a conscientious type lugged his heavy and awkward parachute all the way, which in hindsight he wished he'd left in the cockpit. After covering some miles he came to a small town and managed to find the mayor and talked him into providing him with a car and driver to take him to Calais. He was somewhat amazed that the mayor agreed. He was taken to within walking distance of the port, so continued into the dock area, teamed with some British and French troops, and managed to get himself aboard one of the last ships leaving for England. He had been shot down at around 10.30 am but by 11 pm that night he walked into the mess at Hawkinge to the amazement of everyone, sporting those two black eyes and a smashed nose.

Bunny always looked the part as a fighter pilot. Handsome, although in most photographs he seemed dour, with wavy hair, RAF moustache, he seemed never too far from his pipe. He even appeared film-star-like – although only briefly – in the movie about Reginald Mitchell and the Spitfire, which starred Leslie Howard and David Niven. This was *First of the Few*, filmed at Ibsley in 1941, by which time Bunny was commanding 501 Squadron.

Mike Cooper-Slipper was another pilot I met that first morning. He was six months younger than me and came from Staffordshire. He joined the RAF via the short service commission route in 1938 and had become a member of 605 in February 1940. He had also seen action over Dunkirk.

Ian 'Jock' Muirhead came from East London and had been accepted into the RAF as a 16-year-old apprentice in 1929. Like many such boy-entrants, 'Jock' managed to get himself accepted for a flying course, his first squadron being 151, but then moved to 605 in April 1940. He had also claimed some scalps over France and Dunkirk although shot down on 26 May during a fight with some Me110s. He baled out safely, and got home by ship as previously mentioned.

Jock became the first member of 605 Squadron to win the Distinguished Flying Cross for these recent actions. The award was announced in the *London Gazette* on 28 June 1940 with the following citation:

This officer has shot down five enemy aircraft and has shown outstanding skill, coolness and daring in carrying out eight patrols in five days over N.W. France and Belgium. During the last patrol he was forced to escape by parachute and after surmounting many difficulties succeeded in reaching his unit.

There were one or two regulars on the squadron who had yet to see any action and the rest were made up from earlier auxiliaries, such as Ralph Hope and Douglas Scott. The balance were all VR chaps like myself, so 605 were more or less complete by the end of July. Ralph Hope was in fact a nephew of the former Prime Minister Neville Chamberlain. He had also rowed for Oxford in the 1935 boat race. He had learnt to fly in America whilst working for the family business in New York, and he was a really nice man, one you could easily get on with – a gentleman.

I had my first flight with the squadron on 9 July in P2994. It was a formation trip together with Bunny Currant and Cyril Passy. In the afternoon I was up in L2059 with Sergeants L F Ralls and R D Ritchie. Exactly one month later, Bob Ritchie, while engaged in a patrol off the east coast, called base to report that he had a glycol leak and that fumes were making him drowsy. That was the last we heard and apparently he was overcome, passed out, and dived into the sea off Dunbar. The body of this 24-year old was picked up by a ship and returned to Drem, later to be buried in his home town of Fife.

The station commander at Drem was a chap called 'Batchy' Atcherley. Wing Commander Richard Llewellyn Roger Atcherley, to give him his full title, and his twin brother, David, were fast becoming legends within the RAF, legends that grew as the war progressed. When the war began he was commanding 85 Squadron at RAF Debden, in 12 Group, Fighter Command. Batchy had then been sent to Norway where his reputation was even more enhanced. He was tasked with finding landing grounds for RAF fighters, which were mostly located on frozen lakes. One tactic he employed that I heard of was that in order to create a landing area on a snow-covered iced-up lake, he got some locals to guide a herd of reindeer across the snow, the men being rewarded with some medicinal brandy from an RAF doctor.

After the ill-fated Norwegian campaign, Batchy had been given command of Drem and he used his recent knowledge of

605 Squadron Hurricane

airfield defence and operational efficiency to the full. He arranged dispersal sites for the aircraft, ordering in quantities of old railway sleepers to act as hard-standings among the trees at the edge of the field, and also building rudimentary blast pens around them. Being a grass airfield and prone to becoming wet and muddy in inclement weather, these dispersal points made it virtually impossible for our Hurricanes to sink into any soft earth as they stood waiting for action.

Another thing was his work on what became known as the Drem Lighting System, which was later developed and used extensively by Bomber Command and others. Before this, night flying pilots only had 'glim' lamps, or flares to assist them to get down where there were no permanent runway lights such as those employed on larger, concrete airfields. Batchy devised this system of lights to give a pilot a clue as to his angle of glide as he made his landing approach, red, amber and green giving this indication of a correct or incorrect approach height.

He set this up on the airfield and we pilots were the 'guinea pigs' of the system, which was quite good in a way as we were able to get in quite a bit of night flying experience which we otherwise would not have got, while testing his scheme.

Life went on pretty much the same. We had quite a lot of leisure time on our hands as we were very rarely on a full readiness state. These spare moments were mostly spent exploring the local hostelries in nearby towns and villages, testing the merits of the various beers and barmaids. In those early days officer's messes were not the most convivial of places and we were not encouraged to mooch about in them. Pre-war habits still prevailed at this early stage of the war. There was no bar, only a waiter service for drinks and silence was golden!

The first morning I went in for breakfast, the dining room had these long refectory-type tables down the centre and in front of every place set out for the meal there was a little lectern. The form was for you not to talk to the person opposite you but rather to take a newspaper and prop it up on this lectern, thereby discouraging discourse. Thus breakfast was taken in complete silence, except for the clink of cutlery on bone china, or the spreading of butter on toast, nobody saying a word. This soon changed as the war progressed, but in those early days one was never supposed to hang around.

From time to time someone would organise some form of entertainment for the men and all sorts of people were prone to turn up. This one time a young man called John Gielgud, an up and coming Shakespearian actor, came along. He obviously thought he should play down to the licentious soldiery a bit so he told a few jokes that didn't go down awfully well but he told one particular story which he explained happened when a recruit had first arrived at an RAF station. A corporal had apparently asked: 'Where's your fork and spoon?' To which the recruit replied: 'In my fork'in pocket!' These days that would not offend, but back then, with ladies present too, it was thought quite disgusting. How things have changed. I recall there was quite a discussion as to whether or not we should invite him back to the officer's mess after the show.

The summer weather helped and the more flying experience we all acquired the better we hoped to perform if and when we were sent south. Daily we were hearing reports over the radio of increasing air battles over southern England and although the figures banded about seemed to indicate that Fighter Command were knocking down more Germans than they were losing Spitfires and Hurricanes, we all heard over the service grapevine that some squadrons had suffered badly and their losses made it impossible for them to remain in the south. Squadrons in 12 and 13 Groups were gradually being ordered south into 11 and 10 Group areas so it didn't take a genius to work out that our turn would eventually come.

Before it did, however, the squadron had its first real taste of action in what is now called the Battle of Britain, on 15

August. On this day the Germans decided to launch a massive assault against the RAF by attacking its airfields in the south and, unusually, in the north-east. The Luftwaffe's task in these opening weeks of the Battle had been to engage and defeat Fighter Command, not only in the air, but by hitting its airfields. The Germans had been frustrated somewhat in this task, and while their fighter pilots were claiming more and more Spitfires and Hurricanes shot down, they were still being met in some strength. Surely, they thought, the RAF must be down to its last reserves.

Fighter Command had indeed been hit hard but was still strong enough to oppose the daily onslaughts. Its airfields were coming under increased pressure too but none had been knocked out completely. Early German reconnaissance flights heralded another day of action although if they were coming they did not seem to be in a rush to do so. The sky remained largely empty during this Thursday morning but a clear sky must surely indicate that it would be a good day to come.

It was not till gone 11 am before the radar people began to see a build-up of enemy aircraft over France, heralding today's raids. Stuka dive-bombers arrived first, going for RAF Hawkinge but fighters already airborne thwarted any concentrated attack and the airfield was spared, although the returning Ju87 crews reported otherwise. The airfield at Lympne was another base attacked but this time unopposed by our fighters.

As these attacks began, the Germans, believing that with all the fighting that had been going on in the south, the north of England must be virtually undefended, had decided to launch a raid by Luftlotte 5 from Norway. By now it had become necessary to rotate squadrons from the south and of course, others like 605, were still in the north awaiting developments. The Luftwaffe's bomber crews had been briefed to attack airfields at Dishforth and Usworth, with secondary targets of Newcastle, Sunderland and Middlesborough, while some seaplanes were detailed to fly towards the Dundee area as a feint to draw off fighters known to be defending Edinburgh.

Some 70-odd Heinkel 111 bombers from KG26 headed across the North Sea, escorted by twin-engined Me110 fighters from I Gruppe, ZG76. This raid became something of a nonsense due to poor navigation, the bombers flying too far north initially, so that they were seen to be almost in tandem with the seaplanes. By the time the seaplanes turned back, and the force of Heinkels had been reduced to 63 due to aborts, the 13 Group controller knew that a major raid was on its way.

Spitfires from Acklington were scrambled shortly after midday when the raiders began to turn south to get back on track. Then Hurricanes from Acklington were also sent off. At Drem we were also alerted and we got the scramble call at 12.25. The first group of Spitfires to sight the enemy were given something of a shock. The controller had reported a 30+ estimate of the raiders, but the Spitfire leader reported there appeared to be more than 100 bombers and fighters. Despite the odds the Spitfires attacked and claimed a number of bombers shot down. Other bomber crews began jettisoning their bomb loads and turned east.

Five minutes after this initial combat action, 605 Squadron arrived, or to be more accurate, just Archie McKeller and B Flight. A Flight was being led by Douglas Scott and for some unearthly reason Scott got us completely lost over the North Sea and we never saw any action whatsoever. B Flight however, got in amongst the bombers and did quite well. McKeller and Bunny claimed victories although Ken Law, a South African, was shot down and had to force land on a golf course by the beach near Hartley and was badly injured.

B Flight consisted of Archie, Bunny, Jock Muirhead, Eric Jones, Cyril Passy and Ken Law (actually Ken Schadtler-Law). Eric and Ken concentrated on one Heinkel that Ken finished off, but return fire did for him. Cyril Passy was also hit by return fire and had to force land a mile short of Usworth airfield.

In all McKeller had claimed three bombers, Bunny one shared, Eric Jones another with Law, and Jock, after attacking a group of 25 bombers, spotted another in trouble. Bunny had already knocked out one of its engines and Jock finished it off and put it into the sea, so he shared this with Bunny.

Some years after the war I ran into Ken Law and during our conversation I asked him where he was living. You can imagine my surprise when he replied that he had just moved into Forresters Drive, which runs alongside Croydon aerodrome. Why it was so uncanny was that later 605 Squadron, when based at Croydon, used the houses in this same road, as our dispersal area, as I shall relate later. Quite a coincidence. Ken did not return to the squadron after his injury but he remained in the RAF, retiring as a wing commander in 1968.

After the air battle, Eric Jones wrote home about his experiences. This is his letter:

'I think I can give you some good news today. Yesterday our flight was "at available" which is to say we have to be on the camp and be able to get into the air within 15 minutes. At 11.45 a message came through that the whole squadron was to go up on patrol. Within 10 minutes we were climbing to 20,000 feet and heading out to sea. From there we were directed by the ground and heard that about 30 enemy aircraft were approaching. We cruised about and eventually found ourselves over Newcastle and the Tyne. I began to think we were on a wild goose chase because by this time we had been up for about one and three-quarter hours and we were being told to land at local aerodromes to refuel. There were only five of us left by this time; the others had drifted away. Suddenly, over the leader's machine and about three miles away, I saw the biggest formation of enemy aircraft I have ever seen, bigger than I ever saw at Hendon air display, and then another smaller formation behind them.

'Archie McKeller, my leader, decided to attack the big formation, so we turned and climbed into the sun. At that moment I ran out of petrol and by the time I had turned on to my reserve tank, Archie was 200 yards in from of me. We kept closing until we were about 4,000 feet above the enemy and directly overhead. Then we turned on our backs and dived to attack.

'I found myself attacking two aircraft which were below each other and dead in my sights. As I came down I pressed my firing button and for the first time heard my guns go off. I could see my bullets hitting the aircraft, when suddenly the starboard engine of one of the Heinkels exploded and left a long trail of black smoke. Almost immediately the port engine of the other machine caught fire and the last I saw of those two, as I shot by at 400 mph, they looked as if they would collide.

'I pulled out of my dive and climbed up again well to one side of the formation and looked for Archie. I couldn't pick him out, so I decided to attack a lone

aircraft which was a little way from the others. I went in
from the side and as he went through my sights I followed
him round. Suddenly his nose went straight up into the air,
and then he toppled over and went straight into a spin.
Two parachutes came out as the machine crashed towards
the sea. I climbed up again and waited until I saw another
straggler and then I went in again and pressed the button.
There was a roar and then silence – I had run out of
ammunition – so I dived towards the clouds and as I went
I saw lots of bombs explode in the sea.

'My total bag for my first encounter is one Heinkel
111 shot down and two damaged. We lost two machines
but the pilots are safe; one came back to the aerodrome
last night, the other is in hospital with concussion. My
machine was not hit.

'We had a wizard champagne party in the mess last
night. The whole of A Flight was unlucky; they didn't see
a thing but our flight sent seven down and damaged six.'

Archie McKeller also wrote home, telling his parents of his
part in the engagement:

'Dearest Little Mother, I am very well and very pleased
with myself. On Thursday at 12 o'clock I was sent off
with my flight to patrol Newcastle at 20,000 feet. We all
arrived safely and remained there until 1.30, when I saw
seventy to eighty Nasties in one big formation followed
by a second formation of twenty to thirty. They were
approaching Newcastle from the south. I whipped into
them with my flight. I got three down, with one possible,
and the rest of the boys got five down with seven possible
– possible being when the Hun breaks away from the
formation with engines out or flames coming, but is not
seen to crash.

'By this time there were a lot more fighters, so
everyone gave the Nasties the fright of their lives. I was
very proud. The Air Vice-Marshal came along and
congratulated the flight on their good show. It really was,
as the majority were all new and inexperienced. Two of
the boys were shot down, but without damage to one,
and only scalp and head wounds to the other, so I reckon
it was pretty good going.

'Unfortunately I caught my little gold bracelet on one of the clips of my aircraft during the show and broke it and it is lost, so if Dad is feeling pleased about this news I would like another one, please!!! All my love, Sonnie.'

Once the dust had settled, the tally came out at three destroyed, five probables and one damaged, but this was later adjusted to four destroyed, four probables and one damaged the next day. In all, the Germans lost eight bombers and seven fighters to the RAF, plus two fighters damaged. For this and earlier actions, Archie McKeller was the squadron's second recipient of the DFC, which was announced before the end of the month and gazetted in September:

This officer has at all times displayed the keenest desire to engage the enemy. In his first large-scale encounter against enemy aircraft he displayed a great sense of leadership and tactics in launching his flight against ninety Heinkel 111's. As a result, at least four enemy aircraft were destroyed, of which Flight Lieutenant McKeller destroyed three. He has displayed outstanding leadership and courage.

Gerry Edge was promoted to acting squadron leader at the beginning of September and left us to take command of 253 Squadron at Kenley. His place as A Flight leader was taken by Bunny Currant. Then, it was our turn to move. Orders came through in early September for a trip south. We had been hearing more and more about the major battles down there, so when we finally got the call it was not unexpected. With some excitement and not a little apprehension, we packed our things and prepared to leave Drem for RAF Croydon, in 11 Group Fighter Command.

We left on the 7th. The ground crews went off in a Bristol Bombay transport aircraft with others in a Handley Page Harrow in the morning while we pilots took off after lunch with 18 Hurricanes. We landed at RAF Abingdon to refuel as it would be foolish to land at Croydon with fuel tanks almost empty, in case of an immediate alert. We didn't want to have our Hurricanes destroyed on the ground before getting into action. We reached Croydon at around 19.30 that evening. We had replaced 111 Squadron who had flown north to our old base at Drem. They had only been at Croydon for about five days but had suffered several casualties during that time, and also been mauled in August while at Debden.

The one thing I remember about arriving at Croydon is that I hadn't any brakes, having lost my air pressure after taking off from Abingdon due to an air leak. However, Croydon, being a former civil airfield used by Imperial Airways, had a large grass landing area. I told the others that I would be landing last and so once everyone had got down then I lowered my wheels and came in as slowly as I could without stalling. I just put the thing down at one end and slowly rolled to a stop, from where the ground crew pushed me to dispersal. Not the best of starts, I thought, and of course, my guns would have been out of action too, so just as well we hadn't run into any trouble.

It has to be said though, that we were pretty shocked as we arrived. London had been attacked on this day, the first daylight raid. Up until now the Luftwaffe had mainly concentrated on airfields and aircraft factories. Now they were going for the capital. As we headed in we could see all this smoke while still some 30 miles away, and as Croydon hove into view we could not fail to notice a huge pall of smoke that continued to hang over the city to the north of us. As daylight gave way to darkness further bombing stoked up the fires and created more, so that we could see this red sky in the distance. It was like Dante's Inferno. What had we flown down to? Bunny Currant was later to record: 'My God, we really are in the thick of it, we're really up against it.'

I think we were pretty unique in our accommodation at Croydon. As I mentioned earlier our dispersal – and our billets – were the houses in Forresters Drive that had been cordoned off from the rest of the neighbourhood. All the people who had resided there had, of course, been moved away. Not just because their houses were needed to accommodate air force personnel, but it was going to be dangerous living on the edge of a potential target for German bombers. In February 1940 a Bristol Blenheim had crashed into No.45 and done a lot of damage to it and the house next door. A mother and daughter were both killed, and as fate would have it, their's was about the only house still occupied.

Using Forresters Drive, we had one house turned into an officer's mess where we had a bar in the front room, and dining table in the back room. In other houses we used the upstairs bedrooms for sleeping, each house taking five, two in each large room, one in a box room. We shared the bathroom facilities but we didn't use the downstairs rooms overmuch. Often the kitchen was useful for a brew. A section of houses across from ours was used by the sergeants and senior NCOs.

Each garden stretched out onto the airfield itself and beyond the bottom fences stood our Hurricanes, facing out towards a take-off area. The airmen and ground crews also used houses on the opposite side of the road. In one house the CO had his own room, and for a brief spell I shared a bedroom with Charles English before he was killed.

We did not take long to get into a routine. Each morning we were awoken by our batmen sometime around dawn, had some tea, then some cooks came along and prepared breakfast in the kitchen. We had our meals in the rooms we'd made into dining areas. The NCO pilots did the same in their section of houses. Across the road the airmen had a similar arrangement for eating.

If we were on stand-by or readiness we just sat in the garden as the weather was pretty good, if not, we sat in the rear drawing room, that looked out towards the airfield, with our Hurricanes lined up just beyond the rear fences.

We didn't use the other side of the aerodrome at all; it had already been badly bombed in August. We did use the hangars and workshops over there for heavy maintenance to our aircraft, but the daily work was all carried out at the bottom of the gardens. Later when we had new radios fitted this all took place in the main hangars. Close to the houses we had a caravan that was used by the duty pilot and where an airman would sit and man the telephone link to the operations room. It was quite pleasant to sit out in the gardens in deck or other easy chairs while on readiness, our mae wests (buoyancy aids!) on. We had no illusions that things were going to be quiet around here, and so it proved. The very next day, the 8th, came our first alert and our first serious scramble.

Chapter Three

The Battle of Britain

The next morning we were up before dawn. With the raid on London the previous day and with fires burning all night over the east end of the city, we viewed the coming day with some apprehension. While our resolve was absolute, one just couldn't dismiss what we had seen and heard without wondering what was in store.

The squadron was at readiness after breakfast this Sunday morning, but the German bomber crews were obviously resting after yesterday's efforts. However, some must have been up for around 10.45 we were scrambled, although I was not among them. Four Hurricane squadrons were sent up, 46 from Stapleford, 253 from Kenley, 504 from Hendon and ourselves. We had twelve aircraft and teamed up with eight of 253, that was being led by our previous flight commander, Gerry Edge.

Within minutes they were in contact with about 50 Dorniers, preceded by three Ju88s, the whole lot being escorted by up to 20 Me110s and loads more Me109s above and behind, with another 20 or so below the bombers. When the boys found them they were between Maidstone and Tunbridge Wells.

Archie went down after the Ju88s, while Bunny and A Flight attacked along the port side of a group of 25 Dorniers but before they could really get into position they were engaged by 109s. However, many of the bombers had started to turn back, although they did not drop their bombs. There was now what was to become a familiar mix up of British and German aircraft, everyone trying to do something nasty to each other.

Our CO – Churchill – didn't see the enemy formation. McKeller had yelled for everyone to come on, get stuck in and hit these bastards, but Churchill just kept on going. They were approaching the Germans at a closing speed of about 500 mph. In the end, it was just a case of pressing the gun button, hoping for the best, and moments later they went over the top.

Jack Fleming was flying behind the formation acting as weaver. He had seen the 109s that were flying as close escort to the bombers, but failed to spot the others coming down behind him. His machine was hit and he managed to bale out but not before he had been badly burned. He became one of Archie McIndoe's 'Guinea Pigs' at East Grinstead, in fact for many years he was Guinea Pig number two to Tom Gleave, in the famous club of theirs. He was to be with McIndoe for nearly a year as I recall, but he never flew operationally again. His Battle of Britain had lasted just one day – or indeed – ten minutes.

Jack – he was actually John – had been born in Scotland but his family had gone to New Zealand while he was still a child. Accepted for a RAF commission offered to graduates in British and Commonwealth universities he had sailed to England in May 1939 and after training joined 605 in August. In hospital with his injuries he found himself in a ward of a dozen pregnant mothers. Moved to the RAF hospital at Halton his case was deemed hopeless after he refused to allow doctors to amputate both legs at the hip. Luckily he was found by McIndoe who, seeing that plastic surgery was out of the question, suggested he might try his new saline bath treatment at his place in East Grinstead. With nothing to lose, Jack agreed. Recovery was slow but successful and within a couple of years he was a station armament officer at an OTU, and later, in Canada became Inspector of Bombing and Gunnery at several similar operational training units. He was made an MBE and at the time of the flying and rocket bomb menace in 1944-45, with the rank of wing commander, he was heading one of the special teams tracking launching sites. He was extremely lucky not to be facially disfigured and his hands survived too. I know he had to wear special thick underwear for the rest of his life (he died in 1995) having lost a whole layer of his skin from his body.

Fortunately, Jack was our only casualty in this the squadron's first action from Croydon. When they got back and the pilots totted up their claims, the results were, Bunny one Dornier with a 109 damaged; Cooper-Slipper a 109 destroyed and a Dornier damaged; Alec Ingle a Dornier probably destroyed, and Jimmy Humphrey a 109 damaged. The Dornier bombers were from KG2, the 109s from JG53.

That evening Archie, Humphrey and George Forrester, 'borrowed' the station Bedford truck and drove up to London for a night out and a few hours to relax. The rest of us got an early night.

The next day, the 9th, the squadron was not in action till late in the afternoon. Take-off was at 5 pm and those pilots that were scrambled engaged 26 He111s from II/KG1 plus the usual escort of 109s, this time from JG3, and Me110s of III Gruppe of ZG76, near Farnborough. The formation was successfully broken up which prevented it reaching London. In all eight RAF squadrons nibbled away at these raiders as they passed over Croydon. The reason the Heinkels were seen to turn, was that the 110s went into a defensive circle, thereby leaving the bombers to fend for themselves. Later they dumped their bombs over Purley and Epsom.

McKeller came home claiming three He111s and a 109, while Bunny and Ricky Wright shared a 110. Archie's exploit of downing four in one action naturally provoked much interest from the media, and it was also mentioned in at least one book, *So Few*, by David Masters, who must also have interviewed Walter Churchill who had witnessed the action. By this time everyone knew that Churchill's eyesight was giving him problems in the air. Apparently as the squadron reached 15,000 feet Archie had called Churchill to report enemy aircraft ahead. At the distance they were, Churchill was unable to pick them out, only seeing about six Me109s above with 20 Me110s off to one side.

Churchill decided to try and draw off the 109s and to leave McKeller and the others a better chance at the bombers. Recovering from this skirmish, Churchill then saw McKeller's section up-sun and turning in for an attack. McKeller pressed the gun button and Churchill watched as the Scot's fire blew one bomber up and then this crashed into a companion and ripped its wing off. Meantime the first bomber swung into McKeller's path and it went down pouring smoke from both engines, followed moments later by the third bomber, seen going down on its back.

Back at base the CO had apologised for messing up the initial attack, whereupon McKeller, never slow in coming forward, said:

'Your sight is no good. You are too old – you're an old man!'

'I'm going on flying,' retorted the CO.

'You'll simply be shot down,' was McKeller's blunt response.

'All right, I'll let you lead,' and from then on McKeller generally led, unless he was absent at which time Bunny took over.

Bunny also shared a 109 on the 9th, but with another squadron. Again we lost a pilot, George Forrester. Jimmy Humphrey baled out of his crippled Hurricane and got away with it, landing near Bordon with a hand wound. However, as he came down he drifted over a Canadian army camp and was fired on by the over-enthusiastic soldiers, one bullet tearing through his tunic pocket and leaving a mark on the left side of his body. Once on the ground he was pounced on by several Canadians, who took his RAF buttons, his boots and maps, before sending him off to hospital. His hand wound was repaired but he lost his little finger. He did not get back to us until November and then he was posted off to other duties.

Forrester had joined the squadron up at Drem in early August. It appears that this 26-year-old lad had collided with a Heinkel 111 belonging to the Staff Staffel of KG53, that crashed at Southfield Farm, Chawton, near Alton, minus a wing. George crashed at Southwood Farm, near Shalden, and was buried at Odiham cemetery in Hampshire.

Somewhere about 1990 his brother got in touch; he was Major-General Michael Forrester, CB CBE DSO & Bar, MC & Bar. He had been three years younger than George and had seen considerable service, as evidenced by his impressive list of decorations, in Palestine, Egypt, Greece, Crete, Western Desert, Syria, North Africa, Italy and France, before going onto the Staff of 13 Corps and then commanding 1st/6th Queen's Royal Regiment, ending the war as assistant to the Supreme Allied Commander, Mediterranean forces. Even post-war his list of appointments was equally impressive. He wanted to learn all he could about how his brother had met his end and we were able to supply as much detail as we were able. The Heinkel, coded A1+ZD, went in with three of its crew still aboard while two others managed to bale out.

From time to time I am asked about losing people and friends in the squadron and did I feel it very deeply and so on. Well, of course one felt it but on the other hand I'd only known some of these chaps a few weeks, sometimes less. They were not friends of long standing. Peter Crofts for instance, who was to be shot down in late September, was only with us about two weeks, so one didn't really have the time to get to know him. I'd probably had a beer with him in the mess and that was about it.

By the time 605 got into the Battle we were more fortunate than other squadrons who had fought on during August, for we were able to receive replacement pilots and aircraft very quickly, so we always seemed to be up to full strength and complement. So in 605 at least there was never any thought that we were going to lose this fight. This feeling continued unabated into October too.

The squadron was involved in a 15.45 pm scramble on the 11th and engaged 40 or more He111s escorted by loads of Messerschmitts, between Rochester and Eltham, turning the whole mass back towards the south and west, so London was saved from this bunch.

After they had turned south, we were within sight of Croydon and those on the ground saw Bunny destroy a Heinkel that crashed just a few miles east of the aerodrome. In further attacks he damaged two more. Archie and Eric Jones chased another bomber out over Beachy Head but ran out of ammunition without being able to finish it off. However, they continued to make feint approaches at it, which must have so un-nerved the crew in their obviously damaged machine, that they baled out! This machine, from 2/KG26 lost one of its crew, but three others were rescued from the Channel by German air-sea rescue.

Cooper-Slipper managed to damage another Heinkel, Archie claimed a 110 probably destroyed, while our two Polish pilots, Jan Budzinski and Witold Jozef Glowacki destroyed a 109 and a 110 respectively. Both had come to us at the end of August, after a spell with 145 Squadron.

This raid, I should emphasise, was not thwarted by 605 alone, for at least six other squadrons got in amongst the enemy, giving them a severe mauling. 605's only casualty was the CO, who received a slight flesh wound to one arm. That evening we celebrated the day's activities with a dinner at our favourite retreat, the Greyhound in Croydon.

The next day was reasonably quiet after the hectic events of the 11th. There were a number of isolated reconnaissance sorties flown by the Luftwaffe followed that night by more raids on London. The squadron was scrambled at 13.45 but within minutes, nine were ordered to land again, leaving Red Section, led by Bunny, orbiting base. Circling at 3,000 feet below some cloud they were informed that three bandits were west of their position, approaching from a south-easterly direction at 11,000 feet. With his companions – Cooper-Slipper and Ricky Wright – Bunny began to climb and soon spotted what they identified as a Dornier 215 about six miles north of them, heading south-east at 8,000 feet. The German crew must have seen the danger for the bomber, which in fact was a Ju88, began to turn into them. Bunny was able to lead a head-on attack, which made the bomber's crew jettison their bomb load and make a rapid turn to the south. They chased the Junkers over Hastings on the south coast and the pilot continued to flee hastily out to sea towards France pursued by our three stalwarts, who finally shot him down into the water eight miles south-west of Cap Gris Nez. The machine was from 1(F)/122, the 'F' standing for Fernauftkärungruppe (long distance recce unit). Its four-man crew did not survive.

That evening Gerry Edge came over from Kenley to take dinner with us. It was good to see him again and to know he was doing an excellent job in leading 253 Squadron right on our doorstep.

On the 13th Bunny was officially promoted to flight lieutenant. Again there was little hostile activity this Friday. The weather wasn't too bad – bright intervals with showers, but there was rain over the Channel. The summer of 1940 was not all 'wall-to-wall' sunshine as some people seem to remember. Ricky Wright was credited with damaging a lone recce Ju88 between Tunbridge Wells and Hastings that afternoon. I was with him and got in a few shots at the fleeting machine, and I must have believed I had hit it for I noted 'one Ju88 damaged' in my log-book. Then I found myself in cloud and lost sight of Ricky as he continued the pursuit. I was flying Hurricane R4118, of which more later. According to Luftwaffe records there was a Ju88 from III/LG1 that was severely damaged over southern England and returned to its base with one wounded crew member, although I believe 238 Squadron had a similar claim. The Junkers was, in the event, so badly hit that it had to be written off.

There was nothing much happening on the 14th either, but this was but the lull before the storm which exploded on the RAF on the 15th. The morning had remained fairly quiet but sometime after 11.15 the scramble call came and 605 were vectored onto three formations of bombers, attacking the first of these near Maidstone. Archie destroyed a Do17 and probably a He111. Bunny shot down a 109, two Dorniers and damaged a Heinkel, while Mike Cooper-Slipper [above] bagged a Dornier, with Sergeant H N Howes probably getting another and Pilot Officer E J Watson putting holes in one more.

Mike had quite an afternoon. As he went into the attack he came under return fire from the bombers and had his controls shot away. It must have been a frightening few moments as a Dornier loomed up in front of him, knowing he had no way of avoiding it. Surviving the unavoidable collision Mike found himself spiralling down, the port wing of his Hurricane missing, but he managed to bale out and reached the ground safely at Church Farm, Marden, while his Hurricane (L2012) crashed at The Leas, Yalding, Kent.

The unfortunate Dornier was a machine from 5/KG3 which crashed at Widehurst Woods, Marden. Two of the crew survived by baling out. Some years after the war, Bunny Currant recalled this incident, saying:

'Now, Cooper-Slipper, he was a lucky chap. We attacked a formation of German bombers. I was leading the squadron at the time, and I got there with plenty of height on the port side of the German aircraft which were coming this way, and we did a beam attack from above; I led with Cooper-Slipper being my number two.

'I took the first Vic of bombers, fired at them, broke straight down beneath them, looked up, and when I looked up there was one Dornier going round slowly with one wing off, and alongside it a Hurricane going round very, very much quicker, because it was a little aeroplane, also with one wing off; then a parachute suddenly appeared.

'When we got back Cooper-Slipper was missing. He was only 19 at the time and later he rang up to say he was all right and was down in Kent somewhere, and he came back and brought me a German mae west. What happened was, he actually dived and hit the wing-root of the Dornier, glanced off it upside down, into an inverted spin with one wing off. All he had to do was to open his hood, undo his straps, and he shot out because of the inverted spin, like a cork out of a bottle, quite unhurt. He was very lucky.'

According to the squadron diary, Mike brought back two German life vests and a rubber boat (dinghy!) that were given to him by the Maidstone police. One story was that he landed close to some Kentish hop pickers who were not far off lynching him before he was able to convince them he was English.

Mike was a character in those days – quite mad – but he quietened down a lot in later life. We also had Eric Jones shot down on the 15th but he too baled out over Plaxtol, near West Malling, with only slight injuries. You will remember that Eric left us his memories of 15 August in chapter two, now I can add what he also remembered of 15 September:

'We took off about 11.20, just before lunch and I was shot down half an hour later. The 15th September was of course Battle of Britain Sunday and I think the RAF claimed to have shot down 180 enemy aircraft. It was a very busy day.

'I was shot down by cannon fire from, I can only assume, a Me109 fighter as they were escorting bombers. My aircraft was shot from the rear. I know they were firing with 20 mm cannon because they [later] took a 20 mm nose cap out of my firearm in an operation performed in the evening of the event. I had the nose cap for years until it disappeared from my office. I was not, to my knowledge, fired at by the German bombers that were in front of me.

'I have always estimated that I must have been hit [while] at a speed in excess of 300 mph. I was hit at a height of 18,000 feet, in the Maidstone-Sevenoaks patrol line, whilst commencing an attack on a formation of Dornier bombers. At the time I was in full fine pitch and my throttle was "through the gate" and the last thing I remember doing before trying to escape was pushing the stick forward and to the left to avoid the rest of my flight who were [approaching] rapidly to attack the bombers; the cannon shell entered my left elbow and down my forearm. It lodged just above the wrist, so the throttle was never closed.

'My uniform was completely soaked in glycol so I unleashed my harness and slid the canopy open but it immediately closed as I hadn't locked it. I started to dive towards the earth, pulled the canopy open again and at the same time stuck my head out. The force of the speed of the aircraft – the engine was on full power – sucked me out and I came to in my parachute swinging peacefully backwards and forwards. I managed to get clear of the aircraft at an estimated height of 3,000 feet and lost my boots and gauntlets.

'There was just silence. No aircraft noise and no wind. As I looked around I saw a column of white smoke about a mile or so away, where my aircraft had hit the ground. I was drifting towards a building, Old Soar Manor, and the house next door. I drifted over a line of tall trees and then suddenly I was on the ground, on my back, and watching a green apple roll along the ground. I had landed in an apple orchard.

'I was shot down over a little village in Kent called Plaxtol. It was the only place I really knew in Kent because a group of pre-war pilots from our flying school went down to the thatched cottage of a farm at Plaxtol for a weekend of horse riding. I staggered up and to a gate that I climbed from the front garden of Old Soar Manor. To my relief people immediately recognised me as an RAF pilot and escorted me, with the assistance [of those] next door into the manor where they gave me hot tea and comfort. They bandaged my arm and at my request put me to bed where I immediately fell asleep. I was awakened somewhere between 3 and 4 pm by the arrival of an ambulance driver, and was taken to Wrotham Cottage Hospital, where I met Jack Fleming from our squadron who had been shot down some days earlier.'

Eric did not return to the squadron for some weeks, only to be shot down again in November. He eventually became an instructor in South Africa. Upon his return to England he converted to Mosquito aircraft and, in 1943, actually returned to 605 which was by then flying night intruder sorties over Europe. Later still he became a chief flying instructor at Debret, Canada, till just after the war.

It was about this time that we became aware that something serious was in the air. We know now that the intelligence boys were warning Churchill that an invasion might well be imminent. The Germans had been steadily assembling large numbers of barges and landing craft in harbours along the French coast, and if they were going to come this year, it would have to be before the autumn weather set in. Bomber Command had been raiding the barges in these ports all the time.

I remember one morning we were called to readiness at dawn, that, as usual, was very early, and we were sitting in our Hurricanes on the airfield in the eerie light of morning. Dawn came and there wasn't a sound to be heard. It was a strange morning and an equally strange feeling as I looked along the line of silent aircraft each with a familiar face peering over the rim of the cockpit looking distinctly apprehensive. Sitting about were our ground crews ready to start up the machines, as each fighter had its trolley accumulator plugged in ready for contact. The only sound in my ears was some soft music from Henry Hall's music show made possible because we could tune the aircraft's radio into the BBC with our early sets. It was all very surreal.

Why were we sitting here, in our aircraft, half an hour before sun-up on stand-by? Someone had the answer, or at least, we hoped they did. Was the balloon about to go up? If it was the invasion, then God help us.

In fact nothing happened and an hour after dawn we were told to stand down and get ourselves some breakfast. What the alert was all about we never found out, but it was the only time I felt that we could soon be in for it. There was no other time I had any doubts that we would win in the end.

I am uncertain as to the date of this episode but I'm sure it was after the 15th. On the 16th things once again remained relatively quiet although we did have a morning alert and one of our pilots was shot down and wounded. This was Pilot Officer E J Watson, downed by a Messerschmitt 109 over Detling. Although he was wounded he made a creditable forced landing. Watty came from Dundee and had been a pre-war airman under-training. Following his pilot courses he had been another to join 605 at the beginning of August. I found out much later that he had been shot down by no less a personality than Oberst Werner Mölders, commander of JG51. Watty was his 38th victory in WW2, his 52nd if one counts his victories during the Spanish Civil War and he would go on to amass an amazing 115 in all. Watty did not return to the squadron and I heard later that he was killed in Burma in early 1942, flying Hurricanes with 135 Squadron.

Croydon was a great place to be for us, with London not far away. I could also slope off home, which in retrospect was more dangerous than staying on the airfield. With my parents living so close to Battersea Power Station and the huge Clapham Junction rail complex, the whole place was a potential target. In fact our house was damaged a bit, broken windows, a few tiles off, etc. On one visit I noticed barrage balloons were floating in the air above Clapham Common, on which there were also anti-aircraft guns sited. Kids used to collect shards of shrapnel from exploded AA shells each morning after a raid.

The trains never stopped running. All I had to do was to get myself along to Wadden station, which was less than half a mile from the airfield's main gate, and within 15 minutes I could be at Clapham Junction. From there it was just a short walk to our house, less than five minutes. I always remember my parents' faces when I turned up one morning soon after coming down to Croydon, they still blissfully thinking their one and only child was safe up in Scotland. They were anxious about me then, but of course, I, at 20 years old, didn't even consider how they might have felt. So instead of being welcomed, it was rather a case of, what are you doing here? Is there something wrong? They would probably have preferred it if I had an arm in a sling or a bandage around my head, knowing then that I would be out of danger, for a while anyway.

A few days later Archie McKeller was awarded a Bar to his DFC which was the cause of another party at the Greyhound. He was all but leading the squadron now, with Churchill still nursing his wound. His citation in the *London Gazette* read:

> *During a period of eight days in the defence of London, Flight Lieutenant McKeller has destroyed eight hostile aircraft, bringing his total to twelve. He displays an excellent fighting spirit, is a particularly brilliant tactician and has led his squadron with skill and resource.*

A strange story emerged following an action on 24 September. Jock Muirhead, in Hurricane R4118 and one of our Poles, Witold Glowacki (P3832 UP-P), were patrolling over Beachy Head shortly after 4 pm, when they ran into a Dornier 17z returning from a raid on London, on this cloudy day. This appears to have been a machine from 2/KG76, but as the leader of Yellow Section later reported he saw it fall into the sea five miles south-west of Cap Gris Nez. The problem is that this Dornier did not end up in the sea but was written off after a crash-landing at its base with one wounded crewman aboard. So unless Jock misidentified his prey – only a He111 was reported lost over the sea – the aircraft got home, although written off in its crash-landing.

It was impossible to question Glowacki as he did not return. Probably the explanation is that although the German aircraft appeared to be heading for the sea, its end may not have been positively witnessed due to the arrival of some Me109s. However, the Intelligence Report does make it seem as though the bomber ditched:

'Two Hurricanes (Yellow Section) 605 Squadron left Croydon at 1541 hours on 24 September with orders to patrol Beachy Head, angels 10. While flying east near Beachy Head at angels 12, they saw a Do.215 at angels 14, in cloud, also flying east. These clouds were more in the nature of mist down to 12,000 feet with visibility of about 1,000 yards. Yellow 1 and Yellow 2 climbed and overhauled the Do.215 rapidly, Yellow 1 attacking with a 3-second burst from starboard $1/4$ from underneath, but observed no result. Yellow 2 then attacked from the port quarter with a similar attack. The enemy aircraft then jettisoned 10 bombs from the rear compartment and six from the front, which probably fell into the sea. Yellow 1 then made an astern attack after which both of its engines were on fire; it lost height, and Yellow 2 made a further attack while the enemy aircraft was losing height. Yellow 1 and Yellow 2 followed it down just below cloud base, which in mid-Channel was 1,000 feet, and saw it crash into the sea 5 miles SW of Cap Gris Nez. At this moment 4 Me109s appeared overhead, so Yellow 1 and Yellow 2 dropped down to sea level and crossed the French coast at Ambleteuse. After this, Yellow 1 did not see Yellow 2. The Me109s attacked Yellow 1 over land, so he hedge-hopped east for 15-20 miles, then turned south-west, shook off the Me109s and crossed the coast again between Boulogne and Le Touquet, climbing into cloud at 12,000 feet, and returned to Croydon 1725 hours.

'While low flying, Yellow 1 was fired at by only a few ground defences, the fire consisting of red cannon.'

Jock insisted that his missing wingman share in the victory and of course, we had no idea about what had happened to Witold. He was just over a month short of his 27th birthday and survived being shot down, crash-landing at Ambleteuse, near Marquise. It is not totally clear what happened to him subsequently and from some photographs which were taken at the time, and later came to light, it must have been spectacular, as the rear half of the fuselage was on top of the front portion, but with the rudder facing completely the wrong way round.

Also in the photographs is Witold sitting on the wing, another with him standing by it. The picture that appears in this book shows him with blood around his right eye and cheek, looking understandably dejected, while other photos I've seen have him with some form of bandage round his head and eye and standing upright. All we know then is that he died. Some reports say he suffered an allergic reaction to an anti-tetanus injection, while another suggestion is not particularly palatable. In any event, pilots of LG1 attended his burial at Guines.

I spoke earlier of Hurricane R4118. This machine had joined us up at Drem and Bunny had actually flown it down to

Croydon on 7 September. Several pilots used it, perhaps Jock Muirhead mostly. Jock was flying it on his action off the French coast. Archie Milne would bag a 110 with it on 27 September and I was in it while damaging two Ju88s in September.

What makes this particular Hurricane famous, was that after serving with 605 it then became a training aircraft until finally, after a complete overhaul, it was shipped off to India to help train Indian Air Force pilots. However, by the time it and others like it were made available, the RAF and IAF were no longer using Mark I Hurricanes and it remained in its packing case till after the war.

By then most of this stuff was being destroyed but as luck would have it, R4118 was given to the Banaras Hindu University, a town some 150 miles south-east of Lucknow, and 300 miles north-west of Calcutta. It was given so that the engineering students at the university could receive instruction on the Rolls-Royce Merlin engine. The engine was therefore removed and the airframe left more or less to rot into the ground. After nearly 60 years of heat and tropical monsoon weather, it was discovered by Peter Vacher who was visiting the university to look at some vintage cars which were stored there.

After much haggling and Indian paper work, Peter got it back to England and actually managed to restore it to flying condition. By then its identity had been established and of course, Peter was keen to find anyone still around who might have flown it in 605 Squadron. He found Bunny, Peter Thompson and me. I remember sitting in this rusting hulk shortly before work began, and I thought it an impossible task, but Peter and his team of helpers did it. R4118, back in its full 1940 war-paint took to the skies again in December 2004, 64 years after the Battle and 61 years since it was last flown.[1]

The squadron diary describes 27 September as a 'Great Day for the Squadron'. It began when, after scrambling from our very domestic dispersal area, rushing from our deckchairs in the garden, we found 12 Me110s flying over Kenley at 18,000

---

[1]The full story is told in Peter's excellent book *Hurricane R4118, The Extraordinary Story of the Discovery and Restoration of a Great Battle of Britain Survivor*, published by Grub Street in 2005.

feet. This was the day Archie Milne shot down a 110 flying R4118.

These 110s were in one of their famous defensive circles, and either they were lost or were perhaps waiting for bombers to escort. Anyway we went in and we managed to shoot down several of them. They were heavily engaged by all sorts of RAF squadrons apparently, 17, 32, 602, 249, 46 and even 1 RCAF Squadron, all of whom seemed to claim something. The 110 unit was V/LG1 whose CO, Hauptmann Liensberger, was among those shot down. In all about six 110s went down in this scrap and several others limped back home badly mauled. In fact, I am told that V/LG1 never flew again in the Battle because it had been so decimated.

I had sent fire into a 110 and was just starting to line it up again for another burst, when suddenly there was an almighty bang and my engine blew up. I immediately thought, OK, that's it, time to get out. Anyway I quickly realised that the Hurricane was not burning although there was a lot of glycol coming out – poisonous stuff – so I thought I'd stay with it for a bit longer.

I had done all the right things, turned the petrol off, turned on the oxygen so I could breath, then looked down for a place to land. When contemplating any sort of forced landing one always tries to find the biggest field available and there, right below me was a large open area, so down I went. The engine of course had stopped but the wheels and flaps came down and although I had no idea where I was I put the thing down without further mishap. As I trundled to a halt this airman appeared. I was a bit surprised to see anyone so quickly let alone an airman. I climbed out of my aircraft and the man asked if I was all right and I confirmed that I was, but asked him where I was, and he told me Gatwick. Later I wondered if some German gunner, seeing me falling away with a dead engine and streaming glycol smoke claimed me – that is if he was one of those who got home.

As I landed I could see an Me110 burning by the side of the field but whether this was the one Archie Milne had claimed I don't know. My airman friend pointed to the burning 110 and he asked me if I had shot it down. I replied that I didn't know for sure. Then he said, 'I just wondered, Sir, it blew up and I have this chap's ear, if you would like it.' I declined gracefully, but that was how it was in those days, this man just thought that by offering me some poor dead German's ear he would be doing me a favour.

In all, Bunny, Archie Milne, and Sergeant Jan Budzinski claimed 110s destroyed, Ricky Wright claimed a probable, Cyril Passy and myself both claimed a damaged, so we were all pretty pleased with ourselves. Bunny's combat report gives more details of this action:

> I was Red 1 leading the Squadron which took off at 09.23 hours and ordered to patrol Base, angels 15. As we climbed for height I saw a ragged formation of approximately 14 enemy aircraft (twin-engined) at 15,000 feet, just East of Croydon, flying N.W. They were engaged by A.A. and some of our fighters. When at 8,000 feet we were ordered to watch Croydon and Kenley for dive-bombing aircraft at 7,000 feet. We continued to orbit both bases. A dog-fight was taking place above us at 18,000 feet between Me110s and Hurricanes. The Squadron was then ordered to go up to the dog-fight and give a hand. Squadron climbed to 18,000 feet and attacked in line astern a circle of 12 Me110s, which were now just south of Kenley. I attacked one Me110 from the port beam at 300 yards with one ring deflection and a 2-sec burst. The port engine burst into flames. Enemy aircraft turned left and climbed – I pulled my nose up and gave a 5-sec burst full beam at 300 yards. Enemy aircraft dived with port engine still in flames. I dived behind and gave a continual burst at 200 yards, no deflection, and expended my ammunition. Enemy aircraft pulled up out of the dive, stalled, and dived inverted, both engines on fire, and crashed into a field nearby a large wood and house 3 miles S.W. of East Grinstead. Confirmed by Red 2 and Yellow 1. No return fire experienced. Evasive tactics – turns. Normal markings. I landed at Base 1105 hours.

It is interesting to note that my Hurricane – V6699 – despite this blown engine, must have been quickly repaired by the people at Gatwick for it was flying again the next day, unfortunately with a sad ending.

I seem to remember Alec Ingle flew over and picked me up in a Magister. While I was on my way back to Croydon, the squadron was scrambled again at around noon and got up to

25,000 feet and for the first time found themselves above some Me109s which they were able to bounce. There were nine of them over north-east Kent, flying at 18,000 feet. They went into attack and upon landing, Bunny was not a happy one, for despite the favourable situation in which they found themselves, nobody could claim a kill with certainty. Sergeant Jones put in for a probable, while Passy, Cooper-Slipper, Bunny and Ricky were only able to record 109s as damaged.

When Alec and I landed in the Maggie, I was greeted by Walter Churchill with: 'Hello, I thought you'd had it! Nice to see you. Take the afternoon off.' Although this might sound very generous of him it was the way things had to be. There was no let up in 11 Group of Fighter Command throughout August, September and even into October. As I have said, 605 always had a full complement of pilots but never any surplus so unless something nasty happened to you, you just kept on flying day after day.

Alec Ingle, Mike Cooper-Slipper and Ralph Hope, to mention just three, were all shot down but baled out safely. They were all back in action the following day. As far as I was concerned my log-book tells me that on the 28th of September, the day after my unfortunate incident over Gatwick, I flew four times, two of which resulted in combats. Fortunately in those days psychiatrists and psychologists were in short supply and counselling unknown, otherwise we might all have been grounded due to combat stress. Instead, a few pints of beer in the Greyhound generally did the trick.

While I was relaxing in a bath and thinking how wonderful my CO was, the squadron was scrambled again, at 15.15, and encountered five Ju88s south-east of Croydon and chased them south. In this action one was shot down and they helped to bring down three others, seeing a fifth crash off Winchelsea.

Two new pilots arrived on the 27th, Pilot Officers Peter Parrott DFC and Derek Forde. Both came from 145 Squadron and both apparently had asked to be posted to 605, 145 having been languishing up in Scotland. I got to know Peter quite well. He had been lucky to survive an encounter with a He111 during the Dunkirk show. Its rear gunner had put a bullet into his coolant system, which like mine had begun to stream glycol. He was fortunate to make Dover before having to crash land, writing off a number of sheep in the field he chose, which upset the farmer somewhat. He seemed more concerned about who would recompense him for his lost sheep than Peter's lucky escape.

The next day Bunny got a 109 destroyed but we lost Flying Officer Peter Crofts – in my hastily repaired V6699 – while Flying Officer Ralph Hope had to bale out. He landed in an oak tree, thankfully unhurt.

Peter Crofts was 22, came from London and had joined the RAF via Cranwell as a flight cadet. He had earlier been a Blenheim pilot but responded to the call for fighter pilot volunteers after France fell and following a brief spell with 615 Squadron, joined us at Croydon on 13 September. He fell dead at Red Pale, near Dallington, killed in his parachute as he descended. The East Sussex Constabulary report from the Heathfield station noted that the Hurricane had appeared to explode just before it reached the ground, falling at Earl's Down, which is also by Dallington. His body was later discovered in a field some $1^1/_2$ miles away at South View Farm, found by Nurse Sheldon, who lived in a house nearby. He had received head wounds and both his legs and neck were broken. His parachute was also found some distance away.

His parents later put up a memorial to their son near the spot. Some years later the memorial was in need of attention and in 1974 a memorial cross was erected on the site and dedicated by none other than the present Lord Dowding, son of our 1940 commander-in-chief. Derek Hugh Tremenheere Dowding, who succeeded to the title after his father's death, had been at Cranwell with Peter, and they had trained together. Dowding had flown in the Battle with 74 Squadron. He died in 1992.

In the late afternoon of the 28th, Ricky Wright and I were sent off after a 'bogey', along with Archie Milne, but Archie became separated from us in cloud. Off Beachy Head we ran into a Ju88 that was attempting to bomb some shipping. We both attacked and scored hits on the raider before it too became lost in cloud. I was again flying R4118, that was coded UP-W.

On the 29th we said farewell to Walter Churchill who left us in order to take command of 71 Squadron. This was the first 'Eagle' squadron, manned by American volunteers as America was not yet in the war. Apart from his deteriorating eyesight he was also beginning to suffer from sinus problems.

In early 1941 he took command of RAF Valley and in 1942 he was flying operationally again from Malta. In August of that year he had planned some offensive actions from the island to Sicily and actually led the first one. On the second such sortie he was hit by flak and crashed in flames, being buried in Syracuse War Cemetery.

Churchill's place was taken by Archie McKeller, a popular move, and Jock Muirhead took over B Flight. Bunny was still A Flight's boss, and he was awarded the DFC at about this time. His citation read:

> *This officer had led his flight with great skill and courage in air combats in the defence of London. He has destroyed seven enemy aircraft and damaged a number of others. His splendid example and fine fighting spirit have inspired the other pilots in his flight.*

Thus September ended. The Battle was still far from over or won, but we certainly had the feeling we were winning. In the three weeks since arriving at Croydon, and having watched with some trepidation the smoke and flames over London, we had taken part in some of the most intensive flying any of us had known. All of us knew only too well that each day might be our last, although we tried not to dwell on such thoughts. It was always unreal that we woke from our beds, in a civilian house, in what appeared to be a peaceful England, but that at any moment we might be fighting for our very lives several thousand feet above the Kent or Sussex countryside. The chill of autumn might soon be upon us, but the heat of battle was still hot.

Our reverie would quickly be shattered if some airmen started up a Merlin engine at the bottom of the garden before the tea arrived. Dawn was just breaking and one looked at the clock by the bedside, disbelieving the hour. Surely we had only just gone to bed!

Chapter Four

Dangerous Skies

The official date of the Battle of Britain ran to the end of October 1940, and for us at Croydon and all the other fighter squadrons in and around southern England, there was no let up. The nature of the battle was changing, however. The Luftwaffe's bomber units had been suffering badly during August and September and tactics now altered somewhat. While there were still bombing raids to engage, we began to meet more and more fighters. Hermann Göring was still desperately endeavouring to fulfil his promise to his Führer to defeat the RAF so that an invasion could take place. By this time, however, he and Hitler had metaphorically missed the boat and his plans had been put on hold. Göring was now trying to save some face by trying to knock out as much of Fighter Command as he could before the winter weather started to arrive.

He therefore instructed his fighter pilots to try and engage the RAF, and by flying what they called *Frei Jagd* (free hunting), they were no longer tied to escorting bombers and could seek out, chase and do battle with as many Spitfires and Hurricanes as they could find. The RAF quickly discovered that there was no percentage in combating mere fighters who could inflict no harm on London, factories or airfields on their own, so Keith Park was quite happy not to let this fighter versus fighter tactic turn simply into a war of attrition. Once the Germans cottoned on to this, they began to send over their Messerschmitts with bombs strapped to their undersides, thereby making it a reason for us to tackle them before these bombs did any damage, however insignificant. What damage they could do might be slight but it was not something we, the RAF, could totally ignore. However, this was a dangerous game, made more so because the clear summer skies we had enjoyed were now starting to cloud over, and with Me109s lurking about, it became an even more hazardous place to be.

October began for 605 on a high note for on the 3rd the

squadron was released for the first time since arriving at Croydon and we pilots celebrated the fact by scooting over to the Greyhound for dinner.

Next day it was a mixture of rain and fog that gave us more respite. The only activity in the air was by lone raiders or recce aircraft, but we flew section patrols. On one of these Bunny and Archie Milne were vectored onto a Ju88 of II/LG1 just before 1 pm and shot it down into the sea off Dungeness.

Messerschmitts were over London on the 7th and in a fleeting dog-fight at about 10 am, Archie McKeller, Ricky and Jock each damaged a fighter, but Jock's Hurricane was hit and he had to bale out near Dartford. This day Oberleutnant Viktor Mölders, brother of Werner, a staffelkapitän with 2/JG51 was shot down at Doleham Farm, Guestling, force-landing to became a prisoner.

In mid-afternoon we were off again. We found a group of 15 Me109s but we failed to see another 40 or more 109s above and behind. Archie must presumably have known what he was doing, for he went down on the 15, and not surprisingly some of the upper lot began to come down to bounce us. We got a warning at the last moment and scattered. A dog-fight ensued and McKeller put in claims for four. I got one that fell near Lingfield, and Derek Forde damaged another, but Charles English didn't make it home. He fell near Brasted. His brother R H English would be killed flying with 3 Squadron in May 1941. Some of the 109s we engaged were from JG27 who were escorting bomb-carrying 109s of 4/LG2. JG27 lost two over the land, 501 Squadron putting a third into the sea off Sandgate. 4/LG2 also lost two aircraft.

When we initially heard the 'break, break, break!' we did just that. One never argued when you heard this instruction, or asked questions, so we turned in all directions. English, my No.2, must have been slow in breaking as his Hurricane was hit badly. He tried to get out but apparently his parachute got caught on the tail-plane and he crashed with his machine. Meantime, I went down as fast as I could then pulled out, looked around but it seemed as if nothing had happened. Then ahead of me, for some unearthly reason, was a 109 peacefully going home quite happily. After checking the sky all around me, I closed in and sat behind him, lined his silhouette in my gun-sight and shot him down. It was quite extraordinary, I don't know what he was doing. I think it must have been one of the bunch that attacked us, made a shot and figured he was done. Or perhaps he was one of the bomb-carriers, and having dropped his bomb, was going home for tea. His mind could not have been on the job, he just wasn't looking around. Anyway, he was going south towards home and he didn't make it. You can never relax when you are in action; that does not work. This chap had and paid the price.

Later in the afternoon 605 were flying at 27,000 feet near Biggin Hill and ran into more 109s. Archie bagged one while Ricky, Cyril and Budzinski shared another between them.

We were back in the fray on the 8th too. Bunny led A Flight off at 10.45 and he and I got a Ju88. We were rather unkind to this German crew for they were all alone and we managed to sneak up behind the bomber and shoot it down. Not particularly heroic but effective. We were near Gatwick when we spotted it – a machine from II/KG51 I'm told. It went down into a field at Toovies Farm, not far from Three Bridges.

Unknown to us then was that Tim Vigors of 222 Squadron was on the fringe of our action, as he later reported:

'I broke away from the squadron to attack a Ju88 which was diving to clouds. Hurricanes of 605 Squadron got there first and delivered attacks. The enemy aircraft went into clouds with one engine smoking. I flew on above the clouds and the enemy aircraft came out in front of me. I gave it a five second burst from 400 yards and the second engine poured out volumes of smoke. It turned on its side and dived into cloud. One Hurricane followed it down and saw it crash.'

A couple of days breather, then on the 12th Alec Ingle and Sergeant Harry Howes each shot down a 109, both going into the sea off Dungeness. Unfortunately we lost Sergeant P R C McIntosh. Although hit over the sea McIntosh came down and crashed by Littlestone golf course. Croydon had been a great base for him as he was a local lad and was only a couple of months younger than me. He is buried in St John's churchyard, Croydon.

Then we lost Ralph Hope on the 14th. It was a day of low cloud and drizzle and although 109s were about, so were a few lone raiders. One such raider, a He111, was chased by Ralph who inadvertently flew into the Inner Artillery Zone south of London, where his Hurricane struck a barrage balloon cable, crashed at South Norwood and he was killed.

We were up against more 109s on the 15th. We were sent off to patrol over Maidstone at 28,000 feet, taking off at 08.25 that morning. We found an estimated 'balbo' of around 50 Messerschmitts at 23,000 feet with another eight hovering four miles behind them at around 32,000 feet, all flying roughly north-west.

Bunny was leading and he made a perfect attacking manoeuvre, bringing the squadron through south and then round to the left, thereby allowing the sections in the front to dive on the leading 109 formation. This is my combat report, dictated to our intelligence officer, Flying Officer Price, and typed out by him:

> Whilst patrolling with No.605 Squadron at 28,000 ft, and flying S.W. in sections vic astern, we sighted 40 to 50 Me109s flying N.W., approaching the Thames Estuary, at 23,000 ft. We turned through South and came down in a diving beam attack, developing into a quarter attack. As we were diving on them they broke up. I did a beam attack on one aircraft, but noticed no result. I then commenced an astern attack on another Me109, opening fire at 200 yards. I closed slowly to 100 yards. The Me109 must have then throttled back, as I closed rapidly, firing the whole time, and eventually overtook him. I could see my ammunition striking, and as I passed he stalled, fell on to his back, and went down in a spin.

Three of us were given probables, Cyril and Ricky, getting the other two, while Bunny damaged two and Pilot Officer Jimmy Hayter another. Hayter, a New Zealander, who had flown bombers in France, was yet another volunteer to help Fighter Command, who was then himself shot down. He took to his parachute and came down into the grounds of Great Swifts, the home of Major Victor Cazalet, interrupting a cocktail party, to which he was promptly invited! He continued to have an interesting and varied war, collecting a DFC and Bar along the way.

The day ended tragically as we realised that our second missing pilot, Jock Muirhead had not been so fortunate. He had disappeared in the fight and later came the news that he had been shot down near Gillingham and had not survived. He was 27. We had no firm idea what had happened to Jock but according to eye-witnesses he was coming down with smoke trailing from his engine, seemingly trying to land somewhere. However, at about 1,000 feet or thereabouts the Hurricane suddenly burst into flames. He was seen trying to get out of the cockpit but just didn't make it.

It was almost the same predicament in which I had found myself over Gatwick on 27 September, but on that occasion luck was with me; poor Jock's ran out and he was killed.

The squadron were up against more 109s on Sunday, the 20th, at 10 in the morning. Twenty Messerschmitts were found over Ashford at 28,000 feet, which was some 2,000 feet above us. They didn't hesitate to attack and a scrap quickly developed. Archie was the only one to score significantly, claiming one destroyed and another damaged. Peter Thompson damaged another but one got him, shooting away his propeller. Pilot Officer J H Rothwell had some of his controls shot away along with half the canvas on one side of his Hurricane ripped away. However, both men made very creditable landings back at Croydon. Of interest is Archie McKeller's combat report:

I was leading Turkey Squadron on a standing patrol on the Maidstone line at 20,000 ft. Control informed me that Bandits were approaching me at angels 20. As I have found from experience that these heights are always at least 5,000 ft underestimated, I informed control that I would climb up higher; this was approved. Control then passed me information that 20 Bandits were South of me, heading 340°. Shortly after this, about 20 enemy aircraft flew over us at angels 28, while we were at 26,000 ft and flying S.E. I turned the Squadron to fly West so that I could gain more height and at the same time be into the sun and behind them, also checking up as best I could that there were no more enemy aircraft behind the first lot.

The enemy aircraft then turned and came down to attack Turkey Squadron. I therefore ordered a defensive circle to the right, and before this could be completed the Me109s were down on the last two of the formation. I, however, was in a fairly good position to attack the

leading attacker from astern, my No.2 protecting my tail.
By this time all the Me109s had turned South and were
going home, some of them down to our level. I followed,
attacking the original enemy aircraft, and could see my
De Wilde [incendiary ammunition] hitting and pieces
flying off his wings and fuselage as well as puncturing his
cooling system, as dense glycol steam could be seen
coming from his radiator; he, however, started to climb
and I could not keep up with him. By this time I had
followed up to 28,000 ft. Another Me109 was spotted at
about 26,000 ft. I therefore did a diving beam, following
into an astern attack closing to approximately 50 yards.
I could see that the enemy aircraft was being badly hit, as
pieces were flying off in all directions. It went into a
spiral and crashed near a farmhouse in the New Romney
district.

This latter 109 crash-landed at North Fording House, near
New Romney at 10.20 am and came from 9/JG54. The NCO
pilot had been wounded and he was taken prisoner.

Honours were roughly even on the 22nd. Twelve
Hurricanes had taken off at 14.41 and were ordered to patrol
between the two airfields of Biggin Hill and Kenley at 20,000
feet. We were flying in flights, line abreast, and with a weaver
behind and slightly below the squadron. A Flight was on the
right, B Flight on the left. We gained height slightly. Then over
Tunbridge Wells we spotted seven or eight Me109s a couple of
thousand feet above, flying to the south-east. We began an
attempt to close the gap; I was flying Red Three in Bunny's
section.

The next thing I knew five more 109s were spotted
approaching from the north-east and trying to position
themselves round and behind us. Then two of the Messerschmitts started to dive down from out of the sun attempting
to bounce our rear pair. The squadron began to form a
defensive circle but a fight was inevitable. One 109 opened up
and hit Archie Milne's machine and he had to make a forced
landing near Dorking. He had a slight back wound but in
coming down he fractured his hip-bone. Ricky Wright, Yellow
Two, evened things up by knocking pieces off another 109. He
followed it down, seeing its hood fly off, with other bits and
pieces coming away, but then he lost it in haze near

Dungeness. We reformed above Gatwick and went home. Once back on the deck, and talking over the action, it was decided that the attacking 109s had managed to split themselves from the main formation, and remained as something of a decoy.

Our Canadian found himself in Redhill hospital, and a German pilot who had also been shot down, ended up in the same ward. An auxiliary nurse, Miss Non Williams, with the Queen Alexandra's Royal Army Nursing Corps, had been on her way to the hospital and had seen Archie coming down, so when she later went into this particular ward, there she discovered both men.

She nursed Archie [above] while he remained there and their relationship blossomed, and later they got married and she returned to Canada with him at the war's end. She died sometime in 2004 and he died two years later.

One day in October, a cloudy day, we'd had a running fight with some 109s and I came down through the cloud ready to go home. Fighter pilots are not renowned for their navigational ability unless one has a railway line to follow or can spot some well known landmark. It is easy to become lost. Often what we did when we had flown out over the Channel was just fly due north until we hit the south coast, then continue on till we hit the railway line that ran from Ashford to Redhill. It was dead straight, you just couldn't miss it.

Once there you would find other aircraft doing the same thing, and as the pilots flew along they would begin to peel off for Biggin Hill or Kenley, while we would turn for Croydon. Slight exaggeration I suppose but basically true. This one day I saw the coast coming up and as I passed over it, checked with my compass and thought to myself, that's funny, it looks as though I'm flying south, my compass must be all wrong, and realized I had upset the whole thing during my recent gyrations. Suddenly there was a Boom, Boom, Boom! and black smoke puffs appeared off to one side. I was just questioning the parentage of those gunners who couldn't distinguish between a Hurricane and a Messerschmitt, when I thought, Oh yes they can, I know what's happening, I'm heading for Paris and not London at all. I quickly reversed my course and it felt an extremely long way home and I arrived at Croydon fairly late. The only reception I received when I got back to the mess was from the mess steward who said, 'Sorry, Sir, I'm afraid your too late for lunch.'

It was a beautiful day on 26 October and the squadron flew three times. On the second of these, the boys dived on 16 Me109s they found at 27,000 feet near Mayfield. Archie McKeller got one and Alec Ingle probably another.

At around noon we were off again and again my combat report tells of the action as I saw it:

> Whilst patrolling in pairs with 605 Squadron at 27,000 ft, we sighted 12-16 Me109s flying N.W. at approximately the same height. We attacked from the port quarter developing into a stern attack. The majority of the enemy commenced to climb, a few however, dived down. I followed one of them down closing gradually. At about 17,000 ft he straightened out. I gave him a burst and noticed my ammunition hitting him. He immediately commenced to dive again and I followed him down giving him several short bursts. When at 11,000 ft I closed rapidly to 75 yds, and gave him a 5-sec burst. Pieces fell off the machine and he turned over on his back and dived almost vertically through the clouds. I followed him through but lost him. The position was approximately between Woodchurch and Tenterden.

I was only credited with a damaged although I thought I deserved at least a probable. Nobody did any better, for McKeller, Spud Hayter and Cyril Passy could only claim 109s damaged as well. Cyril had to make a crash landing near Rotherfield with a damaged prop. He was OK but his Hurricane was wrecked.

During the last action at around 15.30, Spud Hayter spotted four Me109s, gave a call and immediately dived after them, but due to a faulty radio, nobody heard him. Finding himself alone with now four angry 109s, they ganged up on him and he was shot down and baled out near Cranbrook. This day also saw the last of our old R4118. Derek Forde was flying it when we attacked a load of 109s and some others came down on us. The Hurricane was hit but Derek got it back to Croydon and landed it safely. It was Cat. 2 damage, but although repairable, it was struck off our strength.

It was at this time that 605 were selected to be the first operational squadron to receive the Mark II Hurricane. All pilots like to think they are getting the best of any updated equipment and we began to look forward to their arrival.

Meantime, on the 27th during an early morning patrol the squadron ran into some 60 Me109s. These odds were pretty much what we were coming to expect and this was not helped by the fact that we were at 20,000 feet, while the 109s were at 25,000. Despite this we managed to make an attack and Archie McKeller and Ricky each claimed one. It was Archie's 20th victory and with the exception of two shared victories while he was flying with 602 Squadron in October 1939, all the others had been achieved since our arrival at Croydon. In addition he had several probably destroyed and damaged too.

In addition to these two 109s, Pilot Officer A M R Scott got a damaged while Alec Ingle reported a probable. He was unable to finish it off because another 109 pilot got him and he had to make a forced landing at Sewell's Farm, Barcombe. He ended up by the railway line and suffered the usual facial injuries on the gun-sight. Some soldiers from a nearby searchlight post came to his aid and patched him up before sending him on his way. His Hurricane, V7599, was in a bad condition. A hit in the oil feed line caused the main problem, and the forced landing had broken the propeller and buckled both wings and fuselage.

After some celebrations following our CO's high score, it is sad to record that within a few days he was killed. It was the first day of November. Bunny, for some reason, was leading the squadron and whilst flying into the sun at 25,000 feet near Faversham, the boys flew over 12 Me109s flying north-west, so turned and dived on them. In the ensuing mêlée Ricky and Rothwell each claimed a probable, while Peter Parrott, Harry Howes, Eric Jones and Peter Thompson all claimed 109s damaged. One Me109 was seen to crash into the sea off Ramsgate but it does not appear that the Luftwaffe lost any

machines at this time. Arriving home it became evident that
McKeller was missing and it was not long before a telephone
call confirmed his Hurricane had crashed near Addisham and
that he had been killed.

We had seen this crowd of 109s and we were way above
them, and we all heard Archie call to go down on them but we
were diving much too fast and the 109s saw us and as they
scattered we went right through them. A quick burst and then
we had overshot and they were gone. In these situations it is
best simply to break off and go home, I did anyway. I was
right behind Archie but it was then that I lost sight of him as
we all made rapid turns. We really had come in far too fast.
Archie, being Archie, no doubt thought to himself, 'No, I'm
going to chase these so and so's,' and that was the end of him.
A great loss.

The fight had been with JG27 at 0815 in the morning, and
it is thought that McKeller fell to the gruppenkommandeur of
its II Gruppe, Hauptmann Wolfgang Lippert. He had fought in
Spain where he gained four victories flying for General
Franco's forces against the Loyalists, and had also fought in
the French campaign before Dunkirk. He had become the
leader of II/JG27 in September 1940 having been awarded the
Knight's Cross. He would be shot down and captured in North
Africa in late 1941 and die of his injuries.

A skirmish the next day saw Harry Howes damage another
Me109, but the good news this week was due to Bunny, who
was notified that he had been awarded a Bar to his DFC:

*Since September, 1940, this officer has personally
destroyed six enemy aircraft and damaged several others,
bringing his total to thirteen. He has led his flight, and on
occasions his squadron, with great success, and shows a
sound knowledge of tactics against the enemy.*

Then we were honoured with a visit from the Duke of Kent on
8 November. In Ian Piper's history of 605 Squadron, *We Never
Slept*, published in 1996, he records the visit in some detail as
it was the cause of some amusement:

The Duke's visit was however the subject of much
amusement after he had a painful encounter with the
Squadron's adopted mascot, the imaginatively named Billy

the goat. The animal had a reputation for chewing the fabric off the parked Hurricanes and was therefore housed in a tent behind the Officer's Mess, being tethered by a long rope so that he could graze outside. The day of the Duke's visit was very foggy and his arrival time kept being put back until finally word came that he would be unable to attend after all. There was nothing for it but to start eating the feast that had been laid on for his tea, when soon afterwards there was a knock at the window of the Mess, and a very flustered airman panted, "He's here."

As the men straightened their uniforms and opened the French windows to greet His Royal Highness he appeared through a gap in the fence and seeing the men pouring out to meet him, he stopped in front of Billy's tent and saluted. The goat was naturally incensed by a stranger stopping in front of his home, so he shot out behind the Duke and delivered a very shrewd blow to the royal behind.

The goat's horns were both long and sharp and he propelled him towards the group of men at high speed. The Duke, somewhat shaken by his encounter with the wretched creature was very good about it and belatedly joined the men for tea, although they do recall him rubbing his posterior from time to time. The punishment for the goat, if indeed there was any, is not recorded.

Derek Forde once got too near to this damn goat and it went for him, but Derek managed to jump back out of range of its tethering rope. Derek later told us he was lucky because, as he put it: 'God that was close. His horn missed my horn by about half an inch!'

Despite the royal visit, the squadron was still on duty and flew twice. On the second sortie we encountered scattered formations of Me109s over Maidstone and Alec Ingle and I each damaged one. My combat report is timed at 09.50:

Whilst on patrol with No.605 Squadron we were told that a number of bandits were crossing the coast at 21,000 ft flying North West. We flew North at 28,000 ft and saw them ahead and to the right. They were scattered over the sky mostly in twos and threes. Some of the bandits climbed up behind us into the sun. I turned into the sun and saw a Me109 crossing in front of me. I gave him a 2-second burst from the beam. He turned South and commenced to dive slightly. I gave him a 5 to 6 second burst from astern at about 250 yards, but saw no result. I then closed to 100 yards, and gave him several short bursts. I then noticed oil and glycol smoke pouring from him, but as I had used up all my ammunition and there were other bandits about I was unable to see the final result. I last saw him at about 18,000 ft diving slightly and heading South.

I gather we had encountered III Gruppe of JG26, or perhaps JG77; both had fighters damaged. One of our Poles who had only just joined us, Pilot Officer Czeslaw Tarkowski, was shot down in this engagement but he managed to survive unhurt although his Hurricane (N2646 UP-O) was lost. He had been flying at the rear of the squadron, guarding our tails, a job that also meant calling control every 15 seconds or so to give them our location. This may have been useful to the ground but it also made it difficult for pilots in such positions to receive every call over the R/T. It really was an unenviable job. Despite most tail-end-Charlies being new and therefore less experienced, they had to be constantly on the alert, continually changing throttle settings, keeping an eye on where we were, and maintaining radio ground control. Little wonder a number were shot down, having not the slightest idea of what had hit them.

On this occasion Tarkowski at least saw his enemy, Me109s flying in pairs. He also recognized the warning call of 'Bandits' and actually fired at one, but then he heard a terrific bang and the whole front of his Hurricane disappeared and fire engulfed the cockpit. Despite the choking smoke that was trying to blind him, he slid back the hood as another burst of gunfire hit his machine. He kicked the stick and with a sudden jolt appears to have been ejected into space and lost consciousness.

He had gone out at around 25,000 feet, very high for a bale out as the oxygen level is way down but luckily he came round at about 16,000 feet and landed safely in a tree near Sissinghurst Court. People helped him down although they thought he was a German, but once his nationality was cleared up, they gave first aid to the burns on his face and he was given a wonderful lunch.

On Armistice Day, Alec destroyed a 109 north of Rye during a squadron encounter with seven Messerschmitts, the fight beginning near Sevenoaks and ranging across Kent. This was a machine from the 9th Staffel of JG53. The German pilot, Oberleutnant J Volk was wounded and baled out to become a prisoner. After the action Alec made out the following combat report:

> I was flying Blue 1. The Squadron was flying at 25,000 ft near Sevenoaks. Several Me109s passed below and F/Lt Currant led the Squadron in to attack. In view of my position I decided, after diving 2,000 ft, that I could not contact these enemy aircraft and pulled up again to approximately 24,000 ft. I headed South East for about 10 minutes and called up control to find out if any further enemy aircraft were at my height. Just as I had made this call I saw 2 Me109s appear in front of me travelling West to East. I attacked the second one and in the ensuing dog fight in which Blue 2 and Green 3 as well as a 253 Squadron aircraft joined, I got in two deflection shots of about 2 seconds each. The evasive action taken consisted of diving, climbing, half-rolling and pulling out and at one time flying inverted for about 5 seconds. Eventually two of the aircraft involved headed the enemy aircraft in my direction in a climb from which he flattened out. I got directly astern during the climb and gave him a 9-second burst closing from 200 to 50 yards. Large pieces of the aircraft broke off from the port wing root and the aircraft caught fire inside the cockpit. The pilot baled out and landed four miles North-North-East of Rye. My No.2 had kept with me all this time and confirms these events as does also Blue 3.

Celebrations for this victory coincided with more booze with the announcement that Mike Cooper-Slipper and Ricky Wright had been awarded the DFC and DFM respectively. Mike's citation read:

> *Flying Officer Cooper-Slipper has displayed great skill and daring in air combat. On one occasion he deliberately rammed and destroyed a hostile aircraft after his own controls had been practically shot away. He has*

destroyed seven enemy aircraft and damaged three others.

I am not sure Mike would have agreed with the deliberate ramming, for he had told us it was '... an accident, not design, a complete and utter accident.' Deliberate ramming sounded a lot more courageous! Ricky's well deserved – Immediate – DFM citation noted:

> *This airman, since 605 Squadron have been at Croydon, has shown great skill and personal courage and a fine devotion to duty. He has been wholly or mainly responsible for the destruction of six aircraft. He has probably destroyed three more himself and damaged a further six. He has led his section at all times with the greatest efficiency, showing fine qualities of leadership and a sound knowledge of tactics.*

It was obviously a time for awards and the announcement of the Distinguished Service Order to Archie McKeller caused a sombre moment. He would have been very proud. Mike was also lost to us following his posting to the Central Flying School at Upavon to become an instructor. He was later to fly in the defence of Singapore and Sumatra and was lucky to escape capture and return to Ceylon. After the war he became a test pilot in Canada and once retired remained in Vancouver until his death in 2004.

The day after this great but sad news, Lord Trenchard made a visit to us and I am sure we kept him well away from our goat's quarters. The enemy were no respecter of high-placed visitors and during his stay the squadron were scrambled and chased eight Me109s out over Folkestone, Peter Thompson claiming to have damaged one, a machine from JG53.

I did not fly on 15 November, a day when the squadron were once more heavily involved with Me109s over the south-east. The boys were patrolling at 09.30 that morning and were vectored to 50 Me109s over the North Foreland area. Once they spotted them, seven or eight split away from the main bunch and turned south, with 605 chasing hard. Later seven or eight more also split from the larger group and also turned south, placing our Hurricanes between both these sections which was not a pleasant situation. The 109s from the second section closed in and attacked, shooting down Pilot Officer Gauze, who was killed, and Eric Jones, who baled out near Tilmanstone, inland from Deal. Czeslaw Gauze had only been with us for a few days. Although Polish, this 22-year old had been born in Brazil. He is buried in Whyteleafe cemetery, just down the hill from Kenley aerodrome.

We rarely if ever knew who we were fighting in these deadly battles unless some intelligence officer found out from a prisoner, and the news filtered down to us. Post-war historians can often research who was fighting who, and who got who. In this particular action it is now known that the 109s were from JG53 and JG26. The former unit claimed one of our Hurricanes, while the leader of JG26's Staff Staffel and gruppenkommandeur, Adolf Galland, got the other, although he does not appear to have had it confirmed. By this time he had over 50 victories.

Shortly before 1 pm the boys were off again to patrol over Gravesend and found nine Me109s at 20,000 feet, which was below them. These appear to have been bomb-carrying 109s from II/JG54. For once our Hurricanes made a perfect attack and Bunny, Ricky and Harry Howes each claimed one, with Sergeant H W Pettit getting a probable, and Pilot Officer A J M Aldwinckle, a damaged. JG54 lost one of their aircraft, while JG26 had two pilots brought down and taken prisoner. Later, two more 109s collided over the Channel, one pilot being killed, the other rescued. News was received later that the 109 claimed by Aldwinckle, who had already seen action with 601 Squadron, was the one that force-landed at Eastchurch, Kent, its pilot taken prisoner. Aldwinckle had an interesting pre-war history, having been born in Argentina of British parents, educated in South Africa and then sent to the college of engineering at Chelsea, London, and at Brooklands. His first job was with Imperial Airways, having become a licenced inspector in 1938. An F Reservist he had learned to fly pre-war and had completed his RAF training by September 1940.

The squadron received a telegram of congratulations from the AOC for this second action, but I assume no reference was made to the morning's showing.

The next few days remained fairly quiet and on the 23rd, Air Vice-Marshal Keith Park himself showed up at Croydon,

and took the opportunity to present DFC and DFM medals to
Bunny and Ricky. Yet again a VIP visit ushered in some air
actions. On the squadron's second, some 109s were
encountered but no engagement took place. On the third
patrol, in company with Gerry Edge's 253 Squadron, Sergeant
Pettit shot up a 109 between Lympne and Ashford. Hit
hard in this attack, the German pilot had surrendered in the
air by jettisoning his cockpit canopy, then began to glide
down towards the Romney Marshes, with Pettit in close
attendance.

However, Sergeant Ken Jones came upon the scene below
him, and assumed the Hurricane pilot was following the 109
because he was out of ammunition. Jones immediately
attacked, whereupon the 109 pilot made a hasty landing. The
Messerschmitt crashed into a row of trees next to Smeeth
railway station, mid-way between Ashford and Folkestone. It
burst into flames but the pilot, from the 5th Staffel of JG53,
managed to extricate himself without injury. Ken Jones, who
had joined us in mid-October, was a particular friend of Pettit,
and probably thought he was doing him a favour by finishing
off this kill.

Over recent days the squadron had started to receive its
promised and eagerly awaited Hurricane IIs. By 28 November
we had a total of nine on strength and this day was the first
time we flew them on a patrol. It is no exaggeration to say that
everyone was pleased with them. They had a Merlin XX engine
which gave us higher speeds and a much better rate of climb.

To add to our pleasure, Gerry Edge arrived on the 29th as
our new commanding officer. He was welcomed by all those
who remembered him from his earlier time with us, and those
who had not yet met him, but who knew of him by reputation.
His tally of victories with both 605 and 253 hovered around
the twenty mark, with several more claimed as probables and
damaged. Amazingly, apart from his DFC, awarded for his
actions with 605 over Scotland and France, he had received
nothing further, despite his claims for two Heinkels on 7
September, four Ju88s on the 9th, two more Heinkels and a
109 on the 11th, plus a Dornier and a Ju88 on the 15th. This
is 11 confirmed, plus one probable and one damaged. He
served with distinction for the rest of the war, in the Middle
East, later becoming SASO to our old friend Batchy Atcherley.

He helped with the planning of the invasion of Sicily, and then commanded 84 Group Control Centre in 1944, taking this unit into Normandy after the D-Day invasion, and later into Germany. He was at least made an OBE in January 1945. After the war he became a farmer in Kenya before retiring to England. He died in August 2000.

The squadron were again in trouble on the first day of December as German fighter sweeps continued over southern England. The squadron was scrambled at 10 am to patrol over Canterbury at 27,000 feet and were once more accompanied by 253 Squadron. They spotted several 109s below them and 253 attacked from head-on. As the German pilots turned away, one presented his stern to a 253 pilot and suffered hits before pulling away.

Our squadron went for two 109s although there were others overhead but they must have decided they could get in an attack before the upper Messerschmitts could do much to interfere. As 605 closed in the 109s poured on the coals and headed away and suddenly some unseen 109s hit us. Harry Howes' machine was hit and he had to dive away and make a crash-landing near Gravesend. Meantime, another 109 came down on Peter Parrott.

Squadron tactics had altered little since the fighting began and while some squadrons had already started to fly in pairs, or in fours in either echelon or in a line astern, we were still continuing with these confounded threes which were really no good at all and often a menace. Our only progress was that we had introduced, like other units, a weaver, who flew and weaved backwards and forwards behind the main squadron, keeping an eye open for the enemy. Peter once recorded:

'Flying in vics of three never changed while I was in 145 and certainly when I later joined 605, we were still flying in vics and were still flying them when I was shot down on 1 December. By that time we had got to the stage of having two weavers, one above and one below the squadron. I was hit when the squadron made a turn and baled out. The funny thing was and this was the measure of the whole wretched vics, the squadron landed back and somebody said, "Well, where's Peter?" Nobody knew where I was and no one had seen me shot down and they had continued on without a top weaver.'

It was not always the case that weavers could stay for a whole patrol even if not engaged, for their continued need to weave about, with the necessary use of throttle adjustments, generally meant they used up their fuel supply much more quickly. I mentioned this earlier when writing about Tarkowski. Mostly of course they warned the leader that they were having to break off and go home, but in this case, Peter had to go over the side before he could give any warning. Fortunately in this instance, it did not cause the squadron further problems.

Peter went down over Uckfield, landing at East Hoathly and the leader of 253, Squadron Leader R R Miller, who had just taken over from Gerry Edge, saw a 109 shoot down a Hurricane and although he went after it and claimed it as damaged, it got away. It appears the 109 pilots were from I/JG3 and they claimed both Hurricanes. One of the victorious Luftwaffe pilots was Hans Stechmann. He would end the war with 33 victories, mostly over Russia, and remain a senior NCO throughout, but he did receive the coveted Knight's Cross in September 1941. From 1942 he was an instructor and then a test pilot.

The Luftwaffe had not finished with us this day, for after lunch 605 and 253 again joined up during a patrol over Maidstone as several raiding plots had been reported. 253 had two of their aircraft shot about, one of which was crash-landed near Ashford although the other got home despite considerable damage. 605 had sighted four 109s near Dover meantime, with more above – the usual tale. Bunny and Spud Hayter each claimed one shot down, Bunny's victim going into the sea. The other 109s remained at height but eventually struck near Maidstone, Hauptmann Joppien of I/JG51 shooting down both Alec Ingle and Cyril Passy. Both of our chaps were wounded and both baled out. Hermann-Friedrich Joppien was kommandeur of I Gruppe of JG51 and his score at this time was around 30. In April 1941 it reached 40 and then 70 before he died in a crash on the Russian front in August of that year. He had received the Knight's Cross with Oak Leaves.

So this day we lost three Hurricanes with a fourth damaged, but luckily we suffered no pilots killed. JG51 had one of its Me109s go into the sea, presumably that claimed by Bunny. It was to be his last victory with the squadron and brought his score to 15 destroyed or shared destroyed, with several more damaged.

The fateful year of 1940 slowly dribbled away. Three days before Christmas we heard the news that Harry Howes had been killed. He had left us to return to 85 Squadron on 9 December and his death was all the more sad because it occurred in a flying accident. He had been with us since 12 September following that successful period of his over France. His Distinguished Flying Medal had been awarded for these actions during the Battle of France but he had shot down at least four more enemy aircraft while with us, with others damaged.

Our NCOs were the backbone of every fighter squadron and everyone was pleased when Ricky Wright's commission came through. If ever we had to travel by train together again, at least we could occupy the same first class compartment.

From time to time we had been able to use the Southern Railway Company's pavilion that adjoined the airfield, and permission was granted once again for the Christmas festivities so that all the men could congregate together, which they did on Christmas Eve. We officers repaired once more to the Greyhound in Croydon, finishing up back in the mess.

On Christmas Day, dinner was taken in three stages. Officers at 13.30, the men at 18.00 and NCOs 19.30. With the men's dinner, the officers and NCOs, as with tradition, waited on them. Fortunately, being so close to home, I was permitted to shoot off back to Clapham to spend the festivities with the family.

Christmas having come and gone, we all began to wonder what 1941 would bring. For all any of us knew, the spring weather would bring a renewal of Germany's offensive against this country. However, the Luftwaffe were now concentrating on night raids and with Fighter Command becoming even stronger with newly trained pilots being turned out from training schools and operational training units, and with Lord Beaverbrook's splendid work in heading the intensive plan for building Hurricanes and Spitfires at a tremendous rate, we felt that another phase of the Battle over Britain would at least be met with force. Luckily that didn't happen, but it took some time for it to sink in that they were, in fact, not coming back for more.

On the 30th, Air Chief Marshal Sholto Douglas, the new CinC of Fighter Command came to talk to us about the future thinking and planning for the new year, especially as we would be using our Hurricane IIs for offensive operations – he said! These would begin in early 1941, so perhaps official thinking was that the best form of defence was attack. We would see.

New Year's Eve was rather stilted as one of our pilots became ill with suspected meningitis so any thoughts of leave or a joyous party were stopped. In the event the chap got the all clear, but by that time, the day was over.

The summer of 1940 had been a momentous one for Britain and for her fighter pilots. Every year since the end of World War Two, Britain has celebrated the famous air victory achieved by 'The Few' and I am proud to have been one of them. My squadron did as much as any other and took the plaudits and the knocks. My comrades in 605 deserve a mention. They were:

Sgt J Budzinski	Polish	KW	Died in USA, c2006
S/L W M Churchill	British	DSO DFC	KIA 27 Aug 1942
F/O T P M Cooper-Slipper	British	DFC	Died 23 Feb 2004
F/O P G Crofts	British		KIA 28 Sep 1940
P/O C F Currant	British	DSO DFC & Bar	Died 12 Mar 2006
F/L G R Edge	British	OBE DFC	Died August 2000
P/O C E English	British		KIA 7 Oct 1940
F/O J Fleming	British	MBE	Died 1995
F/O D N Forde	British	DFC	Died 16 Jan 1979
P/O G M Forrester	British		KIA 9 Sep 1940
P/O W J Glowacki	Polish	VM 5th Class	Died 24 Sep 1940
F/O J C F Hayter	New Zealand	DFC & Bar	Died 3 Oct 2006
F/O R Hope	British		KIA 14 Oct 1940
Sgt H N Howes	British	DFM	KOAS 22 Dec 1940
P/O J S Humphreys	New Zealand		Died 1986
P/O A Ingle	British	DFC AFC	Died July 1999
Sgt K H Jones	British		PoW; Died 1997
P/O R E Jones	British		Died 1994
P/O P Kennett	British		KIA 11 Apr 1941
Sgt P R C McIntosh	British		KIA 12 Oct 1940
S/L A A McKeller	British	DSO DFC & Bar	KIA 1 Nov 1940
P/O S J Madle	British		Died 31 Jan 1984
P/O J A Milne	Canadian		Died Feb 2007
P/O I J Muirhead	British	DFC	KIA 15 Oct 1940
F/O P L Parrott	British	DFC & Bar AFC	Died 27 Aug 2003
F/O C W Passy[1]	British	DFC	Died 1971
Sgt H W Pettit	British		KIFA 2 Feb 1941

Sgt R Puda	Czech		Died Mar 2002
Sgt L F Ralls	British	OBE	Died 1976
Sgt R D Ritchie	British		KOAS 9 Aug 1940
P/O J H Rothwell	British		KIFA 22 Feb 1941
P/O K Schadtler-Law	Sth African		Died 1986
P/O A M W Scott	British		KIFA 2 Jan 1941
S/L D R Scott	British	AFC	KIA 8 Nov 1941
Sgt L C Sones	British		Died Feb 1993
P/O P D Thompson	British	DFC	Died 2 Mar 2003
P/O E J Watson	British		KIA 26 Feb 1942
Sgt E W Wright	British	CBE DFC DFM	Died Nov 2007

Notes:

VM = Virtuti Militari (5th class)
KW = Krzyz Waleczynch (Polish Cross of Valour)
CBE = Commander of the Order of the British Empire
OBE = Officer of the Order of the British Empire
MBE = Member of the Order of the British Empire
KIA = Killed in Action
KIFA = Killed in Flying Accident
KOAS = Killed on Active Service
PoW = Prisoner of War

---

[1]An interesting aside concerning Cyril Passy, concerns the occasion long after the war when he was living in the West Country. Apparently the local authorities decided to mark some roads with the words 'Drive Slow'. Cyril, being a well educated man (Marlborough and Trinity College, Cambridge), took exception to this and went round painting the letters 'ly' after the word slow, so they read 'Drive Slowly'. Not surprisingly he was caught and taken to task but at least avoided a charge of criminal damage.

Chapter Five

Instructor

The new year of 1941 did not start well for 605 Squadron, for on the 2nd, Alec Scott was killed in an accident. The Glaswegian had learnt to fly with the Oxford University Air Squadron pre-war and had joined us in early October. Two days after his arrival he was lucky to survive a mid-air collision, and now he was dead.

Bunny Currant left us in January, posted to 52 Operational Training Unit as an instructor. He had been a great stalwart ever since Dunkirk and I had flown in close company with him on many occasions. His skill and enthusiasm would be sorely missed. He would end the war as a wing commander with the DSO to add to his two DFCs, and I am grateful that I was to stay friends with him until his passing in March 2006.

Exactly one month after Scotty was killed we lost another two chaps, close friends Sergeants Henry Pettit and Ken Jones. They had flown out of Croydon to do a height test come 'battle climb', and just failed to get back. At first it was a complete mystery, and although we knew nothing at the time, I imagine someone would have picked them up on radar, as they must have decided to head south, and once over the coast, possibly larking about, had flown out over the Channel to see if they could find any Jerries.

Unfortunately, the Jerries found them. You can imagine our amazement when, a couple of weeks later, we received news that Ken was reported a prisoner of war. Harry went into the sea and was never found while Ken, his instruments shot-up became lost and disorientated. Low on fuel he spotted an airfield below and managed to put his Hurricane down. As he climbed out of the cockpit, with little activity going on about him, a door to a hut opened and out came a man in a Luftwaffe uniform. He had no way of getting his engine going again, but with great presence of mind, reached for the Very pistol and fired it into the cockpit. Within seconds the machine was burning merrily, but a less than merry Ken was heading off to four years of captivity. He had so nearly handed over to the Germans a virtually undamaged Hurricane Mark II (Z2329).

Then on 22 February, during a standing patrol, Johnny Rothwell, another chap who had joined us in October, suddenly began to spin earthwards from 30,000 feet. Oxygen failure was the obvious problem but he did not pull out and the spin continued until he hit the ground at Upper Bush Lane, Cuxton, Kent. So we had lost four pilots in less than two months with absolutely nothing to show for it. Not a happy time and the weather was awful too.

The gaps in our ranks were of course filled. Bunny's place was taken by Spud Hayter and A W Bedford and Ron Noble were two of our new replacement pilots. Bill Bedford would later see action in Burma, but his name will be forever famous for his work as a test pilot for Hawkers in the post-war years. Perhaps his greatest achievement was piloting what was referred to then as the 'flying bedstead' – the first trials of vertical take off and landing aircraft (VTOL) which eventually developed into the Hawker Harrier. Ron, after flying with other squadrons from England, then Malta, also ended up in Burma, where he won the DFC. 605 had gone to Malta in November 1941, flying off the carrier HMS *Argus*. From the personnel side, it was a completely new bunch of pilots, for none were from the old Battle of Britain crowd.

Two others who also went to Malta were John Beckitt, nicknamed Joe after a famous British heavyweight boxer, and Philip Wigley. Many years later, in 1991 or 1992 in fact, I was taking lunch at the Royal Air Force Club in Piccadilly, when I noticed another diner looking over at me. After a while he plucked up the courage to come over to my table and asked if I was Bob Foster. Having received an affirmative, he asked if I remembered him, and gave his name as Joe Beckitt. I must confess I hadn't recognised him at all but we thereafter remained good friends, and he regularly attended 605 Squadron reunions until his death some years later.

Phil Wigley did well over Malta after 605 was amalgamated into 185 Squadron on the island. With the danger and intensity of the air battles over Malta, it was often difficult to get confirmation of victories, and I see that between February and May 1942 he managed to share in three enemy aircraft destroyed and more than a dozen probables and damaged! He got the DFC for that lot.

Perhaps it was just as well that our time at Croydon now came to an end. No doubt we were due a break, so on 23 February we were ordered to move to Martlesham Heath, in Suffolk. It was a pleasant posting really. Pleasant in that we did not become embroiled in those early Sweeps and Circuses, let alone the highly exciting but amazingly dangerous Rhubarb sorties across the Channel.

With our men and equipment moving by road, we flew to our new aerodrome and found that 605 were dispersed on the far side of the airfield, in other words, the messes and hangars were on the eastern side – the coast side – and we were on the western side at the end of the main runway. At Martlesham we shared the airfield with 242 Squadron, which was commanded by the famous Douglas Bader. Our first job at Martlesham was to cure the problem of overly hot oil temperatures after flying our Hurricane IIs at height. This was overcome with the help of boffins from Rolls-Royce, and so we settled down to await events.

What came next was a spate of hostile raiders that began lurking off the Norfolk coast, looking for shipping or doing weather reccos, or even hit-and-run raids. It was on one of the latter that I had my next bit of excitement.

On 24 March, although it had taken the Luftwaffe a month to acknowledge our arrival, they obviously decided to rectify this situation. Operations rang up very early that morning, just after we had arrived at our dispersal, even before we had had breakfast. We were asked how many aircraft we could put in the air as there appeared to be a raid coming into our area. The telephone had hardly been put down when enemy aircraft came hurtling across the airfield boundary and over our dispersal, dropping bombs as they came. We recognised them as Me110s and I now know they were aircraft from the specialised group of Erprobungsgruppe 210 (Erpr.Gr.210).

There was a great rush to get to our aircraft as can be imagined. Our dispersal hut was situated on the other side of a fairly deep ditch and being March it was pretty soggy and wet. Ricky Wright had been the first out of the hut, running like mad, but upon reaching the ditch, he tripped and fell head over heels, and everybody else managed to trample over him. His language as can be imagined was not very polite and instead of being first to the Hurricanes, he was about last.

With engines roaring we all raced and bumped across the

airfield more or less individually – no formation at all – and we were soon climbing up into cloud, where we quickly became separated. I don't know if we truly believed we would meet up with those Messerschmitts, for they must have been well away by this time, but the thought was there. Anyway, I stooged about on my own, far from confident that I would see anything of the raiders. Getting above the cloud it proved a beautiful sunny morning and it wasn't long before I was some miles out over the North Sea. Consequently, I was now feeling very much bereft of my breakfast, so I was delighted to get a call from control that it was time to return home.

Having one final look round I suddenly glanced back over my shoulder and down, and below to my right I saw a Heinkel 111. It seemed just to pop up out of cloud and its crew were probably just as surprised to see me as I was to see them. It had had nothing to do with the raid, just a lone bomber out over the North Sea either looking for shipping or perhaps checking on the weather, but its comrades in EG210 had stirred up the RAF and now I had interrupted their mission. Just why our radar had not picked it up and warned me I don't know.

I reckoned the Heinkel opened up on me although I'm not totally sure, but anyway I turned round, climbed slightly, attacked him from almost head-on, then got behind him and opened fire again. The bomber began to dive away towards the clouds with me chasing and firing at it. I claimed a damaged having seen smoke coming from its port engine, so I'm pretty sure I did some harm to it. I often wondered that if I had not spotted it when I did, whether the pilot would have been able to get in a proper attack on me, in order for his gunners to have a crack, meaning that I would probably not be here now. My combat report reads as follows:

I was ordered to intercept E/A bombing base and was sent on a vector of 090°. When about 75 miles East of Clacton and above 8/10 – 10/10ths cloud I was ordered to return to base. Whilst turning I was fired at by E/A which had broken cloud behind me. I took evasive action and got into a position to do a diving $1/4$ ahead attack from the port side. I gave him a 2-secs burst whilst closing and after breaking away noticed black smoke coming from the port engine. I then gave him a 7-8 secs burst from $1/4$ astern and he dived steeply through cloud. I followed him through cloud but could find no trace of him.

Landing back at base I soon discovered that the 110s had done some damage to our airfield buildings, including a hangar, and Peter Parrott was jumping up and down about damage to his car that had been in it. It was his own fault for he should not have had his car there in the first place, so he didn't get much sympathy from us. People often left cars in the hangars or nearby them so if the buildings etc were bombed they were often the only things that were written off. Those 110s had certainly come in very low and very fast and were obviously after the aircraft hangars.

At 16.50 on 25 March, Ricky Wright was on a convoy patrol off Orfordness when he ran into two Me110s. He attacked and hit one seeing it climb away into cloud losing oil and trailing smoke from its port engine.

The next day, Derek Forde was on a convoy patrol with Tommy Thompson, Yellow One and Two. They were informed by control that a bandit had come into their area having crossed out over the English coast at Harwich and was approaching them and the convoy. They spotted the enemy machine – a Dornier 17 – and both attacked. Bombs were quickly jettisoned by the bomber crew as its port engine began to leave a trail of smoke. Tommy made three attacks in all, having to throttle back quickly on his last one as the Dornier suddenly dropped towards the sea. One Dornier destroyed.

The rest of the time we were at Martlesham we were on convoy patrols and familiarising with our new Hurricanes. Two days after our bit of excitement, someone shot down a Dornier 17 near a convoy, but one always had to be a bit wary flying these sorties. On one occasion we overshot our rendezvous with some ships heading up the east coast and came in from the east, whereupon the ships quickly assumed us to be hostile and opened fire on us. This was pretty unpleasant but we got away with it. The gunners on these ships as well as the navy boys, generally fired first and asked questions later so one had to be on one's guard, and make sure a reasonable distance was kept.

However, our stay at Martlesham was brief and by the end of March we were posted to Ternhill in Shropshire and several people began leaving the squadron, while new people came in. Archie Milne left and so did Eric Jones, then Peter

Parrott went to CFS for an instructors course. Spud Hayter departed in April to do his stint as an instructor too. It looked decidedly as if it would be my turn soon. On 14 May I spent my 21st birthday at dispersal as there were raiders over Liverpool so we were on stand-by. I remember that very clearly but luckily we were not sent up as the weather was pretty awful.

Then we were moved to Baginton in Warwickshire, which is now Coventry airport, and again everything was in a state of flux, with people coming and going. Then we moved to Honiley and finally I was posted to Usworth, to the Hurricane OTU as a flight commander and said goodbye to 605. By this time virtually all my old comrades had gone.

The squadron later operated in Malta and then the Far East, where it did great stuff against odds but was, like so many other units, ultimately over-run. Its last CO out there was Ricky Wright, and he like many others, was finally taken prisoner. He did, however, survive as a captive of the Japanese and in 1946 was awarded a well deserved DFC for his service in Batavia. In mid-1942 605 was reformed as a Mosquito night intruder unit in England. It continued to distinguish itself over northern Europe, not only seeking out enemy aircraft but also going down on trains and other ground targets, and in 1944, fought against the V1 flying bomb menace. It ended the war proudly as part of 2nd Tactical Air Force.

RAF Usworth, Tyne and Wear, was the place where I had landed after A Flight's abysmal showing back on 15 August 1940, in order to refuel before heading back to Drem. It was, in my opinion, probably one of the worst places you could put a Hurricane OTU, situated as it was on the north-east coast, mid-way between Newcastle and Sunderland, and right in the heart of the Newcastle coal-fields. The weather was usually pretty awful with fog off the North Sea, smog from the coal mines, factories, etc. The runways were not very long, one in fact very short and an anti-aircraft balloon barrage was situated only about two miles away.

To make matters worse, most of the pilot intake we were having now, were part of the Empire Air Training Scheme (EATS), so were coming in from Canada, the USA, South Africa, Rhodesia and so on, where flying conditions had been more or less perfect, thereby allowing almost uninterrupted flight training. Conditions were not so ideal for them now. This successful training scheme had been set up in 1940 when it became obvious that the amount of flying training needed could not be accommodated in the UK. Space was one thing and the unpredictable British weather caused annoying delays. My own training was, as the reader will recall, badly affected in early 1940 because of snow.

I arrived at Usworth and met my new CO, Squadron Leader Dennis David DFC and Bar, a well known Hurricane pilot. He was a great chap, very popular, very gung-ho, so that was a good start. He was a pre-war airman, via the short service commission route, and had flown in France and in the Battle of Britain with 87 Squadron, ending up with 213 Squadron in October. Over France, in ten days he had claimed around a dozen German aircraft shot down, adding half a dozen or more during the Battle.

Dennis told me I would be taking over B Flight and our Nissen hut crew room was on the far side of the airfield. As soon as I could I got myself over there and going into my office the first thing I noticed was about 20 to 30 long wooden poles stuck up in one corner. They were about six foot long with metal spikes at one end. I asked the flight sergeant on duty what they were for and he informed me in all seriousness, that they were for airfield defence. They had been there since 1940 in case an invasion began and the airfield was attacked by German paratroopers. Pilots and ground crew alike would have used the spiked poles to see off the attackers despite them being armed with machine guns, rifles and bayonets. My immediate reaction was that if that had occurred, life would have been interesting, but short.

Also, I was told, that under a tarpaulin at the back of the hut was a gun which, if needed, would have had to be assembled before use. Fortunately it had not been necessary to use it, but an even more fascinating picture came to mind of enemy parachutists floating onto the airfield, with the defenders trying desperately to assemble this gun, a spanner in one hand, a manual of instructions in the other, always assuming someone had remembered where the manual had been kept. There was no ammunition, of course, that was kept in the armoury, so one hoped that in an emergency, someone also had a key to it. Shades of that Burt Lancaster film *From Here to Eternity*, about Pearl Harbor, where the hero was remonstrating with their armoury chap to open up in order to get guns and ammo, with Japanese aircraft strafing and bombing the place.

So this was my introduction to 55 Operational Training Unit, which had only recently moved up from Aston Down. However, things could only get better and I quickly got down to the job in hand, getting embryo pilots to an operational standard before they were sent off to front line squadrons. For the next three or four months it was all pretty intensive flying. People were coming in all the time and away again, most as I recall were from Canada, which was just as well for we were flying Canadian-built Hurricane Xs.

Initially I would give each pilot a test check flight in a Miles Master, a very good and adequate aeroplane after the Harvards these chaps had been flying, then get them onto a Hurricane. Luckily we had a good safety record and I cannot recall anyone dying or getting hopelessly lost, although we did have a few near misses, especially when the weather clamped suddenly, which it was apt to do. The weather of course began to worsen as November and December came, but we managed as much flying as was humanly possible. In due course we got them through and off to squadrons at a reasonably steady pace.

As I mentioned, the majority of these chaps seemed to have been Canadian sergeant pilots and most appeared to be tough, outdoor types, not necessarily your lumberjack image, but great chaps and coming from all walks of life. They were great gamblers too. At any spare time of day, out would come the playing cards and a game would start. I remember one time during a spot of bad weather, I came into the flight hut to find about half a dozen of these guys sitting around the table, a card game in full swing, and out of interest I asked what they were playing. I think they said Scoot or Shoot or some such name, which appeared to be very basic. All you did was to back against a higher card, almost a simple sort of pontoon idea, where you either lost or won a large amount of money.

Upon hearing my question they must have quickly decided they could snag this sucker and I was promptly invited to sit in. I thought I should agree rather than lose face or look the coward, so trying to look keen, I took a seat. Then, for about the only time in my life, I had a run of exceptional luck and every time I needed to pick up a card higher than a Jack or even a Queen, it would turn up. Within a fairly short space of time I had made the equivalent of about two months RAF pay. They, of course, had plenty of money with their RCAF pay being higher than the RAF rate, but if it had gone against me I'd have been embarrassingly broke – even on a flight lieutenant's pay. I am sure they began to wonder what had hit them, but as no skill was needed with this game, there was no real suspicion that I was some sort of hustler, it just happened.

The officer's mess was a bit basic. Usworth had been a sort of semi-permanent station so there wasn't a purpose-built mess, but a friendly sort of building was available. After a day's flying there wasn't much else to do except drink in the mess. The nearest towns were Sunderland and Newcastle, neither of which appeared particularly attractive.

I do recall we had a piano there which was in great demand. Someone would play a few tunes, we'd sing some popular songs of the time, or sometimes other sorts of ditties, the lyrics of which are not particularly printable, but it was all pretty convivial. Our intelligence officer was Freddie Ashton and when he had had a couple of beers, or even if he hadn't, he would suddenly break into some dance routine to the music, either around the table, or even on it. His name meant nothing to us at the time but he later became Sir Frederick Ashton, one of the greatest choreographers and ballet masters, in the world.

Freddie, as we knew him, had been born in Equador and had his early education in Lima, Peru. In 1926 he had been with the Ballet Rambert and in 1933 had become principal dancer and choreographer to the Royal Ballet Company, a position he held until 1970. He was knighted in 1962, was also a CBE, and later received the Order of Merit.

Another incident I remember quite well concerns a chap we had posted in as an instructor. He was of squadron leader rank and was a sort of No.2 to our chief flying instructor. We did not find him particularly communicative, a quiet, thinking sort of chap, who didn't mix at all with anyone. He would eat his dinner and disappear off to his room somewhere at the other end of the mess, and play a violin. Not a mixer at all.

Then one day I got a call down at dispersal asking if I had seen him. I said I hadn't and I was asked to let HQ know if I did, and to keep him talking and occupied till someone came along. And under no circumstances was I to allow him anywhere near a Hurricane. Anyway, he didn't turn up where I was and later it transpired that his batman, when going into his room after breakfast, had found a note saying that he was going to get a Hurricane and kill everybody, or words to that effect, including himself!

When the guy who had rung me, then rang the A Flight office, he was told that not only had they seen him but he had taken off in a Hurricane a short time before, and was somewhere in the vicinity. Fortunately we didn't have guns armed on our Hurricanes, but panic stations ensued none the less. We had a flight lieutenant who was used as a sort of communications pilot, and who was up as well in the Station Rapide, showing some trainees the local area, when this Hurricane showed up and started beating up their aircraft.

The flight lieutenant was quick to realise that this was certainly something out of the ordinary and made a rapid descent for home and got the machine down safely. Finally the Hurricane landed too and the people in white coats came along and that was the last we saw of him. It could have been a nasty occurrence if he'd crashed into the Rapide or even onto some airfield buildings but luckily he didn't.

Our daily routine was for me to give each new arrival the once-over in a Master and when they'd gone solo on a Hurricane they would join in the work of formation flying and discipline, low flying – we did a lot of low flying which was pretty exciting, plus battle climbs to 25 or 28,000 feet. We didn't do any air-to-air firing or air-to-ground, we'd just send them off to do that on a gunnery range elsewhere. I had, in addition, to do a lot of air tests. With so much intensive flying our aircraft needed a good deal of work and maintenance so I was kept pretty busy ensuring they were up to scratch afterwards.

There were all sorts of chaps, as I mentioned previously, and I remember one young American who had joined the RCAF and come by way of Canada to fly for Britain. Having completed his initial training, received his wings and so on in Canada, he came to us for that final polish. Unhappily, I found that he was, shall we say, not very good. We gave him some extra dual flying on the Master, tried to instil into him some extra ability but in the end he was only 'average' or even just below 'average'. I finally got him away in a Hurricane but whilst he was with us he had two accidents, one on the short runway while the weather wasn't that good, and he overshot, ending up in the sand at the end. The second one was during take-off when he swung, failed to correct properly and ended up in a hedge. I really should have scrubbed him and in the end took him to one side and told him that I didn't think he should carry on – for his own safety as much as anything.

He pleaded with me not to wash him out, saying that his parents and especially his father, a wealthy, well known gentleman back in the States, were so proud of him that it would be impossible for him to return home and admit he had failed. Please, he begged let me go on. He'd get it right soon he was sure. So reluctantly I agreed and sent him off hoping he would get it together and telling him to be careful. He lasted about a fortnight. I wish I had been stronger and stuck to my guns and my instincts. But if we had flunked him he may well have tried again with the American air force and the same might well have happened. He was such a nice chap, anxious to do his bit. It was a great pity.

Sometimes it was quite comical if heart-stopping, watching some of these young pilots getting airborne. With our Hurricanes the undercarriage and flaps were operated by a lever on the right-hand side, and sometimes it was a bit sticky to engage. One would take off with the throttle in the left hand, your stick in your right and then you'd have to switch hands. You'd watch these chaps take off, know they were changing hands but the chap had probably forgotten to screw the thing down and as soon as he took his hand off the throttle, it would drift back.

We could all sense what was happening, and the offender would have to swap over again in order to raise the undercarriage. These lads also tended to land all over the countryside because they were not used to foggy conditions, low mist and thick cloud. But eventually they would return, each with a better story (excuse) than the previous guy.

During my time at Usworth, the Japanese had attacked Pearl Harbor, America had entered the war, and while this concerned us in the overall scheme of things, we were not directly affected by it. Little did I know that it wouldn't be too long before I was going to be more personally involved in the air war against Japan.

There was still no thought of losing the war in the long run but by early 1942 there was no escaping the fact that the Japanese Empire was rapidly over-running everything in the Pacific; they were in the Philippines, New Guinea, had sunk two Royal Navy capital ships with apparent ease off Malaya – the *Repulse* and the *Prince of Wales* – and would soon capture Singapore and Malaya, before marching steadily into Burma, their sights in this area firmly set on India.

In Europe and especially in the Middle East things were not going well either. Vast areas of Russia were now in German occupation, the Wehrmacht almost knocking on the doors of Moscow itself. North Africa was faring no better, the Eighth Army being forced back towards Cairo and Egypt. The island fortress of Malta was under heavy air assault but holding out brilliantly while still managing to hit at Axis shipping in the Mediterranean, although Crete had fallen, and Greece had been over-run by Italian and German forces too.

In the Atlantic, German U-boats seemed to be able to sink Allied shipping almost at will, the Royal Navy and the RAF still trying to develop suitable tactics to reduce the submarine menace, if they could not as yet defeat it. U-boats also seemed to dominate and decimate shipping off the American eastern seaboard, now that Germany was also at war with the USA. The only glimmer of hope in this dark scenario was that with America in the war, its industrial might would surely help challenge the Axis forces, while its armed might would, in due time, be enough to save the Allied cause.

During one of my home leaves around this time, my uncle Bert, who had helped me secure my job with Shell-Mex & BP, contacted me and suggested we have lunch at the Royal Automobile Club in London. When we got there he introduced someone he new, an army officer, and I started to get the feeling I was being assessed for something or other. However, nothing happened as a result of this impromptu 'interview' and I soon forgot all about it.

My uncle Bert was still with Special Branch and after the war he told me that on occasions he was involved in security concerns that involved the SOE – Special Operations Executive – that clandestine organisation set up by Winston Churchill to 'set Europe ablaze'. This involved agents and foreign resistance fighters in all the occupied countries. For instance, he recalled the day two Poles had had a car accident near RAF Tempsford, that was, of course, one of the centres from where SOE agents were flown out to the continent, and he had to investigate to make sure these two were not spies themselves. It then struck me that this army bod we had lunched with must have been with SOE HQ, and that I had been looked at as to my suitability for flying agents over the Channel.

Obviously he was not in the least impressed by me, for which I am greatly pleased. While my uncle may have imagined I might be safer flying un-armed Lysander aircraft into France, Holland, or wherever, to off-load agents and to perhaps bring others back, I would not have been enthused. I much preferred the dangers of Hurricane combat to this far more hazardous work landing at night in a foreign field. I'm sure my uncle had my best interests at heart, but it would not have been a job for me, thank you very much!

In March 1942 after some six to seven months at RAF Usworth I received a posting to join 54 Squadron, at a place in northern Scotland I had never heard of called Castletown. I had been happily jogging along thinking that with all my time and experience on Hawker Hurricane fighters, any new posting I would receive would be bound to have these same aircraft too, but as I very soon discovered, 54 Squadron had Spitfires. Not that I had anything against the Spitfire. True I had never flown one but had seen them in action and been in enough conversations with pilots who had flown them to know that everyone thought them marvellous. In any event I was soon to find out for myself.

On 28 March I flew a Hurricane for the last time. For twenty-one months I had been flying them almost daily, during which time I had clocked up 550 hours on them, 200 of which had been accumulated at Usworth, which was far more flying than one usually did on an operational squadron.

So, saying farewell to my fellow instructors, the latest batch of pupils and my flight's ground crews, I packed my bags. I had by now located Castletown on a map, which I saw was to the east of a place called Thurso, right on Dunnet Bay, with nearby Dunnet Head. If one headed north from here, out to sea, the next piece of real estate was the Shetland and Orkney Islands.

I managed a few days of home leave, my parents no doubt pleased that I was heading up north and away from the increasing operations from southern England out over the Continent, and then I caught a train from King's Cross Station heading for Thurso in the Highlands of Scotland. I left in the evening and travelled all through the night, all through the next day, which was an extremely long and tiring journey, in a train that was mostly full of sailors, either going up to Inverness or to Scapa Flow. I seem to remember the train was named *The Jelicoe*, which of course suited the occasion admirably.

We were given a break at Edinburgh where I was able to get off and have some breakfast, then we continued ever north. We went up via Perth and being a wonderful spring day, found out just how beautiful the Scottish countryside can be. The train went to Inverness and then north-east through the highlands – a really magnificent journey.

We arrived mid-afternoon and I was met and driven to the airfield, situated about one and a half miles south-east of the small town of Castletown. It was a satellite of Wick and its importance was due to its ability to cover and help protect the Royal Navy's ships out in the waters of Scapa Flow. 504 Squadron had been the first there in June 1940, just one month after the airfield opened. Quite a few fighter squadrons had come to and gone away from Castletown, and although on a semi-operational footing, it was also a place units could have a bit of a break from operations from the south of England. I also discovered that Batchy Atcherley had commanded it too for a while in early 1941, after being at Drem.

Although I had not heard of Castletown before, I *had* heard of my new squadron. 54 had a long and distinguished record, and it was this record that was to shape its future, although nobody would have dreamed what that was going to be at this time. It had been a fighter unit in WW1 flying Sopwith Pups and then the ubiquitous Sopwith Camel. Pre-WW2 it had been one of the Hornchurch squadrons and had seen action over France, Dunkirk and in the Battle of Britain. A number of its pilots had become well known, both within the service and, due to its coverage in the press, to those at home. Al Deere, Colin Gray for example, two wonderful New Zealanders. James 'Prof' Leathart won the DSO for rescuing the CO of 74 Squadron who had force-landed at Calais in the run-up to Dunkirk, flying over in a two-seat training machine to rescue him, escorted by Deere and Johnny Allen. While Leathart landed to pick up the downed squadron leader, Al and Johnny had fought Me109s overhead. Both men won DFCs for their part in this dramatic rescue mission. Others in 54 who won acclaim in 1940 were Des McMullen, Wonky Way, Jock Norwell and George Gribble.

My new CO whom I met that first day was Squadron Leader Eric Gibbs, who had been appointed a couple of days before me, having been one of the squadron's flight commanders, and then had taken over from Squadron Leader P W Hartley. Gibbs I quickly discovered was a good chap, although his was a rather peculiar appointment. He was several years older than most, if not all the other pilots, getting on for 30. His fighter pilot experience was a complete zero before coming to 54, having been posted to the squadron via Coastal Command, flying both Avro Ansons, and Lockheed Hudsons, operating in the anti-submarine and anti-shipping roles. Not that he had had no fighting experience. On 11 November 1940 he was flying an Anson – not the most warlike of aeroplanes, and better suited for training – off the Dutch coast when he encountered two German Heinkel 115 seaplanes. He is recorded as saying that he and his crew spent 15 minutes exchanging fire with the enemy machines until the Anson caught fire. While extinguishing the flames he spotted one of the Heinkels going into the sea. Just why or how, with all the people available to Fighter Command, he should suddenly be given command of one of the RAF's premier fighter outfits, we didn't know. Although his name was Eric everyone knew him as Bill.

He was a regular RAF officer and later I think it became known that he knew Air Marshal Sir William Sholto Douglas, who was at the time, AOC-in-C of Fighter Command. How well they knew each other I haven't the least idea, but perhaps there was something of the old boy network at play here. Not that it mattered one jot, for Bill Gibbs was a first class leader.

None of the old 1940 chaps who had made 54 Squadron famous were still around of course, virtually everyone was new apart from some of the ground personnel. On the pilot side especially, there was little or no operational experience at all. One or two may have got in a few sweeps over France but basically they were all inexperienced people coming in. The other flight commander was Robin Norwood, who'd been with 65 Squadron in the Battle of Britain, but I never heard

Left: Starting out in life ....

Below: Learning to fly, Anstey, May 1939. Back row (left to right): Ellison, Williams, Bridge, Cotterell, Lewis, Gosling, Parsons, Farmer. Middle: Lake, Petterson, Fenton, Barwis, Worrall, RWF, Kerry, Phillips. Front: Thorogood, Dennison, Hampton, Rees, Tripe, McLean, Wright, Siddons, Smith, Proven.

(Don Lake flew with 219 Squadron, but was killed in a flying accident with FIU in September, 1941. Laurence Thorogood flew with 87 Squadron in the Battle and at the end of the war had the DFC. Don Smith flew with 616 Squadron but was killed in action on 27 September 1940. Claude Parsons flew with 610 and 66 Squadrons in the Battle, but was lost on a sweep over France in 1941.)

Top: All kitted out and somewhere to go.
From the left, Williams, McLean, Thorogood,
Kerry, RWF.

Bottom left: RAF Sergeant-Pilot. I've made it.

Bottom right: Look at me, Mum! I get my
commission.

Top left: My first CO, Squadron Leader Walter Churchill DSO DFC, 605 Squadron, July 1940.

Top right: Gerry Edge, right, flight commander with 605 when I joined, later to be CO of 253 Squadron before returning to 605 in late 1941.

Bottom: We entertain some ladies at Drem in August 1940. From the left: Archie McKeller DFC, Bunny Currant, Cyril Passy and RWF. (*Croydon Airport Assn*)

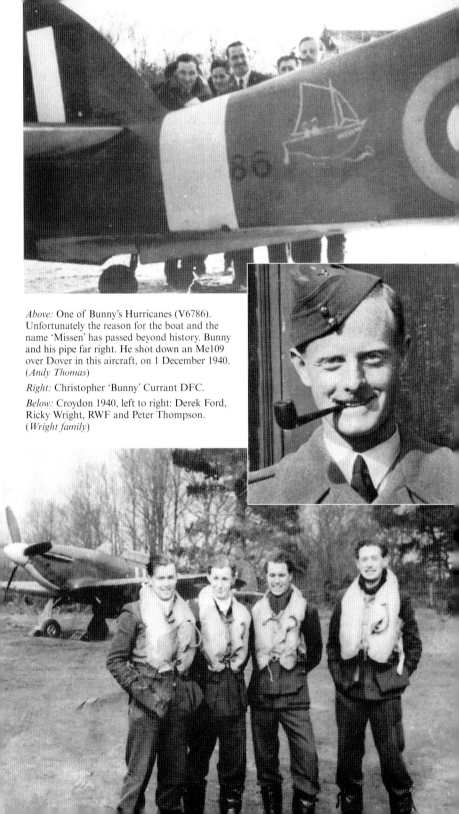

Above: One of Bunny's Hurricanes (V6786). Unfortunately the reason for the boat and the name 'Missen' has passed beyond history. Bunny and his pipe far right. He shot down an Me109 over Dover in this aircraft, on 1 December 1940. (*Andy Thomas*)

Right: Christopher 'Bunny' Currant DFC.

Below: Croydon 1940, left to right: Derek Ford, Ricky Wright, RWF and Peter Thompson. (*Wright family*)

Top: Alec Ingle, with pipe, adjusts my mae west, while Ricky Wright, wearing gauntlets, looks on. (*Chris Goss*)

Middle left: Archie McKeller DFC.

Middle right: At readiness; war was always a waiting game.

Bottom: Pilot Officer Witold Glowaki, from Poland. Crash-landing in France on 24 September, he looks dejected with his head bandaged. Taken to hospital he died that same night, presumably reacting to an anti-tetanus injection. Note the 605 Squadron insignia on the tail-fin (P3832 UP-P). (*Andy Thomas*)

Top left: Peter Parrott was already a combat veteran when he joined 605 Squadron in September 1940. This picture of him was taken and used for a recruitment poster early in the war. He later flew successfully in Italy 1943-44.

Top right: Peter McIntosh, killed in action 12 October 1940.

Bottom left: Flight Lieutenant Ian 'Jock' Muirhead DFC, killed in action 15 October 1940.

Bottom right: Sergeant H N Howes DFM, killed in a crash after leaving 605 Squadron.

Top: Sight-seeing outside Sydney. Left to right: John Lenagen, George Farries, Harold Leonard, RWF, Robin Norwood and Tony Brook.

Bottom: Pilots of 54 Squadron at Richmond, November 1942. Front (left to right): PO G Wall, PO A McIntyre, FO R Beaton (EO), FL E Weatherhead (Adj), RFW, SL E M Gibbs, FL R Norwood, FL D G Jarman (MO), PO J Councer (IO), PO A K Brook, PO G C F Farries. Rear: Sgt Studley, Sgt W Eldred, FS B Mahoney, FS Miller, FS F L Varney(†), FS J C Wellsman(†), Sgt D Monger, Sgt G Horkin, Sgt P F McCarthy (†). († - killed with the Wing)

Top: VIPs at Richmond. At left is G/C A L Walters, then me; Mr A S Drakeford and Dr H Evatt are the two suits with Jimmy Wellsman between them. A/Cdr P G Heffernan OBE AFC is talking to Robin Norwood. On the far right is Sgt Peter McCarthy, who was killed on 5 February 1943.

Middle: They look at our Spitfires. Left to right: G/C A L Walters, Dr Evatt, S/Ldr Ray Thorold-Smith (OC 452 Squadron), RWF, Mr Drakeford, S/Ldr Ken James (OC 457 September).

Bottom: Getting our knees brown at Richmond – RWF, Bill Gibbs, Tony Tuckson and John Lenagen.

Top: One of our new Spitfires arrives at Richmond and the ground crews get busy.

Middle: My personal Spitfire Vc – BR539 – before the squadron and individual codes of DL-X have been applied. Below is the Hunter River, near Sydney.

Bottom: Me standing by John Lenagen's Spitfire BS181 in which I shot down a Dinah recce. aircraft on 6 February 1943, the first Spitfire victory in Australia. John had his girlfriend's name painted on the cowling.

Top: We ham-it up for the press:
RWF, Bill Gibbs, and Jimmy Councer,
taking down my action report.

Middle: More smiles for the camera
chaps. Left to right: unknown,
Wickham, D Wheeler, RWF,
Dennis Monger, unknown, Ian Taylor,
George Farries and Harold Leonard.

Bottom: Some of the boys:
From left, Sgt Jimmy Wellsman,
PO George Ferries, FO Tony Tuckson,
FO John Lenagen, FO D F Evans,
RWF, PO D Downes, PO Tony Brook,
PO F S Young, Sgt David Wheeler,
FO Ernie Weatherhead (Adj),
FL Robin Norwood, PO A McIntyre.

Top: Me showing off in my Spitfire BR539 DL-X, over Darwin.

Middle: Our pilot hut at dispersal, Darwin, 1943. Robin Norwood sits far left while Bob Ashby stands at the side of him having a fag. Tony Brooks is asleep far right.

Bottom: Bob Ashby trying to look interested, 2nd left, while playing cricket at dispersal.

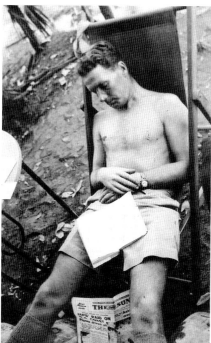

Top: Our DIY accommodation at Darwin.

Bottom left: Our CO, Bill Gibbs, taking it easy. Obviously the newspaper headlines – Japs' Raid on W.A. Coast, Planes Driven off – have worn him out.

Bottom right: Robin Norwood and me impressing the press, again!

Top: Bill Gibbs'
fitter, identified by
the screwdriver, talks
to RWF, McIntyre
and Bill. Bill usually
flew Spitfire DL-K.

Middle: Out in the
bush – Darwin 1943.

Bottom: 54 Squadron
Spitfires await the
next scramble.

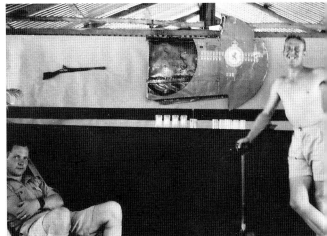

Top: Still waiting! Harold Leonard, RWF, Bill Gibbs, Robin Norwood, and Clive Caldwell, the wing leader.

Middle: Our mess bar at Darwin, with our victory score-board on the wall – the wing-tip from a Japanese Zero. Harold Leonard seated.

Bottom: Showing off – our padre Don Begbie, Bill Gibbs, Tony Brook and Bob Ashby.

Top: Flying Officer Tony Hughes celebrating his encounter with the enemy on 20 June even though he had to make a forced landing.

Middle: A Mitsubishi Ki-21 'Sally'.

Bottom: RWF with B Flight's stalwart ground crews.

Top: Final dining-in night at Ringway, as 3613 Squadron disbands in 1958. RWF and Sir Roy Dobson of A V Roe who was Honorary Air Commodore of 3613.

Bottom: The 50th Anniversary of the Battle of Britain, 605 Squadron re-unite for this picture, in a Birmingham hotel: Front: Archie Milne, Alex Ingle, Gerry Edge, John Fleming, Peter Parrott. Rear: Bunny Currant, Ken Jones, RWF, Mike Cooper-Slipper.

much about his part in it. I took over B Flight, and Robin, who had arrived on 54 ahead of me, had A Flight. It didn't seem to matter much because on the occasions Bill Gibbs wasn't around, it was myself who took command rather than Robin. Perhaps I had more experience than him, but he was a good pilot nevertheless.

Castletown was a big field, not an aerodrome as such. It had temporary accommodation, tents, Nissen huts and so on. The officer's mess was a house in the grounds owned by Sir Archibald Sinclair, who at the time was Secretary of State for Air, a man chosen for the job by Winston Churchill when he formed his government in May 1940. The Sinclairs were a well-known family up in the north of Scotland and the RAF had been given, and taken over, this large manor house which we used, being just a couple of miles from the airfield.

So I was quickly introduced to my new colleagues, Bill, Robin, and the adjutant, a bluff Yorkshireman, Ernie Weatherhead, who was a bit older then all the rest of us. Pilot Officer R G 'Cecil' Beaton was the engineering officer. The pilots were the usual mix of nationalities and the job was to train everyone up to an operational standard, just like we had done in 605 at Drem, with the idea of eventually going south into 11 Group to take part in operations over Northern Europe. My first task was to get up in a Spitfire. Bill Gibbs took me out to one and while I sat in the cockpit, he pointed out all the knobs and tits. It was not so dissimilar to the old Hurricane, and I am pleased to say I took off and landed back without embarrassing myself. Any operational sorties we flew were mostly convoy patrols, perhaps a mock attack on a Hudson when we found one, weather tests, and the like. We even managed some air-to-air firing – all good and interesting flying experience for the youngsters. Youngsters? Several were older than me!

Otherwise we were stuck up in the middle of nowhere, with just Thurso our nearest town of any note, and there was precious little to interest us there anyway. John O'Groats was less than twenty miles to the east of us but there was no reason to make the short journey unless you actually wanted to say you'd been there. So once again it was the mess where we spent most of our free time, particularly as we were flying late into the evenings. Being so far north, the daylight was with us much longer than down south.

One good thing about Castletown was that there was no wartime food rationing north of Inverness, some 60-odd miles to the south. I suppose there were so few people up there anyway it just didn't apply. So there was never any shortage of food, which meant we lived pretty well. I remember going home on leave once and instead of taking all my clothes home with me, I went round the local farms collecting about four dozen eggs, which I carefully wrapped up and put in my suitcase, with just my overnight things. As can be imagined, when I turned up in Battersea, I was very popular with my parents, who, like everyone else on strict rationing, probably had only about one egg a week.

In April the sector commander obviously thought that in order to keep his various station commanders on their toes, he would arrange some surprise beat-ups of their airfields. The first one I was involved with concerned RAF Dalcross, which is about eight miles north-east of Inverness, and was the home of a night-flying OTU training air gunners. Two of us did quite a good low level beat-up over the airfield and hopefully they were suitably grateful for the chance to consider their defensiveness. A couple of days later two of us were again sent off, this time to make a similar visit to Tain, which is on the coast just by Moray Firth. I took Pilot Officer Reynolds with me, and over the sea we dropped down onto the water and came belting in, over the beach, across the airfield's boundary fence and proceeded to execute a superb beat-up of the place. It is so much nicer to do these sorts of stunts when ordered to do so. We did not take too much notice, but as we flashed over we did see that there were a number of aircraft on the ground there, some large four-engined jobs, but didn't give it a lot of thought. At the end of our fun we decided to land there, expecting great plaudits from all and sundry on our magnificent display. As we cut our engines at dispersal, some chap drove up and told us to report immediately to the station commander in the control tower.

We duly complied, and instead of congratulation, we were berated hideously by this man. What in the devil's name were we doing? How dare we beat-up his airfield! He went on like this for some minutes until he asked us what we had to say for ourselves? I knew, thankfully, that I was on solid ground, so confidently informed him that we were carrying out orders given to us by the sector commander. This undoubtedly saved our particular bacon, but he continued to rant on in general terms, obviously very far from happy.

Apparently what he was concerned about was that there was indeed a number of four-engined heavy bombers on his airfield, flown in with some secrecy in order to attack the German battleship *Tirpitz* in Trondheim Fjord, Norway. The sector commander must have known about it so exactly why he ordered the beat-up at this sensitive moment I cannot say. So here was this poor man, keeping tabs on everything for the sake of secrecy, his airfield littered with Handley Page Halifax bombers, and the last things he wanted was two snot-nosed Spitfire pilots doing a low-level beat up. I think his initial apoplexy began as he thought the secret was out and we were in fact German aircraft making a hit-and-run raid on all these lovely bomber targets.

I found out much later, that it had been on the bombing raid, which subsequently took place on the night of 27/28 April, that the CO of 10 Squadron, which was part of the attacking force, Wing Commander D C T Bennett, was shot down. He and two of his crew managed to evade capture following a crash landing, and got themselves back to England, although the other four were taken prisoner. Don Bennett, of course, was to become the leading light in Bomber Command's Pathfinder Force.

We also spent some spare time shooting rabbits, but mostly it was just a matter of relaxing in the mess with a few beers, and life went on quite well into May. I recall one mess night some time in April I suppose, we had invited some of the local lairds and their ladies along, with some army people we had billeted near us, etc., and it turned into a good evening. The station commander was Hank More, and after having downed a few beers, some wine and a few whiskies, he stood up at the end of the meal and started to quote Shakespeare. He thought this was all hilariously funny, especially when he mis-quoted – '...once more into the breech dear friends...' from Henry V, as '...once more into your britches dear ladies...' I am sure the ladies present were quite used to him by this time and it all went down well in a way I suppose. In the end we got him into an armchair and he promptly fell asleep.

I always seemed to be running into small intelligence officers. There was that one at Usworth and now we had one

at Castletown. Our manor house mess had big fireplaces as
would befit this sort of dwelling, including of course, a huge
one in the room we used for parties and get-togethers. This
particular one had a large mantelpiece, which stood some
seven feet above the floor and was deep enough to stand on.
One evening, this I/O insisted we help him on to the
mantelpiece so that he could recite *The Green Eye of the Little
Yellow Idol* to those assembled. At the end of his deliverance,
he received rapturous applause, but after taking his bow must
have quite forgotten how high he was off the floor. He
appeared just to step from his vaulted position, crashed down
in a heap and broke his ankle.

Then, quite out of the blue came the news that far from
being sent to the south of England, we were being posted
overseas, and we would be leaving all our aircraft behind. We
had absolutely no idea where we were going, but our first
move would be to go down to RAF Wellingore, in Lincolnshire, which is just up the road from Cranwell. Any Canadian,
Australian, Czech or Polish pilots on the squadron were all
posted to other units, and with new bods posted in we soon
discovered we were all home-grown British, which did strike
us as somewhat peculiar if not downright suspicious.

We travelled by train and soon after we arrived at
Wellingore we were kitted out for overseas, with tropical kit
and so on. We thought perhaps Middle East, Malta, or even
the desert. Or in fact tropical kit may have been a disguise and
we would end up in Russia or Iceland. We must have been
there about two weeks before we were given home leave, I
suppose embarkation leave really, and we began to depart in
batches. I had seven days at home with my parents, now
suitably worried about my immediate future and doubtful as
to whether they would ever see me again. If the enemy didn't
get me, perhaps some dire tropical illness would.

I was back in time for our final marching orders on 5 June
1942, and on the 16th an advance party left for Liverpool
docks. On the 18th we got on yet another train, still totally
oblivious of our final destination, still clutching our tropical
kit and proceeded to Liverpool. By 3 pm the whole squadron
had boarded the *Stirling Castle* to join convoy F6, which was,
as far as we were concerned, heading off into the unknown.
Bill Gibbs eventually told us of our destination once we were
on board and had set sail. There were a lot of army bods on

the ship and members of two Australian Spitfire squadrons, so that when Bill mentioned Australia as our destination, the Aussie presence was not only explained but given credence.

That evening we steamed out and anchored in the Mersey where we spent the whole of the next day settling in. We were all issued with life jackets and told that we must have them with us at all times. On the 20th the anchor was raised and the ship began to exit the Mersey and head for open sea, in company with several other vessels. Heading north we stopped off the Clyde where we spotted several destroyers arriving as well as more ships and it was not long before the coast began to disappear astern.

So, far from preparing ourselves for battling the Germans either in the south of England, or the desert, we were off to take on the might of the Imperial Japanese Empire on the other side of the world. If nothing else, it was all going to be very different from what any of us had experienced in this war thus far.

Chapter Six

Off to Australia

As we headed away from Britain, with all the thoughts and anxieties that has to bring, we still had no real idea about what our role might ultimately be. Obviously it had something to do with fighting the Japanese who in so short a time since they made their surprise attack on the US Fleet at its base at Pearl Harbor on 7 December 1941, had moved rapidly. Within weeks its army, navy and air force had overcome the Philippines, taken Hong Kong, and captured Singapore almost unopposed. They had then moved quickly up Malaya into southern Burma, and it didn't seem too long before India would be under direct threat. In the Pacific Japan had taken Wake Island, moved into New Guinea, Java, Sumatra, Borneo, had a huge naval base on the island of Truk and was now building an airfield on the island of Guadalcanal, in the Solomons.

Not surprisingly, with the Japanese forces almost at the northern edge of the Australian continent, the Australians were getting panicky about air attack or even invasion in and around the Darwin area. As the Japanese reached Timor and began setting up air bases there, Darwin was a prime objective for them. Because of this it was not long before the Australian Minister for External Affairs, Doctor, the Right Honourable H V Evatt, was sent to America to ask for additional help, even though America was pouring men and equipment into Australia which was the best and logical place from where to springboard any sort of offensive action against Japan. He was able to get a promise of more aircraft but they proved slow in coming.

Doctor Evatt then went on to England to meet with Winston Churchill, asking him to please send some warships to help defend her shores, in particular, an aircraft carrier. However, Churchill had none to spare, what with the Atlantic problems and the naval battles being fought in the Mediterranean, not only to help supply Malta, but to keep

Italy's navy in check. So with no help in that direction, Evatt asked for fighter aircraft – hopefully some Spitfires. Despite the RAF's needs in its efforts to keep the Germans occupied over northern France, while also trying to placate Stalin's insistence that Britain help take the pressure off the Russian front by opening a second front somewhere along the French coast, he was also being constantly harassed to reinforce Malta, North Africa and now Burma and India, with ever more aircraft.

Despite this he no doubt felt that Britain needed to show some spirit to help its Commonwealth ally in her hour of need, so agreed to send a wing of Spitfires out, which would comprise three squadrons. Air Chief Marshal Sir Charles Portal, the Chief of the Air Staff, was dead against it, thinking of the RAF's heavy demands being placed upon it, not only in keeping up the pressure on the Luftwaffe, but the other fronts too. Portal felt that pilots might be spared to go, but not Spitfires. For some time now the men of the Desert Air Force had been flying American P40 Tomahawks and Kittyhawks as well as Hurricanes, so Portal was probably of the opinion that RAF pilots sent to Australia could fly P40s provided by America. Churchill remained adamant, wanting to honour his promise to Doctor Evatt, and insisted that the wing went – aircraft and all.

Churchill got his way and it was decided that the two Australian-manned Spitfire squadrons in Fighter Command, 452 and 457, would be two of the units in the wing, while it was essential that a 'famous' RAF squadron go with them. That is how 54 was chosen, because of its good name and record, even though the pilots who had made that name were no longer within its ranks. That is also how its fame led me to travel to the far side of the globe to do my next bit of air fighting.

It is also why we had lost all our non-British pilots, and even some of the ground personnel, who had chosen not to go because airmen still had the option of saying no to overseas assignments on compassionate grounds. Pilots of course had no such luxury and had to go on overseas postings, like it or not.

Whilst this was happening better news was filtering through from the Far East. In May the Japanese Navy suffered its first setback with severe losses in the Battle of the Coral Sea. This resulted in Japan's abandonment of its planned invasion of southern Papua New Guinea and Port Moresby. In June it was again defeated in the Battle of Midway losing four of its aircraft carriers to just one American carrier (the USS *Yorktown*). The invasion of Midway had also been abandoned in consequence. All this of course made no difference to our journey out to Australia for there was still a lot of war to be fought.

I read recently of comments made by an Australian historian that Britain made no effort whatsoever to help Australia in her hour of need. I think the foregoing indicates that this was far from the truth. Churchill was very conscious of the need to help Australia for both 'family' and political reasons. He just didn't have the resources to do so. The sending of a Spitfire wing was both symbolic and practicable although of course, it would have little impact on the overall strategy in the Far East or South Pacific.

This historian went on to say that in March 1942 the Australian Prime Minister, John Curtin, had to plead with Churchill to release Australian troops fighting in the North African desert, so they could return to help defend Australia. In fact it was just the opposite. It was Churchill, supported by President Roosevelt, who pleaded with Curtin not to withdraw these troops as they were desperately needed in Egypt, a plea which was ignored by Curtin, and by the end of March the 7th Australian Division sailed for home.

By this time the Japanese were marching through Burma and threatening India. Even as the 7th Division were cruising the Indian Ocean, Churchill had one more try, this time to divert them to India, but again this was refused and the troops arrived to the peace and calm of Australia. Although, of course, they were never used in the defence of the mainland they were sent, in due time, to Papua New Guinea to halt the Japanese advance on Port Moresby.

Once out of Liverpool our ships joined up with an even larger convoy as we headed into the Atlantic. We had a battleship with us now, HMS *Malaya*, and she stayed with us for part of the journey. We did lose a couple of our destroyer screen near Gibraltar, having to escort a merchantman to the Rock, but the rest continued south. With the weather becoming increasingly warm, we were soon approaching Freetown,

Sierra Leone, on the west coast of Africa, which we reached on 2 July. As far as we could make out the land was covered in dense vegetation, palm trees near the shore, and mountains rising with some amazing slopes and shapes. We were not, however, allowed ashore but we were able to get up on deck in bathing trunks to shower in the frequent but short rainy downpours. This was wonderfully welcome as there was no air conditioning below decks and those poor souls right in the bowels of the ship suffered considerably the further south we went.

Other diversions while off Freetown included throwing pennies into the sea to watch native children diving off small boats in order to retrieve them, although they soon decided that pennies were rather cheap for all that trouble, and eventually only deigned to dive for sixpenny pieces, or anything else that was silvery rather than bronze.

The *Stirling Castle* was a very nice ship and we soon became used to the shipboard routines. The vessel still carried its complement of stewards and it was more or less run like a peacetime cruise liner. We had doubled up in the officer's cabins, I shared one with Bill Gibbs, Robin Norwood with Ernie Weatherhead, and so on. It soon got to be quite a nice life. What's more the ship was 'wet', so drinks were available. So each evening we would have an excellent dinner, almost to pre-war standards, order our drinks then sit back to enjoy the cruise. The only thing that reminded us of the dangers associated with our journey was our life jackets that were never far from our person.

None of us, as far as I know, had ever left the shores of England so all this and our stay off Freetown, including the heat and the mosquitoes, was totally new to everyone. I recall that early on, we would go upstairs to the ship's lounge after our dinner and we RAF types always seemed to take longer over our food, probably because we lingered longer over the wine. This meant that by the time we adjourned, all the seats and tables in the lounge had been snaffled by the army bods. This state of affairs could not be allowed to continue, we had our honour at stake. So one night we detailed one chap from each dinner table to go up before the rest of us had finished, order up six pints of beer and to spread them around enough lounge tables to accommodate us all. When the army lads appeared, most of the tables had been reserved in this way.

Fortunately the army took it all in good humour and the lounge tables were shared out more fairly from then on.

Aboard the *Stirling Castle* we had six crated Spitfires, while the other 42 were on board another merchant ship. During our journey, the British 8th Army were back almost to Cairo, we were told, and it all looked pretty desperate. Portal was only too aware that there were 48 brand new Spitfires sitting off Freetown, and seized his chance to divert them to where he felt they would be better deployed. Churchill reluctantly had to agree, that the 42 on the other ship could be off-loaded, unpacked and flown across to Cairo. Curtin also agreed, provided others were despatched immediately to Australia. We ourselves were not over-chuffed with the news that most of our fighters were being taken from us, but hoped that by the time we got 'down under' new machines, if not already there by another route, would at least be on their way. How naive can one get? There was nothing we could do in any event and just had to rely on our leaders and commanders to sort things out.

So there we were, some 50 fighter pilots, our ground crews, equipment but only six crated Spitfires, as we sailed from Freetown at around noon on 6 July. Two days later we crossed the Equator at three o'clock in the afternoon, but we did not have any fun and games in 'crossing the line'. The CO's birthday on the 14th was celebrated, Bill reaching the great age of thirty. Our battleship left us on the 17th, but a heavy swell that now developed gave us some manner of protection from any lurking U-boats. On the following day we sighted our first school of whales, complete with water spouts.

Two days after this we were off Durban, South Africa, half the convoy having already peeled off to head into Cape Town. After nearly a month at sea, it was with great relief that we were told we could have some shore leave, where we found rationing non-existent and the shops and bars well stocked with all one might desire. We spent nearly a week in Durban, which was very pleasant. We officers also hired a couple of cars and went on a sight-seeing tour.

The ship took us out to sea again on the 26th, this time being met by a light cruiser for escort, and once again other ships made up the convoy, to which was added a merchant cruiser on the 30th, but then we and the light cruiser altered course towards India. We watched in silence as the rest of the convoy slowly disappeared out of sight. On the last day of July we sighted Mauritius, but had to circle round and round while the cruiser put into port to take on fuel, before we could continue on. Five days later the cruiser left us and her place was taken by a Dutch light cruiser, the *Tromp*.

Not knowing exactly what to expect once we arrived in Australia, it was a pleasant interlude to have a lecture on the place and its people, giving us some insight on what we would meet. One thing was for sure, we would all be called 'poms' in the very near future, perhaps even 'pommy b......s!'

Then the Dutch warship left us, replaced by HMAS *Adelaide*, which was to escort us on the final leg into Melbourne, into which we steamed on 13 August. Without delay we were disembarked and electric trains took us to the town's agricultural showground, where the men went under canvas and we officers were quartered in the government pavilion. This might sound grand but in reality it was only a long double row of hard iron stretchers each with a hessian palliasse filled with straw. We were each given three blankets but otherwise the place was devoid of all furniture. The latrines and ablutions were somewhat limited and about 100 yards away. These were shared by everyone. It did not take long for the officers to find better accommodation in local hotels, in fact this happened the very next day. Bill Gibbs made it his business to try and find local families to accept us poor guys from the home country. The rest of that day was taken up with medical examinations, probably to ensure we hadn't brought anything nasty into the country.

For a few days we were allowed to take some local leave before making our way to an airfield where we could prepare for our war with the Japanese. However, with still only six crated Spitfires on strength, this seemed as far away as ever. On the 23rd we left for Richmond by train, although we had to change at a place called Albury on the New South Wales border because of the different gauges to the railway lines. Altogether it was not a very comfortable journey so we were mighty relieved to get to Richmond on the morning of the 24th. Richmond is about 30-odd miles north-west of Sydney and when using this line things were not helped by the transport officer generally making a habit of booking five servicemen to each three seats. As our adjutant also pointed out after several journeys on it, the cook almost always served the same meal, two long, fat sausages, mashed potatoes and gravy.

Once we had arrived we were given some more leave and squadron personnel were billeted out with private families in both Sydney itself or in the surrounding district. The hospitality was pretty good overall although this ranged from, 'Leave your shoes out and the butler will clean them for you,' to 'don't leave your shoes out, or the dog might run off with them'.

All the Aussie pilots of course, took the opportunity to visit home during these leave periods while the RAF had to find somewhere to live. As we arrived we were met by a number of local Australians and just like evacuee children we were chosen, or perhaps I should say invited, to go and stay with them. As far as I can recall everyone who wanted to was housed in a local home. It was a great gesture and very much appreciated by all the RAF contingent.

Bill Gibbs had remained temporarily in Melbourne where he had much paperwork to contend with and arrangements to make with the Australians. It was a strange set-up in some ways for although we had come out with two Australian squadrons, the Air Ministry in London continued to keep control of the one pure RAF squadron. Therefore, the RAAF, et al, couldn't do too much to assert any control over 54, and this caused a certain amount of friction, so Bill became a sort of liaison officer working between the RAF in England and the RAAF in Australia.

I myself was at Richmond, but Robin Norwood, who I have already explained was not a particularly social type, had found a flat in Sydney, a nice modern flat, and we decided to rent it so that if anyone found themselves stuck in the city overnight as the weeks went by, they could always have a place to flop down. Meantime everyone began to settle down with their respective families. One particular story I remember concerned one of our airmen who had wound up in some place where the family employed a butler. On the first morning he had been woken up and found that at some stage during the night this butler had come into his room, taken his boots, then returned them highly polished, which struck him as very nice but far exceeded his expectations of hospitality. In due time, two of our chaps married daughters of their hosts.

I suppose with virtually no aircraft there was little point in getting down to doing what we had travelled all this way for, so it was nearly 12 days before we had to reassemble at Richmond. It was a large RAAF base where we began our training in earnest, and became re-acquainted with piloting an aircraft. Here we ran into one of the old-school, or certainly the RAAF old-school, in the form of the station commander. He insisted that everyone walk around carrying gas-masks, something we hadn't done in England since after the Blitz, and then got us to dig slit-trenches all over the place. We were told that ever since a Jap submarine had surfaced off Sydney soon after the war started and lobbed a couple of shells onto the shore, he had issued appropriate standing orders in case of an invasion. It all stemmed of course, from the military authorities but obviously it had not been thought through properly. However, it certainly struck a spot with our station commander, and galvanised him into action, but he really went overboard. As far as he was concerned when we arrived and treated everything with a certain amount of incredulity and disdain, he decided we were little short of being a load of hooligans, and pommy hooligans at that. And his Australian visitors, in his eyes, were no better, presumably having been tainted from their time in Britain. I believe I heard the remark once that he thought that the blokes in 452 Squadron went round thinking they owned place, 457 Squadron went about acting as if they did own the place, while 54 Squadron didn't give a hoot who owned the place! He just couldn't figure out the attitude this British wing generated. He certainly didn't want us on his airfield, that's for sure.

Every once in a while he would sound an alarm, whereupon we all had to pretend the place was under attack and go diving into these slit-trenches and put on our gas-masks. All we needed was another pile of wooden staves with a spike on the end and we would have been fully prepared for little yellow men dangling from parachutes, each brandishing a huge, razor sharp samurai sword. We couldn't quite understand all this, and so it caused a little bit of friction in a way, but gradually we learned to ignore it all.

Once we had reassembled at Richmond we began to get down to some serious work despite the lack of aircraft. We were allowed to keep our hands in by flying Wirraways and Ryans, but it was not until mid-September that our first two Spitfires arrived. Everyone took eager turns to fly these two machines, and in between times we were able to slip into Sydney for short breaks from the airfield.

Meantime two events are worth mentioning. Firstly both Robin Norwood and I, plus our adjutant, found ourselves in hospital, stricken low with food poisoning, and secondly the arrival of our first mail from England. The first occurred on the 20th, the second on the 21st, and some of the mail was dated as far back as 12 July 1942. Nevertheless it was more than welcome.

During my time going in and out of Sydney our main watering hole was the Australian Hotel, long gone now, of course. It wasn't a bad hotel although nothing like the hotels we know today. Its claim to fame was that it had the longest bar in the southern hemisphere. It had this huge rectangular room with the bar built all around the four walls. In the middle of the room there were some pillars with seats around them. Perhaps the whole area was about the size of a tennis court.

Sydney had the most unusual licensing laws in those days. Bars opened about nine in the morning and closed at six o'clock each evening; open therefore all day between these hours but dead on six the shutters went up. The Australian Hotel was very popular and up to about 4 pm you could be quietly sitting there, have a drink or two but as soon as the last hour or so arrived the Australian males from nearby offices and shops would stream in and knock back as many beers etc, as they could before the witching hour struck. So from the peace and tranquillity to absolute chaos in those last couple of hours had to be seen to be believed. Women, of course, were not allowed in bars, just a men only arrangement.

One afternoon a couple of us were chatting to some Australian army sergeants and they invited us to a party they were going to. We readily accepted their kind invitation and among some of the people we were introduced to, were two Australian WAAFs, one named Margaret Gilligan who lived in Rose Bay, just down the coast, which used to be an old seaplane base. She and I became quite friendly and we always tried to meet up whenever I got leave. She had lost her parents and lived with a guardian, but she invited me back to have dinner that first night and we started a long and good friendship, but just that, a friendship. She was a great character and we got around quite a bit together whenever I found myself in Sydney. We were part of a bunch that enjoyed each other's company during times of relaxation.

She eventually married an army chap after I left Australia but we kept in touch over the years and I met up with her again in the late 1990s, in Australia, which was great fun. She was a very nice girl. Most of us managed to team up with someone, and being so far from home these friendships mattered a great deal and did a lot for morale. Going into Sydney whenever we could was much preferred to risking a march round the airfield, if ordered to do so by our over-enthusiastic station commander.

I had my first flight in a Ryan, a two-seat training aircraft, on the 9th, in fact it was my first flight in anything since 19 May, three and a half months back. Then I began to fly some dual with some of the new chaps who had replaced our former colleagues in 54 just prior to leaving England. Then we got hold of a Wirraway, an Australian machine that had been designed closely on the lines of the North American NA-33 and had a Pratt and Whitney 'Wasp' radial engine. These had started life with the RAAF in mid-1939.

Finally those first two Spitfires arrived, one – BR572 – I air tested on 14 September. Our original and only six Spitfires that had arrived with us in port had been left in Melbourne and assembled at a place called Laverton, from where they would gradually be flown up to us, or rather, some of us would go there and fly them back. As time progressed, some more Spitfires started arriving from the UK and on 19 October some of our fitters were sent down to Laverton to help assemble quite a large batch that had arrived in crates.

The Spitfires were all Mark Vc. They had what was called the 'universal wing' due to the fact that the wings were designed to enable a variation in gun installation, a different combination of cannon and machine guns. It could also carry bombs if necessary. They looked different to the Spitfires used in the UK in that they had a large Vokes air filter on the 'neck' of the machine, also used by aircraft operating in the Middle East to overcome the swirling sand. Ours were also the first Spitfires to operate in the Pacific theatre of operations.

Six pilots went down to Laverton and once air testing had been completed, took off for Richmond on the 31st but had to divert to and land at Wagga Wagga, some way west of

Canberra, and just over half way to Richmond. This was due to bad weather initially and they were not able to get off again until 8 November. In his diary, our adjutant Ernie Weatherhead, recorded that he personally doubted that weather alone had kept them grounded, the reason more likely to have been induced by the high standard of hospitality.

I myself went down to Laverton at this time and with three other chaps flew up four more Spitfires on the 10th, with an Australian pilot bringing up another. With me were Pilot Officer Harold Leonard, and Sergeants W K 'Bill' Read and B 'Pat' Mahoney. Everything had to be air-tested first naturally, and in addition long-range fuel tanks had to be fitted and tested, so all this took time. Meanwhile the squadrons had begun formation flying training.

One diversion I had was when the Australians wanted to know how the Spitfire compared with the Wirraway and the Boomerang (the Australian CA-12 interceptor), as well as the American P40 Kittyhawk they were using. Well, I could have told them without going to the trouble of holding a demonstration but I did as I was told. I was detailed to fly up to Mildura, a place situated on the border between the States of New South Wales and Victoria. It was a big air base used as an operational training unit among other things. So I took good old BR572, flying via Wagga Wagga and then flew against the Boomerang and Kittyhawk.

All went well and then it was planned that I should fly these Aussie machines against the Spitfire flown by another pilot at Mildura. The tests had gone to plan and just as I had expected. There wasn't any real competition. Turning, diving, rolling, getting on the other machine's tail, no problem at all. The Spitfire could easily out-fly every manoeuvre the other pilot tried against me. However, things were suddenly cut short by a signal saying that in assembling our Spitfires at Laverton, it had been discovered that with some aircraft the aileron wires had been double crossed which in turn had started to cause some rubbing. All Spitfires had to be inspected and the problem corrected in any aircraft found to have this fault. Upon inspection of BR572, true enough, the control wires had been double crossed so that our mock combat tests had to be stopped immediately, and although the fitters said that everything was working satisfactorily this rubbing might well cause a problem in the fullness of time. The odd thing is that despite this grounding order, I still had to fly BR572 from Mildura to Laverton for the problem to be rectified.

Group Captain A L Walters, our wing leader, had come to Mildura too, in order to watch the combat tests, but his Spitfire did not need any attention. We both flew our machines to Laverton and half way there, the group captain suddenly announced over the radio: 'Oh, there's my old school. Let's beat it up.' So I thought, well, that's all right for you but this is the last thing I wanted to do with this aileron problem, so I wasn't overjoyed at the Groupie's enthusiasm to show off above his old school. However, he did out-rank me somewhat, so for the next ten minutes or so we beat up this school, situated up in the mountains, with myself hoping desperately that nothing untoward would happen with these rubbing wires, but we got away with it and it made Walters very happy.

Group Captain Walters was born in Melbourne in 1905, so was approaching his 38th birthday. He had commanded 2 Squadron RAAF soon after the war started and in 1942 had become Director of Operations for the Australian Air Force. It was from here that he was given command of our wing, officially known as 1 (Fighter) Wing, and unofficially as the Churchill Wing. I don't suppose he was actually expected to fly with us if and when we became operational, but he was certainly a press-on type, and in fact did see action with us later on.

On 25 November we lost our first pilot, Bill Read. He was part of a formation practise flight when his Spitfire developed a glycol leak. He decided to try and force land but the engine overheated, caught fire, and despite his low altitude, he determined to bale out. However, he was too low for his parachute to deploy and Bill was killed. He was one of our new intake, having come to us direct from OTU. He was 23, and we buried him at Rookwood Cemetery.

Finally the squadron became operational. This didn't mean we were now ready to combat the Japanese. For one thing they were nowhere near to where we were, but it did mean we could be put on a readiness state in sections – just in case! Or we could, if necessary, fly convoy patrols. This was on 2 December, and the next day we were invaded by a bunch of public relations people and war correspondents. Pictures were taken all over the place and we were all bombarded with questions. It was nice to get away later so that we could fly a

wing and squadron formation fly-past [above].

During December it began to seem more likely that very soon we would be heading north. There was a suggestion we might be going at the end of the month so preparations were put in hand. We even started some air combat training. Despite the month, in Australia it was warming up, for their summers were exactly opposite to what we had been used to in the UK. Things on the ground moved forward and it really did seem that the promise of a move north might well be met. On the 17th an advance party was ordered to be ready to move at an hour's notice from the 19th.

However, Christmas arrived and we all went on leave which was very nice, but not so pleasant for the advance party that had indeed been sent off. Our Christmas day was spent in a heat of 80° Fahrenheit, which was a very different experience.

It was a sultry day that ended with a massive downpour of rain accompanied by thunder.

On the 28th we began packing our 'blues' for storage in Sydney for from now on we would be in tropical kit. The next evening there was a big parade dinner for the wing. Several big-wigs came too, including Doctor Evatt, the Minister for Air, the Honourable A Drakeford, the Australian Chief of the Air Staff and the AOC of Eastern Command, and the station commander. All wing officers and sergeant-pilots attended, and lots more photographs were taken.

Before we left, our intelligence officer showed some extra intelligence by visiting the Australian Comforts Fund building in Sydney and purchased 60 gramophone records to take with us, which displayed some considerable initiative. Once at our new base at Darwin, these records were played each night over the tannoy and it was not unusual to see some of the chaps start to become a bit misty-eyed. One in particular caught them out, that being: 'Every night about this time, Oh! How I miss you.'

On the last day of 1942 the first main party to move left Richmond soon after first light and went to Sydney docks where it embarked on a merchant ship – the *Maetstuycker* – which had no real accommodation for troops. By comparison, our ship that had brought us to Australia had been a palace. Our adjutant had the right idea, and rather than doss down below, he built himself a little nest in the back of one of the lorries parked on the main deck.

Our last night in Sydney was on New Year's eve. Some of us went to a night club in town, because these sorts of places didn't stop drinking at the magical hour of six o'clock. Margaret came along and we shared a table with the CO of 452 Squadron, Ray Thorold-Smith. We had a good time, but it was a sad time too, for he was to be killed flying from Darwin in March. I remember so well wishing him a Happy New Year and after that, because the Australian boys were on a different airfield to us, I never saw him again.

With New Year's day having come and gone, the road and rail parties moved off from Clarenden by train on 4 January and soon afterwards were at sea. It would take them some time to reach Darwin, and I am told, and believe, that their first impression as they disembarked, was that the place was pretty grim. Meantime, the land party went by train from

Sydney to Albury, with every seat occupied and little chance of anything other than a quick cat-nap. The train journey from Albury was a bit better, and this chugged to Adelaide and then on to Alice Springs on the Northern Territory Line. From Alice the accommodation degenerated to cattle trucks, that, it was noted, had not even been cleaned out. It took four days from Alice Springs to reach a place called Birdum, but at least they had a train from there, but only for some of the journey, and soon they were back on trucks for the final leg.

The Air Party left on the 14th, escorted by a Beaufighter and with a servicing party flying in a Lodestar. I have to say we left Richmond with no great regrets. I suppose it was all right there but a bit of a waste of time when all we really wanted was to get ourselves up north, where we hoped the action would be.

Flying to Darwin could be made in one of two ways; up the east coast to Brisbane, across Queensland, landing at Charlesville, Longreach or Cloncurry, and then through the Northern Territories to Daly Waters and Darwin. Or it was a flight to Mildura then fly north, following the one long straight road north, to Alice Springs and then Darwin. We had been given the latter route, so our first stop was to be at Mildura. Of course, we had our 90-gallon overload tanks fitted. Somehow, one pilot managed to lose his and he was forced to land.

I remember that first leg very well indeed because a couple of days before we left we had a bit of a farewell party and several of us had obviously eaten some bad food, and had begun to suffer the effects of food poisoning. A couple of days before heading north I was actually in sick quarters with severe diarrhoea. This was still lingering around a bit on the morning we were due to leave so I said to the Doc that if still suffering like this, sitting for three hours in a Spitfire's cramped cockpit wasn't going to be one of the best places to be. With a smile he told me not to worry and with that he gave me a bottle of white liquid and told me that if indeed I did feel any twinges down below, I should take a swig from it and I should be all right.

We took off and after about half an hour I felt a twinge and a little tummy gurgle so I took a sip from the bottle. This went on and on for the whole trip, and I had practically emptied the contents by the time we landed at Mildura. I was mighty relieved that I hadn't embarrassed myself in mid-air, but of course, the result of this was that I became completely bunged up for the next seven days – absolutely solid!

The flight had taken three hours and five minutes but apart from sipping this stuff, the trip was largely un-eventful. We arrived about lunch time, spent the night there, and with our aircraft refuelled and serviced, took off the next day heading roughly north-west and landed, again at lunchtime, at a place called Oodnadatta, which was nothing more than a tiny airfield stuck out in the middle of the outback. It had taken another three and a half hours of flying. This was purely a refuelling stop, followed by an hour and twenty-five minutes heading further north to Alice Springs, where we spent the night.

Although we were being led and navigated by a RAAF Beaufighter, our route was pretty straightforward merely flying up this single road. Robin Norwood did burst a tyre landing at Oodnadatta, so we had to leave him behind until a replacement could be sent up, but the rest of us continued on and he followed a few days later. Our flying height was only a few thousand feet, in blazing and brilliant sunshine, and I remember that upon arrival at Alice Springs we were soaked to the skin with sweat. Getting out of the aeroplanes and making the short walk to the flight hut, our shirts were immediately covered with black flies. I'd never seen so many flies in all my life. The hut had a double screen door and lobby arrangement and the idea was upon reaching it, someone behind you swatted and brushed off this layer of flies as much as possible, thereby letting you make a quick dash through the first door and closing it behind you before opening the inner door. And that is how we all got in, although of course, some flies were bound to enter too but far less than if one just walked in without this brush off game.

We stayed the night at Alice, I seem to remember we were in tents off the airfield, and then the next morning it was an easy day, just flying up to a place called Daly Waters, a well established airfield that had been used over the years for people flying London to Australia etc. Nice place and it only took us two and three quarter hours. Another night spent there and my best recollection was that the station commander here had a large refrigerator in which he kept about two dozen bottles of beer, ice-cold Castlemaine XXXX, and it was a glass

of beer I will remember for the rest of my life. We only had
two bottles each and it is truly what the Australians call the
old 'amber nectar' – great stuff and it went down a treat. We
were off early the next morning for the last short leg to
Darwin, not wanting to arrive at night, and we got there about
mid-day after just an hour and a half flying time.

Darwin has two seasons, a wet one and a hot dry one. The dry
is beautiful from about April to September/October time. No
rain, blue skies, and you can plan ahead and not have to worry
about bad weather spoiling your arangements. It is hot but not
overwhelming. In contrast the wet season is different
altogether. From November it is really monsoon weather.
There is a lot of rain, particularly in the evenings, typical
tropical downpours, but with reasonable days before the
clouds start building up as the humidity rises. As we arrived in
January 1943, half way through the wet period, although we
landed in good weather, it was hot, sticky, damp, rather nasty
and that really was our welcome to Darwin. The good thing
was that after Alice Springs, the flies were far less of a
problem.

We had arrived on the 17th and were met by our adjutant,
who with his party had already started work on our camp
area. Our new home was in the bush, about three miles from
the RAAF airfield where we would keep our Spitfires. We
bedded down for the night and nothing much happened for
the next two or three days while we settled in and the ground
crews serviced all the aircraft. I must say that we hadn't the
least idea what to anticipate, what we were in for, nothing like
that, but we had not expected to find ourselves sitting around
for so long and doing so little. The war we had come to fight
was starting to disappear in our neck of the woods.

The two Australian squadrons had followed us up along the
same route. 452 had made the journey on the 15th, 457 on the
16th. Group Captain Walters had flown in too but was now in
charge of the wing in all aspects except for in the air. That job
had been taken over by a new wing leader flying, a veteran
from North Africa, Wing Commander Clive Caldwell DFC
and Bar. He had over 20 victories flying over the desert with
250 and then 112 Squadron that had been equipped with
Tomahawks and then Kittyhawks. He was an obvious choice
and the Australians had asked for him to come home.

Although the RAF were reluctant to lose such a fighter, they agreed and after a brief stint in England where he converted to Spitfires and flew a few ops with the Kenley Wing to see how things were done away from the desert, he then left for his home country. Caldwell came from Sydney and despite his 31 years, he had proved himself an exceptional fighter pilot. Once he had arrived in Australia, and with his wing still stooging about at the Richmond area, he went to an operational training unit to test and instruct on the Boomerang, which seemed a bit odd to us, but anyway, he had now arrived to lead us.

Our arrival up north was all supposed to be a secret but I cannot think for a moment that our presence was totally unknown to both friend and foe alike. There were no press or war correspondents about, so perhaps things were really being kept under wraps.

The camp we had was pleasant enough, basic of course, but adequate for our needs. An area had been cleared in the bush and our tents had been set up. We began to build a few huts, and also a couple of primitive messes, which kept everyone occupied. Initially Bill Gibbs had a tent to himself while the rest of us doubled up as usual, Robin and I sharing once again. So there we were and thus began long periods of boring inactivity, waiting for something that never seemed to happen.

We began flying, practising formations and scrambles. We had aircraft on alert and we also flew the odd convoy patrol for shipping coming in and out of the harbour. Otherwise, we just stooged about, improving our accommodation with a pretty fair amount of personal DIY. There was a lot of timber around and most of us became quite adept at this boy scout stuff.

As for the Japanese, well we knew from our intelligence people that they were across the sea in Timor, and expected that if they were going to return to the Darwin area, that is where they were most likely to come from. It seemed amazing that after the initial panic about getting the British to send a wing of Spitfires out to Australia, it had taken almost a year to get us to where we were now. Would we indeed see any action, that was the question? From the initial feel of things we were certainly not convinced, but only time would tell.

Chapter Seven

Darwin

We had been a long time coming. It was now late January 1943 and the war with Japan was now over a year old. By the time the promised Spitfire wing had been organised in June 1942 and it had finally arrived in Darwin, seven months had come and gone, but at last we were in situ and ready for anything – so long as something, anything – happened.

The initial excitement in Australia had started way back in February 1942. With the Japanese forces spreading south and west, and having already landed in New Guinea, things were beginning to look decidedly serious for northern Australia. Further to the west lay Timor, which had been an important staging area for reinforcements from Australia to the islands of Java and Sumatra. Sumatra had fallen already and Java must surely be next. Therefore there seemed little use in holding on to Timor, although initially a force of American and Australian troops were sent to reinforce the island, and actually sailed on 15 February 1942, but it was attacked and forced back towards Darwin. On this same day a force of Japanese carriers, cruisers and destroyers had been ordered to head south and launch a strike against Darwin.

The port of Darwin, as well as being this important staging post for Allied forces that might pose a threat to Japanese intentions further north and west, and also the Philippines that was still fighting, was full of ships and there was a large quantity of aircraft on nearby airfields. Darwin had already had Japanese reconnaissance aircraft snooping about and the tension was mounting. The time for the Japanese attack was dawn on the 19th.

That morning there were 47 ships in Darwin harbour, including the transports that had returned from the abortive attempt to reach Timor. They came in all shapes and sizes, and included Australian and American vessels, and there were also some flying boats on the water – military and civil. At RAAF Darwin were a number of Lockheed Hudsons, some American

P40s that had just arrived, plus the personal aircraft of Major-General Patrick J Hurley USAAF, on a visit. There were also some unserviceable Wirraways with others at nearby Batchelor airstrip, while at Daly Waters were eight more Hudsons. On these three airfields were, in addition, a number of civil light aircraft.

Despite the obvious tension, two clues that something was about to happen appear to have been ignored. A signal from a coast-watcher on the northern edge of Melville Island, which is situated just north of Darwin, reported a large force of aircraft, but this was thought by RAAF HQ to refer to some P40 Kittyhawks that had been sent off to escort a B17 that had been going to Timor but had been thwarted by bad weather. Then a call from a catholic mission on Bathurst Island that abutted Melville Island, also reported an unusually large formation of aircraft heading for Darwin from the north-west, but this too was ignored. So, just like at Pearl Harbor on 7 December 1941, nobody had read the signs and those on the ground, and on the water, had no warning that danger was fast approaching.

The similarity with Pearl Harbor does not end there. Four of the six aircraft carriers used for the Hawaiian island attack were deployed in the raid on Darwin. The *Akagi*, *Kaga*, *Soryu* and the *Hiryu*, having re-equipped in home waters after the Pearl Harbor raid, had headed south towards Australia. By early morning of 19 February they were some 220 miles north-west of Darwin and ready to launch their planes. By 08.45 hours, a total of 188 aircraft, comprising 36 fighters, 71 dive-bombers and 81 high-level bombers, led by the very same leader that went for Pearl, Commander Mitsuo Fuchida, set a course of 148° and headed for Darwin.

The Japanese formation came upon an American PBY (Catalina) flying boat just north-west of Bathurst Island and one of the escorting Zero fighter pilots broke off to attack. Shooting this down in flames, the Japanese pilot headed for Darwin alone and found himself above five patrolling P40s, who were totally unaware of any impending problem. The enemy pilot, despite being totally alone, attacked them, shooting down three into the sea, and wounding the pilot of a fourth, who succeeded in crash-landing back at his base. This was quite an overture to Darwin's first aerial assault.

Japanese bombers and dive-bombers now headed in,

preceded by a number of low-flying Zero fighters that commenced a strafing attack on the ships. Moments later enemy bombers began unloading their ordnance on both town and harbour from 14,000 feet. An oil storage tank was set ablaze, buildings demolished, and ships were hit, sunk and damaged. Dive-bombers now proceeded to make their attack on ships and airfields. Some American P40s endeavoured to get off the ground but were overwhelmed by attacking Zeros, losing pilots and planes. More aircraft were strafed on the ground by the Zeros and left on fire. Three USN PBYs were also sunk at their moorings.

It was all over by 10.40 but Darwin was left in utter confusion. Military personnel and civilians lay about dead and injured. Fires raged, filling the sky with black smoke and dust. Believing this might well presage an invasion, many people evacuated the town. Yet more raiders were to come.

Just before noon more bombers headed in, bombing Darwin airfield again which was devastated. Buildings and hangars were wrecked, plus the last two P40s. Men headed into the surrounding bush and some days later over 250 were still unaccounted for. The Qantas hangar was also badly damaged. The raiders flew away, reporting that as far as they could see, any threat from Darwin in the near future was out of the question. The Japanese were now able to assault and capture Timor without fear of any intervention from northern Australia.

Having achieved their object of destroying or at least neutralising Darwin, the four carriers returned to the Celebes to refuel and re-arm. The *Kaga*, *Soryu* and *Hiryu*, headed for their next target, Ceylon. Here again the carriers achieved great success with minimal loss, raiding Colombo on Easter Sunday, 5 April, as well as the Royal Navy base at Trincomalee. They sank two HM cruisers, the *Dorsetshire* and *Cornwall*, amongst other losses. A couple of days later, at sea, the British carrier HMS *Hermes* was attacked and sunk along with the destroyer HMS *Vampire* and the corvette *Hollyhock*. In May the Jap carriers again returned to home waters and the following month headed eastwards across the Pacific towards Midway Island. Heading for this target their luck ran out. They were spotted on 4 June by patrol aircraft which preceded devastating attacks by US carrier aircraft. Between 09.00 and 17.00 that day, the Japanese lost four carriers to the American's one carrier loss (the *Yorktown*). It has been said that this was the turning point in the war against Japan. As all this was happening, we had been leaving England aboard the *Stirling Castle*.

While the 19 February attack on Darwin was devastating, others followed that were less so, but this was mainly due to there being far less to bomb and destroy. The town itself had been totally evacuated, and when we arrived there in January 1943, it was all but deserted and in the total control of the military. Further raids came during March 1942, some against the RAAF airfield known as '4 mile'. On the 22nd raiders attacked two civil aerodromes, while the 28th and 30th saw further raids on 4 mile. Some American P40s came into the area after this first raid and did claim some success against an attack on Anzac Day, 25 April 1942. Meantime, the Japanese kept a constant eye on anything that happened around Darwin, in order to make sure there was no build-up of men or equipment that might herald any sort of action from the area. Other places were attacked by aircraft too, including the coastal town of Broome, 650 miles to the south-west of Darwin, on 3 March 1942 with many casualties inflicted. Few later raids were as large as these early ones, sometimes just two or three bombers, and several others were made at night. It all helped to keep the Australians guessing – and watching.

A list of further Japanese incursions spread from June to November 1942, so the whole area seemed on almost constant alert. The Australians were well aware that they were extremely vulnerable. Their Prime Minister, John Curtin, had sent a cable to Winston Churchill in February 1942, which stated:

> 'Australia's outer defences are now quickly vanishing, and our vulnerability is completely exposed. With A.I.F. troops we sought to save Malaya and Singapore, falling back on the Netherlands East Indies. All these northern defences are going or gone... We feel a primary obligation to save Australia, not only for itself, but to prepare it as a base for the development of the war against Japan.'

This then had been the pre-curser to Doctor Evatt's pleas for help and assistance from both the USA and Britain, and for

Winston Churchill to promise Spitfires. However, as I
mentioned in the previous chapter, the war had moved on
considerably since these early raids of 1942, but we were here
now and would see what we should see.

Number 1 (Fighter) Wing was now in Darwin. However, we
were not all in one place. 452 Squadron were initially based at
Batchelor and then at the beginning of February at Strauss,
about five miles from us in Darwin. 457 Squadron after some
days at Batchelor, moved to Livingstone. We in 54 Squadron
had our camp-site at a place called Nightcliff.

The aerodrome was just a short drive away to the south-
west, and although it was known as Darwin, because it was
four miles from Darwin town, was often referred to as '4
mile'. It had earlier been the home of 52 Operational Training
Unit. There had been some Kittyhawks here but they had
departed by the time the wing arrived.

452 Squadron was commanded by Squadron Leader R E
Thorold-Smith DFC, the chap I had wished a happy new year
just before we left Sydney. His name was Ray but he was also
known as 'Throttle'. He came from New South Wales and
although I am not sure I knew then, he was in fact a month
younger than me. Pre-war he had been a medical student but
had become a pilot with the RAAF and in England had joined
452 Squadron as a pilot officer. During the summer and
autumn of 1941 he had flown many sorties over northern
France and had shot down six or seven German fighters and
won the DFC. By March 1942 he had risen to squadron
commander, just in time to bring 452 to Australia.

It was the first RAAF fighter squadron to be formed in the
UK, with mostly Australian personnel, in April 1941.
Equipped with the Spitfire Mark II it had moved to RAF
Kenley in July and the following month changed its equipment
to the Spitfire Mark V. During the rest of the year it was part
of the Kenley Wing.

Squadron Leader Pete Brothers DFC had commanded 457
Squadron when it was formed in June 1941, again with
Spitfire IIs. However, it did not see much operational work as
it was based at RAF Jurby on the Isle of Man until March
1942, when, with Spitfire Vs, it moved to Redhill, in Surrey. It
had only just started operations over France when the call
came for it to move to Australia. Pete Brothers handed over

command to Squadron Leader K E James. Ken James was an Australian, from Victoria, and oddly enough, was just two months older than me. In that brief period that 457 were flying over France he managed to share the destruction of a FW190. He too had risen from pilot officer to commanding officer. Unlike Thorold-Smith, Ken would survive the war.

Bill Gibbs therefore, had ten years on both of his brother COs, while our new wing leader, Clive Caldwell, was about a year older than Bill. Overall command of all air defences at Darwin was in the hands of Air Commodore F M Bladin, who at 44 years of age was older than all of us. We all mixed together pretty well nevertheless. I liked Caldwell and think the feeling was mutual. He did a good job with the wing and considering he didn't know any of us, he slotted in very well. I suppose his record spoke volumes as far as we were concerned. His predecessor, Walters, had done the initial ground work although he lacked experience. In fact he only learnt to fly the Spitfire after we had arrived in Australia. As a wing leader it was absolutely crazy, but to give Walters his due he never led the wing in action, and after Caldwell took over, his role was mainly one of being around as senior Australian Air Force officer, and when he did fly he would slot himself in as a number two in a section.

At the end of January, Group Captain Walters wrote to HQ North West Area requesting allocation of squadron code letters for our Spitfires, and proposing that 54 have the two letters TA, 452 DL and 457 XB. Confirmation was soon received, but allocating letters DL for our squadron, QY for 452 and XB for 457. 54 had DL pre-war but had changed them to KL in September 1939. In England 452 had used UD, while 457 had had BP. Its new XB was later changed to ZP. Walters had also requested that he and Caldwell be allowed a wing leader's prerogative of having their personal initials painted on their machines, ALW and CRC.

It was a known fact that our arrival, or to be more precise, the arrival of Spitfires into the area, gave everyone there a great uplift of spirits. We may have liked things to have been a little more permanent by way of buildings and maintenance hangars but we soon adapted to the conditions. Our engineering officer, Cecil Beaton, was a great chap and worked wonders keeping our Spitfires in repair and serviceable. We were lucky in that 54 Squadron was at the old RAAF base. Although it had been badly bombed in those earlier air raids, one hangar had survived and most of our maintenance was carried out in it. The other two squadrons, being out in the bush on airstrips cut out of the jungle, were all under canvas, aircraft and men.

One problem we did encounter with our new Spitfires was one with the constant speed mechanism. The problem was that it would go into fully fine pitch without giving the pilot the slightest warning and could blow up on you, which did happen. After the first couple of episodes, which fortunately the blokes involved got away with, it was mostly corrected, but I am pretty sure we lost a couple of chaps in one of the March air battles due to it. I know Robin Norwood had it happen to him once.

Despite having lost all our non-British pilots back in England, the squadron make-up of pilots was still a very mixed variety of men from the UK. I have already mentioned Gibbs and Norwood, from Sussex, and some of the others were as follows:

Flying Officer J A Tuckson, who came from Surrey
Flying Officer J D Lenagen, from Trinidad
Pilot Officer G B Farries, a Lancashire lad
Pilot Officer A K Brook, from Kent
Pilot Officer A McIntyre, from Sussex
Pilot Officer I Taylor, from Glasgow
Pilot Officer G Wall
Pilot Officer H Leonard, from Wembley, Middlesex
Flight Sergeant F L Varney, from Crawley, Sussex
Flight Sergeant B Mahoney, from Kent
Flight Sergeant Millar
Sergeant J C Wellsman, from Twickenham, Middlesex
Sergeant D M Wheeler, a Hertfordshire lad from St Albans
Sergeant W Eldred
Sergeant G Horkin, from Yorkshire
Sergeant D Monger
Sergeant P F McCarthy, from Gravesend, Kent
Sergeant A E Cooper, from Worcestershire
Sgt Studley

Some had interesting backgrounds. For instance, Tuckson's

father was a pilot, guiding ships through the Suez Canal, while Wheeler's father was a vicar, which led us to refer to him as 'The Bish'. Dennis Monger, after the war, became an outside broadcast man for the BBC and covered all the Farnborough air shows along with Raymond Baxter. Baxter did all the commentating while Dennis was the producer. He was quite a character and I well remember his love of whisky, especially when he would come into the Shell enclosure at Farnborough to drink our booze. When he retired he went on a cruise but died on it with a glass of whisky in his hand. I am sure he would have thought of no better way to go.

In addition to Ernie Weatherhead, our bluff Yorkshireman, and R G 'Cecil' Beaton, our medical officer was Flight Lieutenant J D Jarman, who hailed from Welsh Wales, while our intelligence officer was Pilot Officer C R 'Jimmy' Councer, a Kentish man. The padre was Flight Lieutenant Donald Begbie.

By late January, early February we had got ourselves organised as best we could. We lived in the bush in our tents, while building our huts. If we had been in Burma they would have been called *bashas*. We were now flying practise formation sorties and trying to be ready for any action that might present itself.

Then on the 5th, we suffered our first loss. In the afternoon the squadron was flying a formation but when coming back to land, two Spitfires collided on the runway. Sergeant Peter McCarthy, aged 20, was killed. The other pilot was not hurt. However, the action we had been waiting so long for, came the next day, the 6th.

By this time I had my own Spitfire, BR539, that was coded DL-X, and it was a machine that I would have for practically my whole time in Darwin. However, it was having a major service on the 6th, so I flew BS181, DL-Y, a machine normally flown by John Lenagen. He had a girlfriend down in Sydney named Yvonne, so the 'Y' was a nice aircraft letter to have, and he also had the girl's name painted on the engine cowling.

We were often told that Australian coast-watchers were constantly on the look-out for hostile aircraft and if seen they would radio to RAAF HQ and give us the warning. We did however, have radar. The Australians had established a

reasonable radar site on the north-west coast which seemed to work pretty efficiently and we did get quite good notice of stuff coming in. Once we got this co-operation down to a fine art we generally got height before the Japanese reached the Australian coast, but it didn't always work.

The squadron record book (Form 540) for 6 February 1943, notes our first success since arriving in Darwin:

> A memorable day for the squadron, since it marked our first real kill in Australia. F/Lt Foster destroyed a Dinah light bomber [above], apparently engaged in recce., about 34 miles W.N.W. of Cape Van Diemen at 1250 hours. F/Lt Foster was White 1, and both he and his No.2, F/Sgt Mahoney, saw the Jap hit the water in flames. General Jubilation.

[Cape Van Diemen is right on the north-west tip of Melville Island.]

This action was really a great piece of luck as far as I was concerned. It was just shear chance that it was my section that was on readiness that morning and were scrambled, when this hostile plot was located on the radar screen, and we were sent off. In fact my section was made up of four aircraft, with George Farries and Dennis Monger being numbers three and four. We were away at 12.05 but the other two quickly became separated from Mahoney and myself and they landed back within ten minutes.

Mahoney and I sped out to sea, vectored onto the 'bandit' which was still some way off. Having mentioned earlier that over the last year quite a number of raids had been made around the Darwin area, of interest is that this incursion was recorded as number 49. Not all bombing or strafing raids of course, just anything hostile that had received attention from the defences, whatever the outcome.

After the sortie, Jimmy Councer debriefed me and then typed out the following report:

From: Intelligence Officer, 54 Squadron, Darwin.
To: Intelligence Officer, No.1 Fighter Wing.
Date: 6th February, 1943.
Reference: Composite Combat Report: 54 Squadron.

White section Capstan[1] RAAF Darwin. Up 1205 hrs. Down 1320 hrs. White Section scrambled with orders to proceed to Charlie Angels 30. White 1's radio transmitter unserviceable to ground but could hear White 2. White 2 could hear ground but not White 1. When at 24,000 feet over Charlie, ordered to patrol Arsy (Roman Catholic Mission, Bathurst Island) angels 25. This was found to be just in a thin layer of cloud. Next vector 350, "bandit 8,000 approaching from E." White section decreased height to 12,000 and when approximately opposite Fort Dundas were ordered to fly on reciprocal course, "bandit approaching from 9 o'clock".

White section returned to Arsy and orbited, and were then vectored 280, "bandit 2 o'clock, 5 miles ahead". The next vector was 360, "bandit angels 17, 10-12 miles ahead", and on this vector E/A (enemy aircraft) was sighted about 1250 hrs. flying S.W. Courses conveyed to about 1,000 yards when E/A apparently first observed our aircraft, and made a steep turn, heading approximately N.W. and climbing to 22,000 ft. at estimated rate of climb of 600 ft. per minute. At 22,000 ft. Indicated Air Speed of White 1 was 225 and he was just overhauling the E/A.

White 1 closed in quarter astern at 17,000 ft. and observed Jap markings. There was no fire from the E/A and no guns were observed. White 1 closed to 300 yds. Dead astern and slightly below E/A, followed by White 2. White 1 fired two quick bursts at 300 yds., the first of which caused cannon strikes to be seen on port engine

[1]Capstan was the code for Spitfires in order to keep them secret from the Japanese.

without apparent result. The E/A here appeared to be gaining slightly, and White 1 fired a third short burst with cannon and machine gun without result. White 1 was then able to gain slightly more and at 200 yds. fired a fourth burst, observing strikes on port engine spreading to the fuselage and starboard engine. A fifth burst, followed by a long burst closing to 100 yds., resulted in further strikes raking the E/A, the port engine of which caught fire, the flames spreading to the rest of the machine.

The enemy spiralled down in flames and was seen by both White 1 and White 2 to hit the water burning fiercely.

Length of bursts. (1) 2 secs.; (2) 2 secs.; (3) 1 sec.; (4) 2 secs.; (5) 5 secs. Approximately. No deflection used.
Ammunition Report:
Machine Guns: Port inner 290 Incendiary; Starboard inner, 287 A.P. Port outer 291 Armour Piercing; Starboard outer 293 A.P.
Cannons: Port: 29 Ball, 28 High Explosive Incendiary. Starboard: 29 Ball, 29 High Explosive Incendiary.
Camouflage: Enemy aircraft was coloured a greyish blue; there were red roundels on underside of wings and on side of fuselage. Markings on tail-plane apparently black and white lines; could not be distinguished with clarity. From pilot's description E/A is considered to be type DINAH, but it was observed that the underside of fuselage was swept up almost to a point at the tail, and the engine nacelles appeared to be slightly larger below the wings than indicated in R.A.A.F. Diagram P1/1.
Pilot of White 1 Flt/Lt R.W. Foster, RAF, who claims one E/A destroyed; of White 2, Flt/Sgt Mahoney, RAF. Our casualties nil. No damage to our A/C.
Weather: 10/10 cloud at 25,000 ft. Scattered low cloud 3,000-5,000 feet. Visibility excellent.

C R Councer F/O
Intelligence Officer,
54 Sqdn., RAF

p.s. The first Enemy Aircraft to be shot down by a

Spitfire in Australia.

[Candy was our squadron call-sign, so on this day I would have been known as Candy White 1 – a great help had my radio been working properly. Pat Mahoney was Candy White 2.]

Not unnaturally I was the hero of the hour and duly took the plaudits from my fellow pilots after I had landed. This bit of excitement caused all sorts of interest as can be imagined although initially it was kept quiet publicly for it still had not been released that we were here. However, as always the press somehow got hold of the story within a few days (they came on the 10th) and the reporters and photographers were soon milling about.

I was photographed quite liberally: in front of the Spitfire in which I had done the deed, with Bill Gibbs as CO of the squadron involved, with Jimmy Councer our intelligence officer, and wearing my mae west as if I was reporting in moments after I had landed. Then with a smiling bunch of pilots with me grinning wonderfully in front. It must have lasted more than the required 15 minutes of fame one is allotted according to Andy Warhol!

The Dinah was the Allied code word for the Mitsubishi Ki-46, Japan's two-seat reconnaissance machine. Most did have a single 7.7 mm rear-firing machine gun but if this one did, or if the gunner fired it, I certainly had no recollection of any return fire. It was known for its graceful lines and this was what helped it fly at a goodly speed. It was generally this speed that helped it get out and away from trouble. It could also cover a lot of ground as well as speed. Usually the crews would be in and out almost before you knew it and the radar boys had to be on the alert, not only to spot one, but to get aircraft airborne quickly and vectored expertly if they were to have any chance of interception. I had been lucky, not only to be vectored proficiently, but then able to close in before the enemy crew spotted me.

Of course, we had no way of knowing at the time which Japanese unit this machine had come from, and it was years later that its identity was discovered. It was a machine of the 10th Sentai JAAF, 70th Chutai. One has to refer to it being a

Japanese Army machine (JAAF) because the aircraft we encountered could be either army or navy. In this respect it was like the Americans or indeed the British, both countries having separate air arms, although Japan's army air force units were more closely allied to the ground troops and in the main came under army control. This Dinah was apparently the first of 18 losses this unit was to suffer in the war.

With Darwin town being virtually deserted, there were obviously few places we could go for any form of entertainment. The gramophone records that Jimmy Councer had purchased in Sydney just before we left were therefore in great demand and had pride of place in our mess building. One particular record that seemed to be played incessantly was Bing Crosby singing 'I'm dreaming of a White Christmas'. Considering the time of year and the heat I can't imagine why this particular song was played so much, unless it made the lads think of snow and mentally cooled them down. The original stock of records were supplemented from time to time as chaps were given leave to take a break in Sydney and those inclined to be generous, or who were fed up with Bing Crosby, would bring back a couple of the latest tunes. We had a radio of course, and once we were established, mail from home came up fairly regularly.

Few Australian civilians were about, just a scattering of cattle stockmen and some essential workers to keep things ticking over. What entertainment we found all had to be self made. Our days were spent at dispersal, having motored down from our camp each morning. The weather was improving all the time, so at least it was generally warm and sunny.

The docks had been taken over by the Australian Navy and Bill Gibbs soon made contact with them to see if we could be of mutual help, although it would be true to say we were looking for more from them than they from us. Nevertheless, we were offered the hand of friendship and on several occasions were invited to dine with them. They certainly seemed to be able to get everything they wanted and asked for, so there was always plenty of good grub available and the drink flowed well too. Bill had already discovered that they had control over all supplies coming into Darwin and being a wise old guy – there is no good getting old without getting wise – had pounced on this chance to improve our lot.

From time to time some dignitaries would descend on us from Sydney, and we even had the odd chap from the UK. One such who had come out from England, was Group Captain Richard Grice DFC. He had got his award in France during World War One but more recently he had been station commander at RAF Biggin Hill during the Battle of Britain. In fact he would hop up to see us several times and I think he was the senior RAF officer in Australia at this time. The usual way up from Sydney or Melbourne for these people was by Sunderland flying boat, via Brisbane, then across the Northern Territories to a place called Groote Island where they would land on the sea. Of the others who called in, most arrived early on while we were still a novelty, but then their visits tended to die off, and it was only people like Dick Grice who would fly up more regularly.

As already mentioned, our food, while adequate, was not over sumptuous. One morning at Nightcliff, out in the airmen's tented area, one of our fitters came back from the mess tent and yelled that there were eggs for breakfast. His words were met by the usual derision and disbelief, but it turned out to be true. Dick Grice had flown up with 60 of the precious things from Melbourne, but it only happened the once. Some of the more enterprising airmen of both nationalities supplemented the foodstuffs by introducing fish traps, a sort of netted enclosure fixed on the shore. Once the tide went out the fish that got caught were retrieved and given to the cookhouse. I must say that it was sometimes hard to distinguish our British airmen from the Australian ones, for many had swapped headgear. With tropical kit came the obligatory pith helmet, and these were exchanged for the Digger's slouch hats. Often, if you didn't recognise the face of the man you were talking to, you'd only discover his nationality when he spoke.

We did occasionally suffer from one of those discomforts that plague westerners who find themselves in the tropics, that oddly sounding irritation, prickly heat. This particular affliction usually gets you between the legs or perhaps under the armpits. The only cure we had was some stuff called Whitfield's Ointment, which we would put round the affected area although it was akin to burning oneself to death. So every evening as the sun went down, someone, somewhere, could be seen sitting in front of their tent or hut, legs wide apart and, having applied Whitfield's would then have to waft air over the treated spot with a towel, or even a fan if you were that way inclined. God, did it sting. There was no worry about seeing you doing this, or rubbing the ointment on, for we all seemed to get it at some time or other. Fortunately with no women about to chase, there were only some Australian army nurses to be found anywhere around the Darwin area, one didn't have to cancel any dates if one became afflicted with this torment. Perhaps some newcomers might initially wonder why some of these chaps were standing about rubbing themselves between the legs and then, grimacing while they wafted a cool breeze over their nether regions, their grimace very slowly turning to a look of relief, but they soon understood personally the reason why.

When we were not scratching and wafting, one thing we did occasionally when we had some free time was to go off duck shooting with our navy pals. The place was teeming with wild life where we were, and I remember going out once into some swampy area. The poor old ducks had never come up against human beings intent on their demise with firearms so we had a bit of an advantage with our 12-guage shotguns. The guns were generously supplied by the navy, for as I said earlier, these sailors had everything.

Often we would take tents and supplies with us and stay out overnight, or even a couple of days if we could. It was not only a good way to relax away from the tedium of the airfield, but it helped supplement our somewhat meagre diet. I cannot profess to being any great shakes as a marksman, although the spread of a shotgun blast had certain advantages over a rifle. On this occasion I had become slightly separated from the other members of our hunting party and found myself by the side of an expanse of water. Suddenly two ducks flew right over me and without much thought but perhaps some inner instinct, I raised my shotgun, fired both barrels, one at each, and both birds nose dived into the water, about twelve feet from the shore. I couldn't believe my eyes. What an 'ace shot' I thought. Why wasn't there anybody about when I needed a witness to such shooting? It took me a few moments to realise that I had bagged a nice brace for the pot and had just started to creep into the water so as not only to retrieve my two floating meals but to bring back the evidence of my 'kills', when there was a sudden 'splonch' and a swift movement in the water. The noise was made by a ruddy great crocodile that poked its snout up just long enough for it to snaffle both birds and take them under. I was back on the bank in less time than it takes to describe it. I could only return with a good story but no confirmation or dinner.

I suppose I should have guessed that all the furore with the press because of my sudden fame at downing the first Japanese aircraft by a Spitfire over Darwin, would not fail to dog me, and so it proved. It was not long before my face, words and exploit began to be spread in various newspapers both in Australia and at home. Unknown to me at the time my mother began collecting as many of the newspaper clippings she could and stuck them on pages in an 8″ x 12″ book-keeper's cash-book. She proudly showed them all to me upon my return home. Some of the titles of the pieces were quite remarkable.

Londoner Got the First.
A Londoner, Flight.Lieut. A W Foster, RAF, was the first Spitfire pilot to shoot down a Japanese plane on the Pacific front, said a Reuter cable today from Australia. He had already shot down three planes and shared honours for a fourth, in Britain and France, before he went to Australia with the new Spitfire squadrons.

I was to get used to reporting errors. Not only did they get my first initial wrong, but they also said I had fought in France.

Londoner Shoots Down Jap Plane.
A Londoner, Flight Lieutenant A W Foster RAF was the first Spitfire pilot to shoot down a Japanese airplane on the Pacific War front, it was revealed to-day in a despatch from "Somewhere in Australia", says Reuters.
    Flight Lieutenant Foster, describing how he came up behind a Japanese reconnaissance airplane and shot it down into the sea, said, "I do not think he even knew I was there."
    All Darwin is thrilled by the arrival of the Spitfires which are piloted by veterans of the Battle of Britain.

Again my first initial is wrong, and then, pretending to adhere to the secrecy of where we were, by saying 'somewhere in Australia', it goes on to mention Darwin, and to give the impression that the town is full of grateful people, when in fact, as I have said already, it was more or less a ghost town.

First Spitfire Pilot to Bag Jap. And so on.

Some weeks later, pictures and an article were published in the *Australian Women's Weekly*, centre spread. There were pictures of a number of pilots and ground crews, with yours truly climbing out of a Spitfire, with side-arm *de rigueur*. The article was entitled: English Spitfire Boys in the Never-Never. It was written by Bill Moore, a war correspondent, whose opening gambit was: *White skinned lads look like bronzed Australian surfers now*. The words that he began with were no better:

> There's a little bit of England wedged into a slice of thickly timbered bush-land that forms part of rugged north-western Australia. That little bit of England is the courageous unit of Spitfire pilots and ground crew who left the misty green countryside of their Motherland to join Australian Spitfire units in tackling Jap air invaders who swarm in from the stratosphere over the Arafura Sea.
>
> Mere lads with pink-and-white complexions have in a few months of their life in balmy, tropical sunshine become as suntanned as the brawniest surfer on Australian beaches.
>
> They have tossed aside the sweaters and mufflers they were wearing in bitterly cold south of England air stations last year, and to-day work and play in shorts and boots as thoroughly acclimatised as the Australian troops who are defending this area.

I will not go on, but this vein continued. Had Mr Moore ever been to England? Did he think it was freezing cold all the time? Was wode still daubed on British inhabitants? Did my parents and friends think I and my comrades were living in a holiday resort where the sport activities included shooting down Japanese aircraft for kicks? Still, I hoped the Australian ladies lapped it all up so we could have even better welcomes when we were able to take some leave in Sydney. Little did I

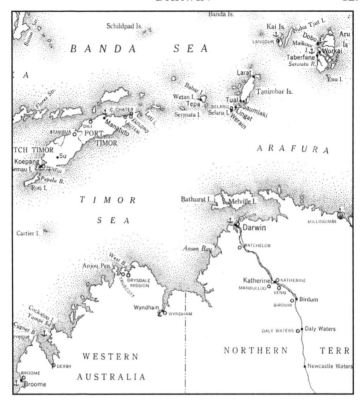

know then that in just over a year hence I would be leading a team of war correspondents who would churn out similar stuff from Normandy!

As time went on my mother would collect some other great and wonderfully written diatribes on our activities over Darwin. It is funny to look back on these cuttings now but in 1943 it was war-winning blarney and read with immense pleasure that gave heart and comfort to the civilian readership. So long as it looked as if we were winning this war, then it did the trick. The war was still struggling on over many battle fronts, but at least there appeared to be a tiny light at the end of a dark and dismal tunnel.

Chapter Eight

Dog-Fights over Darwin

My good fortune in bringing down that Dinah on 6 February 1943, was the first time a Japanese aircraft had been reported anywhere in the Darwin area since the 21st of January. It seemed obvious to us that someone had told them that we had arrived and they had sent an aircraft over to take a look-see. The next day they sent another one but this was in and out before anyone could react properly. Another Dinah did operate over the sea on the 21st, but some way out to sea.

This Dinah did, however, fly close to the ship that had brought our sea party up from Sydney, the *Maetsuycker*, that was making her way up again, from Freemantle. This suggested an attack on her, and Spitfires were sent off to patrol over her, led by Clive Caldwell, and the section also included Robin Norwood. One odd thing about Robin was that on the ground he had a distinct stammer, but in the air, when talking over the R/T there was absolutely no sign of this at all. Before the Spitfires got to the area, a Japanese bomber did in fact go for the ship but its bombs caused neither damage nor casualties.

Ending their patrol, Caldwell and the others landed at an airstrip that was usually only used for emergencies, and the wingco embarrassingly tipped his Spitfire up on its nose on landing, bending the propeller. There were no repair facilities on this strip, so the only course of action to straighten out the offending blade was to employ some brute force with a 9lb hammer. According to Caldwell, this event took place not on 21 February but on 6 March. Whether he is correct or the records are, is not important really, but the basic story remains true.

On the 26th a report did come in that Japanese aircraft had been spotted at Penfui, an airfield at Koepang, on Timor, so we were alerted to be at readiness at first light. However, the next day the weather was so bad that no flying took place anywhere in the region, but the only incursion came on the

28th, a Jap machine obviously making a weather assessment. The weather was still bad our end, and although two Spitfires were sent aloft, they saw nothing.

As we were to find, and what our brother fighter pilots in Burma had already discovered, the Japanese air force generally advertised an up-coming raid in two ways. Firstly they sent over a Dinah reconnaissance aircraft, and then, if our own recce machines went out to take a look at known Japanese airfields, rather than being devoid of aircraft, their bombers and fighters would be seen on the ground. The Japanese usually managed to keep their aircraft out of danger by flying them away and therefore out of range of air attack from Allied bombers. It was a good way to preserve strength of course, but if their aircraft were suddenly seen or reported back at their forward airfields, then there was obviously something up.

It was a poor tactic for them but a good one for us, and I often wonder if their leaders were totally oblivious to this free advertising of their intentions. They must undoubtedly have had some sort of spy system operating on our side although it would seem difficult for any orientals to blend in anywhere in northern Australia. Our initial presence was kept so secret that they couldn't have read about it in news reports or even newspapers. The only way perhaps was that while we were at Richmond and it was common knowledge the Spitfires had arrived, it would have equally been obvious when we suddenly left. Anybody watching trains, the docks or even roads, would have seen clear indications that not only was the wing on the move, but it was heading in a northerly direction. As Darwin would have been the most obvious place to send us, it would not have taken a genius to work out roughly when we would be arriving there, at which time the Japanese would certainly try to confirm this by aerial reconnaissance.

The two Dinahs on the 6th and 7th did not presage any air attacks on the northern Australian soil, but we were nevertheless kept on an even keener alert, expecting something might happen. That, however, was not to be, and in fact nothing else occurred for the rest of February. We had come such a long way and taken so long to be in a position where we could finally do something, but the Japanese were not playing ball. So February was a real anti-climax, and I think we had started to relax slightly until those incidents between

the 26th and 28th. However, as March began things changed dramatically on the second day of that month.

The weather was fine, which no doubt encouraged the Japanese to have a go. Their target apparently was the airstrip at Coomali Creek, which is about 15 miles south of Livingstone. Officially it was raid number 52. The bombers comprised nine Mitsubishi G4M bombers [above], known by their codename as 'Bettys' (although other reports indicated single-engined 'Kates' [Nakajima B5Ns], from, we now know, the Japanese Navy's 753 Kokutai. They had an escort of 21 Mitsubishi A6M Zekes [in other words Zeros] of the 202 Kokutai, led by Lieutenant-Commander Takahide Aioi.

The enemy aircraft were intercepted while they were still over the sea, about 30 miles west-north-west of Port Charles, Darwin. My squadron engaged them in company with one of the Aussie squadrons, and in some confused fighting Clive Caldwell and Bill Gibbs each claimed one fighter shot down, with the wingco claiming one of the bombers. Pilot Officer Ashby claimed a bomber as damaged. We had no casualties although Bill got a bullet in the radiator and glycol system but he got the machine down without much of a problem, being relatively close to our airfield. Upon inspection Bill found another bullet had hit the cockpit and had actually slammed into his head-rest. Close! 457 Squadron had also been airborne but did not make contact.

I gather that Groupie Walters, flying behind Caldwell, found a machine on his tail and at first assumed it to be another Spitfire, until, that is, it began shooting in his direction. However, his reaction was to think the enemy fighter was actually firing at Caldwell. Then tracer shells began zipping over his cockpit canopy and quickly broke away. He had warned Caldwell of the danger, and when they landed, Caldwell had told Walters that he should make sure he looked after himself and not worry about someone else's plight. I thought that a bit unkind. Caldwell would have sung a different tune had he been shot up – or down – without that warning call. Sergeant Eldred had a narrow escape, having to out-manoeuvre no less than four Zero fighters ganging up on him but he made it.

The Japanese apparently did not recognise our fighters as Spitfires, reporting that they had battled with P39 Aircobras and Buffaloes. Considering the Buffalo was a stubby radial-engined fighter, one has to wonder why they should not recognise the slim-trim lines of the Spitfire. I think it was the next day that our intelligence people heard that four enemy aircraft had not got back to their base, so perhaps a claim made by anti-aircraft gunners may be accepted. I don't know if anyone actually saw any of the enemy machines go into the sea, but certainly none came down on land. The Japanese also sent another recce machine over on the 3rd but it was not intercepted. The funny thing was that about this time, the army detonated an unexploded bomb nearby, and as the airmen were sitting down to lunch, they thought the place was being attacked.

Zero fighters had strafed the Coomali airstrip and destroyed an Aussie Beaufighter on the ground and damaged some other aircraft. Although 452 were not scrambled on this occasion, two pilots who were at readiness, saw a couple of Zeros zipping past and couldn't resist taking off to pursue them. Over the radio they heard of the attack on Coomali and having lost sight of the Zeros, decided to take a look at the airstrip. They flew across low and slow at first in order to let everyone know they were 'friendly' but then unwisely decided to beat-up the place. Having just been attacked those on the ground were exceptionally 'not amused', so much so that both men were carpeted for their impromptu demonstration of flying dexterity in front of Air Commodore Bladin. Luckily, Caldwell was present, and managed to persuade Bladin that while silly it was nothing more serious, but both men had their pay-books endorsed, which was better than the court martial that might have been given.

One of these two chaps was Flying Officer A P Goldsmith DFC DFM, from New South Wales. He was a veteran of Malta, one of a couple of Malta pilots that had been acquired by 452 Squadron. Known to everyone as 'Tim' he already had more than a dozen German scalps with several more damaged over the Mediterranean island and would add more over Darwin.

The following day we heard over the radio that RAF Spitfires were now operating over Darwin and had been in a fight on the 2nd and shot down six enemy aircraft, so the secret was officially out.

One of the Australian pilots in 457 Squadron shot down a Dinah on the 7th. It fell not far from Darwin and several people saw it falling in flames and into the sea off Lee Point. However, it was not all sweetness and light. Those problems with the Spitfire I mentioned earlier struck during this bit of excitement, four having to get down fast. Three made it safely but the fourth crashed, and the pilot, Flight Sergeant E M Moore, was killed.

Once again there was a lull in the action, and we reverted to our waiting game. The problems with the Spitfires occupied most of our discussions, and I read somewhere that the wing had more than a dozen aircraft involved in accidents since coming north. These ranged from collisions to bad landings or forced landings, and the majority resulted in aircraft written off.

The days dragged on until the 15th. That day was an eye-opener. Raid No.53 it was and came on a hot sunny morning, with particularly bright sunlight. The raid was mounted by 22 Mitsubishi Betty bombers, plus 27 Zero fighters flying escort. Radar picked up the plot some twenty minutes before being seen nearing the south-west tip of Bathurst Island just before 11.00. Their target was the dock area and the nearby oil storage tanks. Bombs fell, causing damage and casualties, while the American Headquarters building received a direct hit, with others falling on railway tracks and the oil tanks. Only two of these contained oil, but they certainly burst well. Our squadron diary has the following notation:

> Big Japanese raid this morning consisting of 22 bombers and an unknown number of Zeros as escort. The formation coming over in bright sunlight was very reminiscent of the Battle of Britain, and most of us had not seen such a sight since that time. They dropped a

surprisingly small number of bombs on Darwin town and set two oil tanks on fire, producing a spectacular blaze and smoke.

The squadron on this occasion comprised:

F/Lt Norwood	BR544	F/Lt Foster	BR539
Sgt Studley	BR532	Sgt Cooper	AR620
F/Sgt Varney	AR619	F/Sgt Biggs	BR536
F/O McNab	BR528	F/O Mawer	BS305
S/Ldr Gibbs	BR545	F/O Taylor	BS220

Combating this raid, as far as I can remember, was a complete shambles. Although we had warning about it, we were sent off in dribs and drabs. We did not take off as a squadron but in flights, and were immediately grabbing desperately for height as fast as we could, and were still below the bombers when we spotted them coming in over Darwin, and bombing the oil tanks. I can't say why this happened for I'm sure we had adequate warning. I remember this particularly well because in order to try and get at the bombers, I pulled up and opened up with my cannon and promptly went over into a spin! The recoil from these guns, just as I was about on a stall, just took away what forward motion I had and I just fell over and down. It was very frightening at the time and it took a few seconds to realise what had happened, but I quickly recovered.

Then I picked out the bombers again and followed them out to sea and to the best of my recollections there were no Zeros with this particular bunch ahead of me, because I made a pretty long distance approach on them and would certainly have noticed Japanese fighters if they had been around. I claimed hitting a couple of them, and later, one of these was graded up to a destroyed. Jimmy Councer came over and said they had made an assessment of all claims and came to some conclusions.

The other flight, led by Robin Norwood, I believe was used as top cover to 452 Squadron, and they did run into fighters escorting another group of bombers, and tangled with them. Trying desperately to close with these bombers, and when going 'balls-out' as we were, it was not good tactics. In these circumstances, with some aircraft going faster than others, you tend to go in, not as a nice section of four or six, but all over the sky. I do recall looking down and seeing the oil tanks burning fiercely, so the Japanese had already dropped their bombs by the time we got up to them.

The squadron diary also records our claims. Robin, Mawer and Biggs were credited with three Zeros destroyed with Robin also given a probable, while Taylor got two more damaged. I had put in for one bomber probably destroyed and one damaged, but as I said, our I/O later raised my probable to a destroyed. 457 Squadron had got into the act and also made claims, one by Tim Goldsmith, having taken off with permission on this occasion.

Our losses were not light. Four Spitfires were destroyed, two from my squadron. 452 had suffered the loss of 'Throttle' Thorold-Smith, while another pilot had baled out. From 54 we lost Sergeant Bert Cooper, who it will be remembered had survived that collision with Peter McCarthy earlier in the month, and Flight Sergeant F L Varney.

Cooper was 28 and a married man. He had seen some operations over France in 1941 before joining 54. His fighter fell into the sea and although he was seen to bale out he struck the tail of his machine. He was picked up but was dead already having broken his neck. Francis (Frank) Varney, aged 20, died in hospital the same afternoon, two months short of his 21st birthday. We were never sure what had happened but he had tried to attempt a crash-landing on the beach and hadn't made it. There were no bullet holes in his machine. He had come down only a few yards from the hospital at Kahlin and was on the operating table within a matter of minutes, but he failed to respond.

Thorold-Smith and some of his pilots had been at RAAF Darwin the previous evening on night readiness and night flying practise, and were in the process of flying back to Strauss at the time the incoming raid was announced. They had then altered course to help with the interception. Two of Throttle's men had to drop back and down due to oxygen problems. It seems the oxygen supply had been pretty much used up during their night flying and it hadn't seemed necessary to replenish the bottles for the short flight back to their base. None of the pilots would have been on top form having been up all night in any event. The others saw the bombers and then got tangled with the Zeros, for Throttle had not hesitated to engage.

Whether Thorold-Smith had then suffered oxygen failure too, and lost consciousness, or was shot down by a Zero is unclear but his machine was later found in the sea. Its wheels were still retracted and the propeller still in coarse pitch. If he was trying to ditch he would have changed that to fine pitch, but then again, no alert pilot would have chosen to ditch a Spitfire Vc that had the big Vokes air filter up front. This is why it was suggested he had become unconscious and gone down the way he had.

More than twenty years later a memorial plaque was unveiled at the Queenscliff Surf Life-Saving Cub, near Manley, Sydney, to the honoured memory of Thorold-Smith. Clive Caldwell attended, and so did Ted Hall, who as a flight lieutenant, had been in his CO's section on that fateful day in March 1943.

That evening there had been a dinner previously arranged with the Australian Navy boys. We had been getting along famously with them. They fed and watered us very well when we were invited to these get-togethers, and overall we had struck up quite a rapport.

However, on this particular evening when we arrived for dinner, while they were reasonably polite, we soon found out that for most of the day they had been helping to fight the many fires in the dock and town area and had also suffered a number of near misses as bombs fell in scattered clumps among them. This of course, was after we had boasted and assured them that now the Spitfires were here to defend the place, all would be well. They were a bit cool to say the least, especially as the bombers had already dropped their bombs before we even got close to them, and they were on their way out. However, I am pleased to say that after a few beers and pink gins all was forgiven and our relationship soon got back onto its former footing. They also came to dine with us a few times, and we even managed to get some reasonable food together but they always provided the booze.

It was after this raid that the RAAF and RAF released a lot of pictures of us and our Spitfires, while the newspaper reporters, restrictions having finally been lifted, wrote articles as if we had just won the war. The amount of coverage by the Australian press far out-weighed what we had achieved. As ever inaccuracies crept in. For instance our intelligence officer

was described as a veteran fighter pilot from the Battle of
Britain and Ernie Weatherhead was also recorded as being a
pilot. One of the news cuttings was found and kept by my
mother in her collection, and it was in this one that Jimmy
Councer not only became a pilot but was not even allowed the
correct spelling of his name:

> Spitfires in Action Now in Australia – Canberra,
> Thursday.
> *Mr J Curtin, Australian Prime Minister, announced to-
> day that Spitfire squadrons are now in action in
> Australia. It was Spitfires that shot down six out of 15
> Jap fighters which attacked an aerodrome at Darwin on
> Tuesday.*
>
> *Spitfires had been in action in Australia only once
> before, on February 6, when they intercepted a Jap
> reconnaissance bomber off Darwin. Flight-Lieut Robert
> Foster of London, Flying Officer Grouncer, and Flight-
> Lieut Tony Tuckson also from London, are among the
> pilots of the new Australian Spitfire squadrons.*
>
> *Mr Curtin disclosed that the Spitfires resulted directly
> from the last mission to Britain of Dr. Evatt, Australia's
> Minister for External Affairs. He expressed Australia's
> gratitude 'for this splendid gesture on the part of the
> United Kingdom'.*

A similar headline disclosed: Spitfire Londoners in Australia,
again mentioning Jimmy, Tony and myself. Why the reporter
felt it important to mention only chaps from London in his
piece is beyond me. This snippit also mentioned that we had
brought our own ground staff and equipment. The fact that
we had lost most of our Spitfires before we arrived in Sydney
and that many of our ground crews were in fact Australians,
did not apparently register with him.

Our remit, of course, was purely to help defend Australia,
but General Douglas MacArthur, who was the American
supreme commander in charge of all Allied forces in the South
Pacific (the Australians no doubt handing over this control
with some reluctance) didn't think much of any of us by all
accounts. I don't think the Aussies thought much of him either.
As far as MacArthur was concerned it was Americans that
would fight their way back to victory and he didn't want help

from anyone else. If it was deemed necessary he would use Australian soldiers in New Guinea and so on, but only reluctantly. He certainly never gave them any leading role.

I don't think he liked us either, for every time the Japanese attacked Darwin and we shot down a few enemy aircraft, the Aussie press went wild, yet hardly reported any successful actions by the Americans. Nobody wanted to know.

After this March raid all became quiet again. It was another anti-climax as we had imagined the recent action would herald some concerted effort by the enemy to try to knock out Darwin's harbour, but everything died down once more.

Life went on and we started doing a bit of night flying in April, which with a full moon and the cloudless day season now with us, was quite pleasant. To fly under that inky dark blue canopy with its twinkling stars, the land and sea bathed in bright moonlight, was wonderful really. Sometimes the odd enemy aircraft would come over at night but we never shot anything down during these dark hours. Radar might have been able to put us near to a plot but it really needed airborne radar to find an aircraft in the dark. You might be able to pick up a glow from hot exhaust stubs, but you really had to get close in order to see them.

We began some sporting activities with the arrival of more settled weather. Cricket, football and so on, which helped to combat the boredom. We virtually had no illness to speak of amongst the squadron personnel and our medical officer, Doc Jarman, had the cushiest job going. He had a couple of hundred young, fit, healthy men, no local problems with mosquitos, malaria, or things like that. There were no women about, loose or otherwise, so nothing to catch in that area, so apart from dishing out the 'hot stuff' for our prickly heat, nobody needed his services. We just didn't fall ill.

On my 23rd birthday we had a pretty good party to celebrate. I received a cake from an aunt of mine who lived on the other side of the continent, near Perth. We continued to stay on stand-by or at readiness, which in hindsight was pretty ridiculous with three squadrons of Spitfires all being on some kind of alert but there was nothing much else to do anyway, except wait around and fly practise sorties and fly air tests to keep our hands in. I suppose that with so few raids, everyone was reluctant to be far away and not ready, in case the

Japanese came. By mid-afternoon you knew nothing was going to happen anyway as the Japs would never dream of attacking at so late a time, knowing they would have to return to their bases in a darkening sky.

The enemy made their next visit on 2 May with 25 bombers, and 27 escorting Zeros that had come forward from Kendari in the Celebes. This coincided with me going on leave so I missed the excitement. Periods of leave had now started on a rota system and I went off to Sydney with a couple of other lads, flying down to Adelaide in a Lockheed Electra, then east to Sydney. We were able to catch up with old friends and were having a good time but news quickly came that another raid had taken place.

There has been a lot of controversy about this raid. The long and the short of it was that the wing lost a lot of aircraft, not all due to enemy action. I was later told that Bill Gibbs had landed with only about two gallons of petrol left and others made forced landings having run out of fuel totally. The losses we heard about in Sydney sounded very high and the press made great play about it, and caused much of the controversy. I think it also gave General MacArthur another chance to have a go at us, and he seized it with both hands.

We would not have been very professional if we had ignored the advice we had been given by the Americans concerning their experience in fighting the Japanese in the air. Japanese fighters were highly manoeuvrable. Quite apart from the aircraft being specifically designed to be light, they carried no armour plating behind the pilot, did not have heavier self-sealing fuel tanks, and did not carry radios, relying on hand signals between pilots. All this made them even more nimble.

The Americans in their P39s and P40s had quickly found that to attempt any sort of turning battle with the Zero fighters met with almost instant disaster. Before you knew it the enemy pilot had turned inside you and was pumping lead in your direction from behind. The Americans had quickly changed tactic to one of dive and zoom, and forgot all about the turning game. Keeping the throttle open in these combat situations, once a fight started it was then a case of zooming up, and diving down, make your firing pass, pull up and zoom for height again before repeating the exercise. This way you had a better chance of surviving the encounter and of inflicting some damage on the opposition. So what had happened on Sunday 2 May?

According to 54 Squadron's diarist, all the pilots who had not already motored over to the aerodrome were summoned there as a big raid was apparently impending. Three sections were immediately scrambled to intercept at 09.45 while a further eight Spitfires were sent off at 10.10 to provide air cover over base. The latter had only just become airborne when a formation of 21 Mitsubishi Betty bombers, with an escort of Zero fighters, over-flew the aerodrome. The bombers proceeded to disgorge an estimated 40 bombs among the buildings, while others exploded in the nearby bush-land. However, one of the latter managed to smash a water main thus rendering the campsite waterless. Luckily those among the buildings only produced blast damage and nothing more serious or permanent. What was galling to those on the ground was that as the Japanese flew over, there wasn't a Spitfire in sight, the base cover machines having, presumably, been summoned elsewhere.

Bill Gibbs and the other pilots did eventually get amongst the raiding force and made several claims, with one pilot shot down, while the pilots of 452 Squadron also made contact, making claims too, but lost three Spitfires. Flying Officer George Farries was the pilot in 54 Squadron, but he was able to bale out safely. Of the Australians, Flying Officer 'Tim' Goldsmith DFC DFM and Pilot Officer K J Fox both took to their parachutes. Flight Lieutenant P StJ Makin had to make a forced landing. 457 also made combat claims, but Flying Officer G L C 'Joe' Gifford was shot down and killed. Our George Farries came down in the sea and was rescued from his dinghy by a Navy Walrus amphibian aircraft.

While these losses were bad enough, they were made worse by several pilots having to make forced landings all over the place. In 54 Squadron, Sergeants G Spencer and Cavanagh, managed to force land, while Flying Officer Ian Taylor made a crash landing. Flying Officer Gerry Wall ditched off shore, just failing to make the beach. George Spencer (in BR536 DL-H) made his landing on the beach and his Spitfire suffered from the incoming tide. 452's Sergeant R S Stagg baled out, Sergeant W E Nichterlein force-landed, while in 457, Flight Sergeant W 'Bill' Hardwick had to force land too. None of these latter problems were caused by enemy action. Flying Officer A C 'Sandy' McNab was heading back to base with two pilots of 457, whereupon he suddenly pulled up after his two companions had seen him pointing down into his cockpit, spiralled down and with no apparent attempt at baling out, had ditched. The other two circled the spot but there was no sign of the pilot in the water.

The problems were mostly technical, or because the pilots had run out of petrol. Gerry Wall, after landing in the sea in about three fathoms of water, managed to get out of the cockpit although he had to leave his flying boots which had become jammed under the rudder pedals. He swam to what he thought was a small island, only to find it was a coral reef, and one that was rapidly disappearing as the tide came in. Patrol boats were out looking for downed pilots and he was fortunate in being able to attract the attention of one boat by signalling with his chromium-plated whistle attached to his mae west. Taylor, out of fuel, lost his engine just short of the runway and scrunched into the ground, thankfully unhurt. Sergeant Fox had developed engine trouble before the action began and was seen to bale out of his Spitfire, which was pouring glycol, and moments later the machine exploded in the bush. Those watching on the ground imagined at first that it had gone into the squadron's camp site. An ambulance brought him back to the airfield, uninjured. Cavanagh's Spitfire had also suffered engine trouble, forcing him to crunch down on the beach.

Squadron Leader Ron MacDonald, who had replaced Thorold-Smith as the CO of 452, was flying his first mission with the squadron, as number two to Caldwell. He experienced failure in both his cannon and dropped out, and Ken Fox took over his spot. As he did so he fired at a Zero that had swung in behind the wingco's Spitfire, but was then hit by fire from another and had to bale out. Ross Stagg of 452, and Flight Sergeant Bill Hardwick of 457 both had problems with their propeller's constant speed unit, resulting in engine failures, so had to exit the proceedings. Ross was posted missing, and in fact he wasn't located for 15 days, but was miraculously found on the banks of the Finniss River, some 27 miles north-west of Rum Jungle, which was about 40 miles from the coast. He had finished up in his dinghy ten miles out to sea after baling out. Paddling ashore near Point Blaze on the

southern end of Fog Bay, he then spent the next two weeks trying desperately to find his way out from the saline coastal flats and swamps, east of the bay. He was to spend several months in hospital following his ordeal.

As can be imagined, there was quite a furore following this action. In all 14 Spitfires had not returned to their three bases and originally these were assessed as three by enemy action, although the pilots had been saved, two probably due to enemy action, pilots lost, four due to engine failures, and five due to fuel shortage. Naturally Clive Caldwell [above] was taking the immediate flak from all quarters and he later wrote the following report:

At 0940 hours at Strauss Strip, No.452 Squadron with which I was at Readiness was ordered to 'scramble' to 10,000 feet over Hughes where No.54 and No.457 Squadrons would rendezvous with me.

By 0945 hours 12 Spitfires of No.452 Squadron, led by myself, were airborne, formed up and proceeding as instructed.

The rendezvous was effected with precision without any avoidable delay on a course of 270 degrees, the Controller, No.5 F.S. [Fighter Sector] being duly advised.

No.54 Squadron brought 10 A/C, No.457 brought 11 A/C to the rendezvous.

The Controller informed me that a formation of 20

plus bombers escorted by a large number of fighters was approaching from W.N.W. at approximately 20,000 feet their target being judged as Darwin. The Wing turned starboard and climbed as rapidly as possible into sun towards Darwin.

When East of Darwin at a height of 22,000 feet, the Controller informed me that the enemy bombers were now near Pt. Charles but at a height of approximately 25,000 feet with fighters above, height unspecified.

The Wing turned to port and continued to climb rapidly with the sun on our starboard beam, Darwin below on the port beam.

With the Wing at a height of 26,000 feet in a position approximately 10 miles N.E. of Darwin, the enemy bomber formation was sighted passing West Point at 10 o'clock to us and above. The Tally-ho was given and the Controller advised of our position, course, and height. As the bombers crossed the harbour the escorting fighters were observed above the bombers at 27,000 feet. I advised the Controller that we were not in a position to attack except at a disadvantage before the target was reached and in order to assist the A.A. defence that the enemy bombers were at our height. The fighter escort extended above the bombers to a height of 31,000 feet and could by now be plainly seen.

Bearing left, the Wing continued to climb and attained 30,000 feet up sun of the target as the bombers unloaded in the scrub near R.A.A.F. aerodrome Darwin. Had the bombers turned left away from their target we were now in a position to engage them head on with slight average advantage of height plus the sun in our favour.

The enemy however, turned right from the target and levelled out at 32,500 feet and the Wing turned West, flying at an indicated air speed of 185 m.p.h. and moved to intercept as the enemy crossed the coast on their way out.

At this stage the Wing was in sound formation, Squadrons in sections abreast, Wing in Squadrons abreast. As we proceeded Westward, the enemy being kept in view, No.54 Squadron lost position and dropped astern.

When the enemy, losing height crossed the coast just

East of Port Blaze, No.452 & No.457 Squadrons were in excellent position to attack. No.54 Squadron however, despite orders to close up were still some considerable distance astern and therefore not in a position to be used in the co-ordinated attack that I required. 7-8 minutes elapsed before No.54 Squadron again came into position to carry out the duty detailed to them. The attack was made forthwith in the following manner:

The Wing was positioned a clear 10,000 feet above the enemy top cover and approximately 12,000 feet above the bombers, with the sun on their starboard quarter.

The enemy formations of the bombers (21 counted) flying in two broad Vics abreast. Six fighters above and about 1 mile in front of the bombers.

One Vic of 3 fighters on the left of the bombers and a flight of 4 fighters on the right of the bombers as direct escort.

Above and behind the bombers were three Vics of 3 fighters. On the port quarter and above the bombers was a flight of 8 fighters which appeared to be flying in fours or pairs. Below and behind on the starboard side were several fighters in no particular formation. Estimated 32-35 fighters total.

The leaders, section leaders and pilots of the squadrons in the Wing were instructed carefully by me as to their respective roles from the time the enemy formation turned away from the target, enemy disposition of forces appreciated, when I decided on the attack I would deliver.

No.54 Squadron (code name *Candy*) to attack the fighter cover, while No.457 Squadron (code name *Skeeter*) attacked the bombers. No.452 Squadron (code name *Troppo*) following No.457 Squadron. To keep their tails clear during their attack on the bombers, engaging as many fighters as possible and cover their withdrawal back up on the sunward side. ('Skeeter' was Ken James' nickname; 457's CO.)

The program was initiated very successfully, but the ultimate result owing largely to a number of contributing factors was not up to expectations, despite our advantage of sun, height and speed.

No.54 Squadron engaged nine enemy fighters only.

Four A/C of No.457 Squadron did not penetrate to the bombers. No.452 Squadron engaged and were determinedly engaged in return by a number of Haps and Zeros; some of the pilots however, penetrated to the bombers.

Within 10 minutes of engaging I warned all pilots to check their fuel and if short to break away from the combat area and return to Darwin at low revs. on a course of 110 degrees. The engagement from first to last extended over a period of 20 minutes, and when I personally broke away at the end of this period I could see no other Spitfires in the immediate vicinity, though several were in view to the Eastward, one or two of which were circling dinghies. Flying to Darwin on low revs, after detouring slightly to inspect dinghies/parachutes in the water, I landed at Darwin having been airborne 1 hr. 50 mins, with 5-10 gallons in my tanks.

Appreciation of Factors Governing Results
Enemy Tactics
The enemy bomber formation was losing height away at a speed of approximately 250 m.p.h. (an estimation).

The enemy fighters, chiefly Haps did an excellent escort job and were well and determinedly flown, supporting each other in a manner generally suggestive of experienced and practiced pilots used to working together.

Their direction shooting was good on the average. A great deal of tracer was used by them, a practise which I personally do not agree with for our fighters.

Failure of Armament
A very high percentage of both Cannon and Machine gun failures due to faulty ammunition, frozen guns etc, mitigated very seriously against good scoring on the part of the Spitfires. In some A/C no guns fired at any stage due to these causes.

Engine Failure and Technical Faults
1 A/C returned to base 10 minutes after rendezvous due to complete R/T failure.

1 A/C returned to base due to engine failure prior to engaging.

2 A/C crashed prior to engagement due to engine failure, both A/C lost.

1 A/C about diving to engage experienced engine failure and crashed. A/C lost.

1 A/C crashed short of fuel due to faulty petrol gauge showed 10 gallons just prior to cutting out.

War Standing of Pilots

Of the 95 pilots on the strength of this Wing, only 37 had had fighter combat experience prior to coming to this Area. Some half dozen only could be classed as 'experienced'. Of the remaining 58 pilots without previous fighter combat experience, 45 had had no operational experience whatsoever.

In the engagement under review, three pilots only, including the Wing Leader, had had previous experience against escorted enemy bombers.

This general lack of experience has in no way affected the keenness of the Pilots whose 'moral fibre' standards are of a high order. On the contrary several of these inexperienced pilots were led away by their keenness and the natural excitement of their first combat to the extent of forgetting both time and fuel, and their way home despite adequate and repeated warnings. As a direct result of this four Spitfires were lost.

General Observations

On the occasion of the raid on Darwin of the 15th March 1943, Spitfires intercepted the enemy just before they reached their target. This interception was carried out by a part of the Wing only and even that part was not properly rendezvoused or organised.

On this occasion (2nd May 1943) tactics employed were to advantage with the Wing properly organised before engaging the enemy. The time factor involved in carrying this out did not permit interception before the enemy reached their target, by a margin of four or five minutes.

When the Wing did attack it was from an ideal position with every possible advantage. This opinion is shared by all the more experienced pilots engaged in the operation. The time factor involved in effecting a Wing rendezvous would be appreciably improved if No.54 Squadron now based on No.52 Operational Base Unit, RAAF Darwin were to occupy Sattler Strip. This, under similar conditions to the 2nd of May, would permit interception some five to seven minutes earlier at the same height.

It is appreciated that American Squadrons frequently made a practise of independent or 'piece-meal' interception during their tour of duty in this Area. It is not considered desirable to sacrifice the obvious advantage of a full Wing interception for the using of a few minutes involved attaining rendezvous and organised battle formation for co-ordinated attack.

C.R.Caldwell, Wing Commander, Wing Commander Flying No.1 Fighter Wing, RAAF Darwin.

Despite Caldwell's report defending the wing's actions it all left a nasty taste. It didn't phase the wing overmuch, although the losses were upsetting. Down in Sydney myself and the other two guys on leave received signals to report back to Darwin as quickly as possible and we took the train to a place just up the coast called Newcastle, where they assembled new Spitfires which continued to arrive in Australia by sea. Group Captain Walters had also been down on leave too so he joined us with abut half a dozen other pilots and we all flew replacement aircraft back north, via Brisbane, Charville, Cloncurry and Daly Waters.

The newspapers were full of reports of the air battle, and the fact that the wing had suffered somewhat. This, plus General MacArthur's dig, didn't go down with the propaganda people who thought that being too honest only gave the Japanese the good news that the Spitfires had suffered at their hand. It appears that the wing did over-claim a tad, but the Japanese we were to learn much later, claimed 21 Spitfires shot down. Over-optimistic of course, but overall, not too far short of what we had actually lost through all circumstances.

Despite the immediate flap, and our recall from leave, there was no follow-up by the Japanese but I suppose everyone felt a bit safer with ten or so new Spitfire replacements being flown in. The next raid was not until the 10th. Two small sorties on the airfield at Millingimbi, where the Beaufighters of 31 Squadron RAAF lived, along the coast some 280 miles east of us did little damage. However, 457 Squadron were scrambled and engaged the second attack, claiming two Zeros shot down with two more damaged. They lost one Spitfire but the pilot got away with it. After this, it was proposed that each squadron take it in turns to keep a flight of aircraft at this airfield in case of further attacks.

On the 11th the air raid warning went at about 11.30 and 54 Squadron scrambled but it turned out to be two Lockheed P38 Lightnings returning, but not flying their designated route. The next day the squadron sent pilots and aircraft to

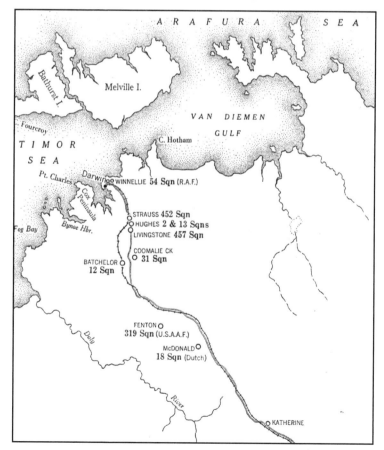

Millingimbi, and amazingly Jap Zeros did turn up on the 13th but made no attempt to come down and strafe the place. Our Spitfires scrambled but by the time they gained height the enemy fighters were well out of range.

Robin Norwood managed to intercept a Dinah on 23 May, but it proved too fast for him and although he believed he had scored hits on its tail, it did not slow down and finally left Robin way behind. Things were still bubbling away, for on the 28th another raid was plotted. The wing scrambled but found nothing, and the plots may well have been a small force of aircraft that attacked Millingimbi. 457 Squadron engaged this small force of eight Mitsubishi Ki-21 Sallys and six Zeros, claiming three enemy aircraft destroyed and another damaged. However, they lost two Spitfires in this action, both pilots being killed. Another pilot, Pilot Officer B Little, had a lucky escape, actually hitting the ground during a low-level chase after a Zero. Little had actually landed back at Millingimbi unaware that the place was under attack but when he did realise, immediately took off again. He chased the Zero for ten minutes well below 300 feet. With his Spitfire damaged he was forced to make an emergency landing but somersaulted three or four times, losing both wings and his propeller. He clambered out of the wreck virtually unhurt and walked the three miles back to the airfield. One of the Australian pilots to make a claim was Flight Lieutenant Peter Watson, from Melbourne, who many years later would become president of the Spitfire Association of Australia, and a man I would meet quite by chance in London 47 years later, of which more anon.

Thus May came to a close. Would June prove any better?

Chapter Nine

Zeros at Six-O'clock

June 1943 started quietly for us and continued so for several days. On the 10th the squadron took a turn at readiness at Millingimbi, three pilots plus three ground crew going there. By the 15th the moon period was with us again, which entailed another period of night readiness, but fortunately we only used half the squadron on such duty, each flight taking it in turns. Although we were on duty, we were allowed to snooze, but fully dressed, in a small hut and every now and then one of the cooks would provide us with tea and wads.

The duty Flight was nearing the end of its stint on the 17th when a call came just after 9 am to scramble after a Japanese reconnaissance aircraft that radar had spotted just north of Hughes. It was already going away from the direction our Spitfires were coming from so unfortunately there was no way we were going to catch it.

There is another story that concerned the night hours. Two of our NCO pilots, Jimmy Wellsman and David Wheeler, had just been commissioned which naturally heralded a bit of a party. Our latrines had been built a fair way from the main camp area, out in the bush, and David felt the call of nature after several beers so headed out into the night, flashlight in hand.

Reaching the latrine building, which was no more than a native-type hut we had constructed over a row of 'thunder-boxes' he dropped his shorts and was sitting quietly minding his own business, if you'll excuse the pun, and was spending his time shining his torch into the various dark corners, when he spotted two eyes shining back at him. After a sharp intake of breath, he finally recognised it as a snake. Not daring to move he nevertheless edged the beam along its body, following with some incredulity its continuing length. Once he reached the tail end he estimated that it was a 15-foot python that had decided to crawl in and take a nap – and he had woken it up!

In one swift movement David grabbed his shorts – and his

courage – pulling them up as he made a dash for the door, then came rushing back to the party, pretty much excited by his experience. Naturally we all tore down to the latrine, everyone full of booze and bravado, and unaware that a python was pretty harmless, quickly bumped it off. Within minutes we had dragged its massive length back to the party and began using the corpse as if it was a skipping rope. David later confessed that if nothing else, seeing those eyes and then the length of the beast, did wonders for his constipation!

Some of us played Bridge on occasion. One evening in early June I recall being one of a team of four to play four others from 452 Squadron. With me were Doc Jarman, Jimmy Councer and Flying Officer Bill Hinds.[1] We were easily defeated which did nothing for our ego. One table went down 1,400 points, the other 4,000! We bravely suggested a return match.

We were also building a new officer's mess in early June, and pride of place was the salvaged wing of a Japanese Zero someone had fished out of the sea. By all accounts it was from a Zero Flying Officer Mawer shot down on 15 March. It had its red 'meatball' for all to see, and one of the ground crew painted the squadron crest on it. We also added some tiny glasses of whisky, a 'nip', each representing a Japanese aircraft the squadron had claimed. Some of the chaps painted similar 'nips' on their aircraft. The new mess was up, painted, and running by 14 June.

We were also getting new pilots. Pilot Officers Garden and Appleton, with Flight Sergeant Kelman and Sergeant Lambert arrived on the 17th. Many years later, Bill Appleton and I were in the same aircrew association bunch in Bexhill, Sussex. This was the same day that a radar report suggested that a large force of enemy aircraft were approaching and 42 of the wing's fighters were scrambled. In the event only two hostile aircraft were seen, high flying and very fast Dinah reconnaissance machines which no one even got close to.

By this time, and certainly after the disasters of 2 May, our poor old engineering officer, 'Cecil' Beaton, had his work cut out. I am certain we had hundreds of Spitfires down in Melbourne but it seemed the devil of a job to get more up to

---

[1]Bill Hinds came from Ashford, Kent and was 22 years old. He was to be killed in action on 7 September 1943, intercepting enemy aircraft over the Hughes-Batchelor area.

Darwin. It made no sense at all, so why it was so difficult to get replacements on a regular basis heaven only knows. Luckily, as far as we knew, we didn't lose anyone through poor quality of the aircraft, other than those constant pitch problems which by now were more or less solved. My aircraft was never a problem. I flew BR539 (DL-X) from start to finish and only flew other machines when mine was having a major service or inspection. Quite remarkable really.

On the 19th we received another signal, warning us of yet another build up of Japanese aircraft across the water at Kendari, so we prepared for further action. We got to bed early and were at readiness by 08.00 on the 20th. It was no false rumour and at four minutes to ten the next morning, a Sunday again, we were scrambled. Officially this was raid number 55. The 'runners and riders' were as follows:

S/Ldr Gibbs	BS164	G/C Walters	BS166
F/Sgt Wheeler	BR484	P/O Appleton	BR544
Sgt Lambert	BR484	F/O Leonard	BR532
F/Lt Foster	BR539	F/O Tuckson	BR570
P/O Garden	BS181	F/Sgt Horkin	EE636
F/Sgt Wickman	JG731	F/O Hughes	JG795
F/Sgt Huggard	BS235	Sgt Holmes	BR530
Sgt Laundy	EE605	F/Sgt Ashurst	EE670

Flight Sergeant Kelman took off ten minutes after this scramble, which made an odd number of pilots, and the reason for this and the delay, are unknown to me. I see that both Garden and Appleton were on this sortie, not bad for newcomers of just three days. The words 'deep-end' and 'chuck em in' come to mind.

Having gained height and heading out over the coast we encountered two formations of bombers with their usual Zero escort, and then began a running fight from the south of Melville Island, over Darwin, and back out to sea again, heading west. The first formation was estimated at around 21 bombers and a similar number of Zeros. They dropped bombs on the RAAF Administration Centre at Winnellie. The second formation consisted of around 19 bombers, and they flew right over RAAF Darwin, dropping bombs among the buildings, while some of the Zero escort made strafing runs. Some extensive blast damage occurred on the Darwin airfield, the photographic and parachute sections being hit, but there were no casualties. At Winnellie some slight damage was inflicted and they did have some casualties, caused by some 40 daisy-cutter bombs. There was also damage to an oil dump and some nearby railway installations.

For the first time we met, not Betty bombers, but Nakajima Ki.49 'Helens' and Kawasaki Ki.48 'Lilys'. These were Japanese army aircraft, so that what we were seeing as navy Zeros were in fact army Nakajima Ki.43 'Oscars'. All very confusing, especially when the eye sees what the mind is expecting. The force consisted of 22 Oscars of the 59th Sentai led by Major Takeo Fukuda, and 18 Ki.49s from the 61st Sentai and nine Ki.48s of the 75th Sentai.

The Japanese tried to confuse us still further by sending in one wave at high level while the second bunch flew in at low level. The interception of the high formation was reasonable but the lower group caught everyone by surprise. I saw this second lot going out after the attack appeared to have ended, and while I was actually making an approach to land. I think it was Harold Leonard who managed to bag one of them as they went. I had already attacked one bomber which left a trail of smoke from its engines when I came up against this Zero – or should I say Oscar.

In fact we surprised each other. I had just pulled away from the bombers and was coming down, and just as I started to pull up again, sitting right across from me was an enemy fighter with its red meatballs shining in the sun. So I decided to have a go at it and I'm pretty certain I hit it but the pilot was soon turning inside me, almost straight away. They were so quick those fighters and it was impossible to turn with him, so I broke off as quickly as I could and made for home.

One could only really go for these enemy fighters if you had height and speed, but on the same level in was impossible unless you managed a complete surprise attack, but this guy had seen me at the same time I'd spotted him. It was an interesting few moments.

Our CO, Bill Gibbs, developed engine trouble soon after he became airborne and had to land again, luckily before any strafing took place. Perhaps this is why Kelman had taken off – to make up the number. Remaining in his Spitfire after landing, Bill proceeded to give a running commentary of events to the controller over his radio. As luck would have it,

Caldwell had suffered radio transmitter failure after he had taken off and had handed over to Gibbs, leaving me to lead 54. With Gibbs having to land too, the wing was led by Ron MacDonald of 452 Squadron, although Caldwell remained in the air and went into action with the wing. One funny thing about Gibbs while on the ground is that while he was listening to one of his pilots who had twice reported he was closing in, each time Gibbs yelled: 'For Christ sake open fire!' The third time this pilot said he was – still – closing in, Gibbs got so frustrated that he yelled again for him to fire, and inadvertently pressed his own gun button. As his cannon opened up, sending a stream of shells across the airfield, there was a hurried scattering of ground crew personnel.

Our only casualty was Flying Officer Tony Hughes who had to force land on the beach near Lee Point and although he was not hurt, his machine was seriously damaged. 452 Squadron lost two pilots, Sergeant W E Nichterlein and Pilot Officer A T Ruskin-Rowe. There was one other casualty for 54 on this day, but it had nothing to do with the raid. One of our ground crew, AC1 Ted Gess was shot in the back while sleeping on his cot by his tent-mate who was messing about with a gun, and died almost instantly.

The wing claimed several victories even though their claims were made wrongly for Betty bombers and Zeros. Even Group Captain Wally Walters put in a claim for a fighter. 457 Squadron also got into the action and claimed a victory plus some damage to others and suffered no casualties. Oddly enough, Walters was ordered back to Sydney shortly after this scrap, and I have to wonder if the 'powers' down there were not enthusiastic about him flying in action.

The next day saw yet another Japanese reconnaissance aircraft in evidence, and it was seen quite clearly from the ground as Australian AA fire opened up but it was pretty high and nothing got near to it. This was probbly the Japanese trying to see what damage they had done on the 20th, or did it presage another raid? As it happened, we were scrambled on the 22nd, being sent off because of a number of radar reports indicating another force was approaching, but nothing developed and despite being in the air for some considerable time, we were eventually ordered back to base. Actually this had been a fighter sweep by Oscars of the 59th Sentai again but the leader, Captain Shigeo Nago, reported seeing no sign of any Allied aircraft whatsoever.

Because of the new tactic employed by the enemy on the 20th, one high formation and another at low level, each Spitfire squadron had to provide a small standing patrol over the south coast of Bathurst Island each morning in case this low-level stuff was repeated, and not being picked up on radar. For the next few days everyone seemed on tenterhooks and with more reports of Japanese aircraft over on Timor, it seemed as though we would see the enemy again soon, but almost a week went by before something tangible happened.

Some weeks later my mother was able to stick another newspaper cutting in her album:

Spitfires Smash Mass Raid on Darwin
Spitfires intercepting a force of 48 Japanese bombers and fighters which attempted to raid Darwin, north-western outpost of Australia, in daylight, destroyed nine and damaged 13 for the loss of two, says today's communiqué from General MacArthur's Headquarters.

The Spitfires caught the raiders more than 40 miles from Darwin, shot down several before they reached the target, and then followed in to take a further toll.

The attacks continued as the Japanese raiders made towards home. Many of the Japanese were 'limping' away from Darwin's defenders and were not expected to reach their base.

In any case, the Spitfires had destroyed the greatest number of enemy planes they had ever accounted for in a single action in the South-West Pacific.

The pilots who helped to repulse the Japanese raiders included Flight-Lieut. Foster of London, who shot down a Japanese bomber and damaged a Zero fighter.

He then followed nine Japanese bombers out to sea, where, although his ammunition was exhausted, he continued radioing their position until Flying Officer Harold Leonard, of Wembley, came up and shot down a bomber. Two bombers were also shot down by Flying Officer Tony Hughes, of Cardiff.

Flight Sergt. David Wheeler of St Albans nearly ran into a Japanese bomber when he dived to score a probable kill. One bullet landed behind his head before the bomber disappeared in a trail of smoke.

A small-scale raid came in on the morning of the 28th, dropping bombs near to a factory north-west of the town but didn't achieve much in the way of damage. All three squadrons were up, but only Caldwell and 457 found the nine bombers and 27 fighters as they flew out. They claimed a couple of fighters and some damage to others but the Zeros shot down one of their pilots and another had engine trouble. Both crash-landed without injury but their Spitfires received damage.

Raid number 57 occurred on 30 June. This time the enemy's target was the airfield at Fenton, and an estimated 27 Betty bombers and at least 18 Zeros and Haps made up the raiding force. The wing was scrambled, led by Clive Caldwell, and 54 Squadron took off at 11.25, and flew on his port side. In total there were 41 Spitfires up and 54 Squadron comprised:

F/Lt Norwood	BR544	F/Lt Foster	BR495
F/Sgt Horkin	EE636	F/Sgt Huggard	BR537
Sgt Holmes	BR530	Sgt Laundy	BR490
F/Sgt Harker	EE670	S/L Gibbs	BS164
P/O Wellsman	BR528	F/O Thomson	EE605
Sgt Fox	BR538	F/S Wickman	JG731
Sgt Monger	BS218	P/O Mahoney	BR484

The wing intercepted the enemy formation before and after bombing and a number of claims were made by 54, 452, 457 and the wingco, but we didn't get away without casualties. We lost one killed, two baled out and one force-landed, while 452 had one pilot killed, one baled out and a third crash-landed.

Several combat reports of this action survive, including the one I dictated, which Flight Lieutenant F H Quinn, the wing's senior intelligence officer, compiled as follows:

'I took off with No.54 Squadron as leader of Blue section, rendezvoused over SATTLER at 6,000 feet and climbed in an Easterly direction in formation with the remainder of the Wing. At 18,000 feet we turned about and shortly afterwards were told to climb over BATCHELOR. We were advised that the enemy were approaching PERON ISLAND at 22,000 feet and were given a vector of 270°. We continued climbing in this direction and were again informed that the enemy were approaching on a Westerly course at 25/30,000 feet. The next report received stated that the enemy had crossed the coast South West of PERON ISLAND. WINCO thereupon drew our attention to the enemy bomber formation which was then at 10 o'clock below and 12/15 miles distant crossing ANSON BAY and heading towards BATCHELOR at approx. 25,000 feet. We were then at 32,000 feet. Five fighters were discernible ahead and slightly above the bombers and six to eight in a similar position to the rear, both being about 1,500 feet above the bombers which they were escorting. At this juncture I did not observe a top cover.

'No.54 Squadron were ordered to go into the bombers and attack on the starboard side, and No.457 Squadron to attack them on the port side, and No.452 Squadron to engage the fighters. My section dropped behind the remainder of No.54 Squadron and I was obliged to make an individual attack from the port beam. As we were diving down five fighters pulled round from behind the bombers and followed us down. We made our initial attack too far out and from 30,000 feet. When we were at 27,000 feet on the way down the fighters before mentioned reached a position behind us and followed us until we reached our target which was then flying at 25,000 feet or more. We did not take evasive action. I attacked the port formation opening fire slightly out of range as the fighters were then on my tail and I was uncertain when I would have to break.

'I closed to 75/100 yards firing a 6 to 7 second burst and as I broke I observed both engines of the extreme port bomber streaming white smoke and the starboard engine of the Number Two bomber on the extreme port vic also emitting smoke. I had originally intended to attack the middle of the three bombers on the extreme port side formation and allowed 2 rings deflection until the bombers passed right through my sight. I claim to have hit both these aircraft. My No.2 followed me in but was engaged by fighters. As I broke from this attack I felt a thud behind the cockpit and my engine began vibrating with revs. and boost fluctuating. I thereupon dived away and on returning to base discovered that the cause was a severe glycol leak.'

I had taken off at 11.20 and landed at 12.30. To my report, Quinn added that:

'White 4, (Sergeant Horkin) observed Blue section attack and saw the extreme port bomber which F/Lt. Foster attacked drop the left wing and go over on its side as though peeling off. Both engines were in flames and it was smoking heavily. He also saw another bomber on the extreme port formation of three aircraft lose formation and fall behind and below with one engine smoking. A similar observation was passed by F/Lt. R. Norwood.'

Flight Sergeant Huggard was my No.2 during this engagement, and in his combat report he said:

'I followed F/Lt Foster and fired at one of the port leading section of bombers from 60° to 40° from beam astern closing to 250 yds, and allowing $1^1/2$ rings defection. I saw no strikes but am confident that I hit the E/A, and this should be confirmed by cine-film. I broke away and went down doing aileron turns to avoid the fighters and at 20,000 ft when about to pull out felt my aircraft violently hit and did more aileron turns to 4,000 ft. When I pulled out I saw that my air system and A.S.I. were out of action. I saw 2 burning wrecks on the ground about 18 m W. of Batchelor. I climbed to 8,000 ft but my windscreen was then getting badly oiled up and having informed Controller I returned to base.'

My Blue 3 was Sergeant S C J Laundy, and he had quite an adventure this day, as he told Jimmy Councer a couple of days later, while in No.1 MRS Hospital, by the Adelaide River:

'I followed F/Lt. Foster and Flight Sergeant Huggard and observed them to make a stern quarter attack on the bombers and [I] made a beam attack on the extreme port bomber of the formation, giving a 3-4 second burst with $2^1/2$ rings deflection, range 400, closing to 150 yards. As a result of my attack the port engine of the Betty started smoking badly. I broke down and came back on the same side, observing the bomber I had attacked falling back out of formation. I heard Wingco refer to this A/C on the

R/T, his remark as far as I recollect being: "That one's done for anyway. Leave it for now and attack the others." This A/C is claimed as probably destroyed.

'I then delivered another beam attack, range and deflection as before, on the leader of the port vic. I observed strikes in the region of the cockpit, and the E/A went over sharply on one wing as though to peel off, then straightened up again and seemed, as I broke violently straight down, to be rejoining the formation. This A/C is claimed as damaged.

'I came up again on the starboard side of the enemy formation and noticed that the extreme starboard vic had fallen back a little. At this point I heard on the R/T: "There's a Zero going down," and observed two A/C going down, one of which I thought was a Spitfire, but could not be sure. I climbed to about 2,000 feet above the bombers, and then, hearing a report of E/Fs, at once attacked the extreme starboard bomber of the starboard vic. Attack was made from beam as before, closing to 150 yards, and the starboard engine and the leading edge of the mainplane of the E/A burst into flames and burned brightly. This A/C is claimed as destroyed.

'I waited to see the result of my attack for a second too long, and as I broke down I felt the tail of my aircraft shudder violently and temporarily lost control. I managed finally to straighten out and tried to get the hood off. The quick release came out about six inches and then stuck, and I had to use both hands, finally getting the hood to slide back, but at the expense of another spin on the part of the A/C. When I finally succeeded in straightening out again the altimeter showed 1,250 ft., the engine was smoking badly, and full revs and boost gave only just over 1,500 revs. At this point I saw flames coming from the side of the A/C, and being unable to turn over I baled out over the side, hitting my right arm and shoulder on the tail-plane. As I went out I saw a Japanese bomber coming down fairly near me.

'I landed, cut [myself] free from my harness, and decided to walk eastwards to strike the main road. On this day I estimate that I made about 6 miles. On walking next morning after a most uncomfortable night in the bush, I decided to remain where I was during the heat of the day and go on in the afternoon. It seemed worth while to give a shout, which I did, and it was answered. I fired my revolver to show my position, and was found by two R.A.A.F. airmen, shortly afterwards being joined by a party of American soldiers on the search for Japanese who might have crashed. I found that I was then 4 miles west of Adelaide River.'

Robin Norwood was leading White Section and his No.2, Flight Sergeant C Harker, also got shot-up by a Zero as he related in his combat report:

'I followed F/Lt. Norwood and attacked the leading vic of the formation, giving $1^1/_2$-sec. burst full beam allowing 1 ring deflection. I realise that this was under-deflection and think my fire must have hit the second vic, but saw no results. I continued down and then climbed into the sun after F/Lt. Norwood, telling him of my position. I then felt my A/C hit in region of cockpit, probably from a fighter astern about 10° angle off. I did not see the A/C which delivered the attack. I did a steep aileron dive to treetop height, then levelled out and pursued an A/C heading N – it might have been either a Spitfire or an E/A. My radiator temperature then went right up and I decided to force land which I did in long grass S. of Byrne Harbour. I gave my approximate position to F/O Thompson, whom I contacted by R/T, and was then sighted by Troppo 15 who got a fix on me. I was also seen by F/Lt. Norwood who was on search. I lit a fire to burn the long grass to facilitate landing of a Tiger Moth, but wind changed suddenly and fire turned back on my A/C which caught fire and was burned out. I was picked up by Tiger Moth after about 5 hours.'

Another loss was Sergeant W Holmes, who baled out. He had just attacked the bombers and was diving beneath them when:

'...suddenly my windscreen became covered with oil and smoke arose from the cockpit. I did not feel the A/C hit nor do I know from whence the fire came unless from the bombers behind that I had attacked. At 18,000 feet, glycol began to come in on the cockpit floor and I asked for a homing which was given. The engine continued running well for a few minutes, then temperature went right up and I descended to 10,000, turned over and baled out. I did not see what happened to the A/C. I landed among trees and was much jarred on hitting the ground. I arranged my parachute in form of an arrow to show the way I had gone, and made for the river I had noted on my way down. I walked for 4 hours, being sighted by a searching Spitfire on the way. I swam the river, turned west, and met a military patrol after about $1/4$ hour.'

Our fatality on this day was Jimmy Wellsman. Reported missing we all hoped that he, like our other chaps who had either baled out or crash-landed, would within a few hours or a couple of days, walk back into the mess, looking tired, happy and perhaps a little sheepish. No such luck. In fact it was not until 21 August, three weeks later, that we finally heard of his fate.

The wreck of his Spitfire was found by an army patrol on the border of the Great Reynolds River swamp area, about 30 miles west of Batchelor. Nearby was Jimmy's body, virtually unmarked, and lying face up, arms outstretched. On 1 October it fell to me to command the burial party, the coffin bearers being six of the squadron pilots. The service was of course conducted by our padre, Don Begbie. Jimmy had only just returned to us from a spot of leave. He had enthused about seeing a film in Sydney, *The First of the Few*, that had been all about the birth of the Spitfire and the life of its designer, Reginald Mitchell. He said he had been very self conscious afterwards, walking out of the cinema in his uniform and RAF wings.

On this occasion I had been flying Spitfire BR495 and another document to survive was our armourers' report on the amount of ammunition fired by those aircraft involved in this combat of 30 June. Our Spitfires carried one 20mm cannon and two .303 Browning machine guns in each wing. Each cannon usually had 60 shells installed, while the Brownings had 320 rounds. My 6-7 second burst had discharged 30 high explosive incendiary shells and 30 ball shells from each gun, while the machine guns on the port side had fired 150 rounds. My outer starboard gun had also fired 150 rounds but due to a mis-feed on the starboard inner gun, only 10 rounds fired. Apparently one .303 round in the belt had been pushed too far in and this had caused the jam. So my burst had loosed off all my cannon ammo. This is not surprising for although the cannon fires at a slower rate than the machine guns, and one can select to fire either machine guns only or cannon and machine guns, most fighter pilots, once they have managed to get in a firing position, tend to hit the target with the most power – the cannon shells – and then use any remaining machine-gun bullets if another target presents itself. Some clever-clogs, once they became very experienced air fighters, might say they first got their guns on target by using just the machine guns, and only then employed their cannon. All very well and good but most of us just blazed away with everything before the opportunity was lost. Often you did not get a second chance to fire.

For the next couple of days things once again became quiet and the squadron's only task was to fly convoy patrols over some ships coming into Darwin, but which had been attacked by a couple of Rufe floatplanes. These aircraft were in fact Zero fighters but fitted with a single large float hanging beneath the fuselage and two, smaller stabilizing ones under each wing, enabling the machine to operate from water.

The day after this a Japanese reconnaissance aircraft made its appearance and then a plot of enemy aircraft some 30 miles out came onto the radar, but nothing developed. However the next day, 6 July, the Japanese came once more. They were after Fenton again, sending over 22 bombers and an escort of 26 Zero fighters. They came in over the coast south-east of Anson Bay, but 54 Squadron were in a bit of a fix owing to the deplorable state of our aircraft. There had been no replacements for some time and this morning we were down to just eleven serviceable machines. Seven were sent off initially:

F/Lt Norwood	BR544	F/Sgt Studley	BS166
F/Sgt Harker	BR545	F/Sgt Spencer	BS305
F/Sgt Horkin	EE636	F/Sgt Huggard	BS182
P/O Lenagen	BS218		

Four more that remained responded to another scramble call

(Gibbs, Wickman, Hinds and myself) but soon after take-off Flying Officer Hinds had to break off with yet another glycol leak of the type that was dogging our aircraft. He was unable to make the airfield so force-landed. Three of the original seven could not keep up with the others and although the four remaining found fighters they were unable to do much about them before they were well away. The whole thing ended with three Spitfires in serious trouble. Flight Sergeant Horkin, although he spotted enemy aircraft, was now flying an almost unmanageable aircraft, and was even contemplating taking to his parachute but finally managed to get it back to Darwin and land. Two other pilots did not fare so well and had to force land but the pilots were OK.

The few of us who were able to get in amongst the raiders attacked the Betty bombers with 457 Squadron tackling the escort. Although we were down to seven aircraft we found ourselves in a good position to attack. They had been spotted after crossing the coast and obviously heading for Fenton. On this occasion we found ourselves on the starboard side of the bombers with the fighters on the port side and up-sun, which made it hard to see them. We were ahead and above the bomber formation so we were able to make a quarter head-on attack.

In this manoeuvre and from a few hundred yards out, the tactic was to pull the Spitfire into a tight turn until the nose of the aircraft, and therefore the gun-sight, were ahead of the target and as you opened fire, you eased off the turn, allowing the bomber to fly through your line of fire. On this occasion, as I pulled away, I saw the enemy aircraft burning ahead of me, and claimed it as destroyed.

The Zero pilots were certainly no push-over and managed to hit the wing from our six-o'clock position. Two Australian squadrons suffered accordingly. 457 had three pilots killed, while 452 had one pilot bale out and another force-land. We had Flight Sergeant Wickman bale out too. He returned two days later after getting back from the bush. One of 457's boys, Pilot Officer F R J McDowell, remained missing for two weeks before they found his body. His son was born a month later. He was part of the squadron's Blue Section of four but one pilot had to abort when his radio failed. The other three must have been bounced by Zeros for they were not seen again. Naturally search parties began looking for the three missing men, but all they found was a Spitfire of 452 that had been missing since 20 June. Flight Sergeant Tony Rowe's body was still in the cockpit.

One reason we were so low on aircraft I gather was that a ship carrying eleven Spitfires for the wing had been sunk by a torpedo. By this time the Australians, while keen to get more aircraft to northern Australia, were of the opinion that they would prefer American P38 Lightnings rather than Spitfires. They certainly had a greater range than our aircraft. However, their chances of getting the Americans to give them P38s were not good. The wing continued to ask for Spitfires although from now on they did not say 'please' but instead started to used the words 'imperative' and 'immediately'. Someone must have been listening for three replacement Spits were flown up to us within a couple of days.

On 18 July further reconnaissance aircraft appeared and one was shot down by 457's CO, Ken James, way to the east of Darwin. The enemy pilot, one of two bodies found at the crash-site, was named as Captain Shunji Sasaki, the commanding officer of the 70th Chutai. His crewman had been Lieutenant Akira Eguchi. Both appeared to have attempted to abandon their doomed Dinah but had left it too late for their parachutes to deploy. We were perhaps a little surprised they had tried for we knew Japanese airmen rarely attempted to save themselves to become prisoners. Perhaps they had jumped, knowing they wouldn't make it, rather than crashing with their aeroplane.

By the time August came very little was happening and boredom once again returned to plague us. On the 13th a party was put on to celebrate the fact that it had been one year since 54 Squadron had arrived in Australia. Just to be bloody-minded, or so it seemed, the Japanese chose this evening to mount their first night raid since January, so our party was interrupted. We had some pilots doing night flying practise and these plus a couple from 452 Squadron were sent off after them but found nothing. Some bombs fell near Fenton and Coomalie Creek but no damage was done, except to our party merriment.

Talking earlier of the Dinah recce aircraft reminds me of the time three Australian pilots in 457 Squadron chased one for some time and although all three took a shot at it, they did not manage to shoot it down. So we in 54 made some bows and arrows and flew them over to their base and dropped them over the airstrip. They went down with a note saying that they might find these useful against Japanese aircraft if they ever got close enough again. On 17 August, 457 actually shot down three of these aircraft, which was quite a feat. The Aussie lads flew the bows and arrows back, dropping them on our airfield with another note, this one saying thank you very much, they did come in extremely useful! The three victorious pilots were Peter Watson and Ken James, while Flight Sergeants R W Watson and J R Jenkins shared the third.

One has to say that if nothing else the Japanese were persistent. If losing three recce aircraft on the 17th had not been enough, they sent over another in the late afternoon. Caldwell was airborne with a wingman and they were vectored onto the Dinah, Clive having said that if they got close enough to attack, the number two should go in, as this lad had yet to open his account. Well, they got close and Caldwell slipped below the Dinah thereby letting his wingman attack. To Clive's disgust and annoyance, this pilot fired from way back – 600 yards or so – without a hope of scoring any hits. Caldwell slipped back behind the Dinah, closed right in and with three quick bursts sent the aircraft down to explode on the sea. As he circled the spot he observed three bodies float to the surface face down, and it was not long before he saw some sharks closing in towards them. The kill was Caldwell's last of the war.

Another night raid on the 20th did little except excite everyone to get aircraft up, all to no avail of course. This was almost the swan-song from the enemy, and in fact the next serious incursion over Darwin did not occur till 7 September 1943. However, it seemed to be little more than a Japanese fighter sweep and recce over the Hughes and Batchelor area. It seems that the Dinah machines were now being escorted by large numbers of fighters due to the recent losses they had sustained. 457 Squadron were scrambled while we in 54 were put on stand-by for about a quarter of an hour, and then scrambled, with me leading and with 452 in company.

We were jumped by Zeros and we lost Bill Hinds. We had been scrambled and told a raid was coming in and this was the only time that all our radio communication was jammed. I was leading because Bill Gibbs was away from base and although vectored towards the hostile plot, jamming started, and then suddenly, from the west came about 20 Zeros. They were above us and coming round behind when we spotted them. Someone called: 'Zeros at six-o'clock, Leader.' We were still, even at this stage, often flying in those silly vic formations and my instant reaction was to signal battle formation and echelon out as we turned to face the opposition, which we did.

We were still turning and climbing into them as they came in, but there was no use hanging around so I ordered: 'Break! Break!' and broke away. However, the Zeros picked off Bill Hinds and two of 452 Squadron. Bill was killed but both the Aussie lads baled out. The other aircraft in the wing became engaged and in fact claimed several enemy fighters shot down.

I came in – I think unfairly – for some criticism for not breaking off straight away but my instinctive reaction, seeing the Zeros coming round, was to turn into them, which I did. There was no percentage in just diving away for if we had done so they would have undoubtedly been able to come down on the slower chaps behind. Even Caldwell, who was flying at the head of a section in 452 Squadron, asked me why I had not broken off and I said I thought it was too late to do so without exposing our aircraft to the Zeros. He agreed with me in the end. All combat is a matter of split-second decisions and you either come out smelling of roses or you don't. The radio jamming had not helped and many years later I learnt that it was a deliberate action by the Japanese and the first time they had tried it.

This was in fact the last time I saw a Japanese aeroplane. I was now time expired and within a few days I was given leave to go to Sydney and consequently left the squadron. I spent the last couple of weeks in Darwin still waiting for further raids, and keeping my flight in order but by the last week of September, it was time to go.

Two events happened during this period. First I was awarded the Distinguished Flying Cross, which was a bit of a surprise but I was proud to have been singled out for this honour. Bill Gibbs would also receive the DFC, and he and I were the only two RAF blokes so honoured, although several of the Aussie boys also got DFCs. I received a load of telegrams following this announcement, from my mum and dad, from Margaret, and one from Mr Anderson, my old boss in the buying department at Shell who had first encouraged me to join the RAF. Another came from Bill Gibbs himself who was on leave in Melbourne, also hoping that the booze would last out! Mr Bisset, our host on many occasions down in Sydney wrote: 'Wizard Show, have a drink of milk on the Bisset.' As if!

The second thing, a short time later, was less welcome. It was the news that my father had died. This was equally unexpected and quite a blow. He had continued to struggle into work, wearing himself out stomping into and out of London on his crutches. I knew he had not been well of late but did not know how serious it might be. I am sure my parents had been anxious when they had seen me off at Euston just prior to my leaving for Australia, wondering if they would ever see me again. Even if I entertained similar thoughts, the immaturity of youth does not normally allow young men to dwell on such matters. It might be different if I was leaving a wife and perhaps kids, but I was still young, free and single. Now, of course it dawned on me that those fond farewells meant a lot to me, for it was the last time I saw and hugged my gallant father.

I flew down to Sydney in an Electra via Mildura. I hung around for about ten days, visiting friends and so on and as usual when I reported to headquarters to see what they wanted me to do, nobody knew anything about me, what I should do, where I should go, or indeed, if there were any orders at all. By this time I had had enough. I wasn't the least bit interested in a suggestion I might instruct at Mildura, and the Australians didn't want me due to the situation I mentioned earlier, that RAF personnel were nothing to do with them, we were under RAF control from England. So, having sat around for some time, and at a loose end, really wasting time, I asked about the possibility of going home. Nobody seemed to object, probably it was the answer to a problem, so, I was given a medical to ensure I hadn't picked up anything untoward during my stay and with an all-clear prepared to depart.

I waited around in Melbourne on extended leave until finally, on 14 February 1944, I boarded the USS *Matsonia*, in company with two other 54 Squadron bods, George Farries and Jock Garden, who had both received injuries in accidents – not flying accidents. We left Sydney, the only RAF personnel on board, and headed north-east towards San Francisco.

The squadron and the wing continued to operate from

Darwin but the main fighting was over. October saw no action at all to speak of, and while 457 damaged a Dinah in early November, and then claimed two Betty bombers at night a few days later, that was the end of the air fighting. In 1944 the squadron went over to some offensive operations, and so did 452 and 457 for a while. In April they began to fly Spitfire Mark VIIIs from Livingstone. Caldwell was taken off flying at about the same time as me and was awarded the DSO for his leadership. Later in the war he commanded a wing at Morotai Island, part of the Moluccas group, north-west of New Guinea. He died in 1994.

Bill Gibbs continued to command 54 until January 1944, having been awarded the DFC the previous November. Post-war he remained in the RAF, transferring to the secretarial branch before retiring in 1953. He died in 1972. Robin Norwood left the RAF in 1946 and died in 1970.

Chapter Ten

Back to Europe – and to Normandy

Our ship headed out across the South Pacific and on 1 March 1944 we arrived in San Francisco Bay, nudging past the infamous Alcatraz prison as we passed beneath the awe inspiring San Francisco Bridge. Apart from we three British airmen, the ship had been crammed full of American GIs returning home from the Pacific, so that as we docked, there was a massive crowd of yelling, screaming, waving people. There was music too, the one I remember particularly being 'California Here I Come', made famous by Al Jolson. Once allowed to disembark and elbowing our way through this seething mass of people welcoming home their sons, fathers, sweethearts and loved ones, we were shipped off to an island in the bay. It was an army depot where everyone went following their arrival to the States. Thankfully we were only here for a day or so.

Whilst there, like everyone else who had been out in the tropics, and vulnerable to all sorts of diseases, not to mention women, the first thing that happened was that we were all put side by side in long lines. This took place in a large hall and once we had quietened down, we were ordered to drop our trousers and underpants. Then, standing there with all our manhood dangling for everyone to see, a medical officer appeared, looking very smart in his clean, well ironed uniform and gleaming buttons. Slowly he walked along the line of men, with a stick in one hand, which he used to raise each man's penis and make a quick observation before withdrawing the said stick and moving on to the next man in line. There were about 150 chaps in this line, and although it must have taken some time for him to carry out his inspection, he must have been quite an expert, for he did not linger overlong on any one of us. It has often struck me afterwards what he might have replied when a member of his family asked him later: 'What did you do in the war?' His reply would have been interesting, especially as he and his little stick must have been kept pretty busy considering the large number of soldiers, sailors and marines coming and going. He must have been doing this day after day.

Anyway, we were passed out 'clean and clear' and so were allowed to go ashore into San Francisco. We were befriended by some UK organisation that was tasked with looking after British service personnel in transit from one place to another. The three of us were put up in one of the best places in town, the Sir Francis Drake Hotel, where we had a great time for four or five days. We were looked after very well and we were free to explore the city at our ease and enjoy all the available entertainments and the great variation in food and drink. After the limited fare we had had in Darwin, eating out in the US was both an experience and a luxury unknown to us in austere Britain.

Then we were told to return to the bay island in order to collect any belongings we had left there in storage, and we were then told we would be taking a train right across America to New York. This was quite an adventure. It took us four days in all, four days of comfort, good food, lots of wonderful scenery to take in and enjoy, and of course, a great way to relax and let the world zip by your window.

George, Jock and I had a four-berth sleeping compartment and when not eating or gaping at the scenery, we spent time playing cards and so on, a really enjoyable experience. We went through the mighty Rockies, across vast verdant plains, past forests and lakes, saw lots of wild life – a splendid time.

We changed trains at Chicago and once we arrived in New York we were sent to Staten Island by ferry, again to be checked out and given the 'all clear'. No little stick this time though. Once that was over we went into the city where we were handed over to some more British people and they put us into another splendid hotel, the Lexington Plaza. What amazed us was that our rooms were situated on the 15th floor and none of us had ever been in such a high building in our lives before. Looking out of our bedroom window, we were surrounded by these massive structures. Awe-inspiring, as can be imagined.

Our time in New York was well spent. We were entertained, taken to see the night life and had a couple of very nice young

English ladies to make sure we had everything we needed, and to ensure our time was as relaxed and as comfortable as they could make it. Obviously we took in all the famous sights: the Empire State Building, the Statue of Liberty, Broadway, Central Park, the Bronx, and so on.

One evening we took a trip down to the famous Greenwich Village area to listen to a chap who wasn't all that well known at the time, not to us anyway, called 'Fats' Waller. These two girls had insisted that we see him perform and I have to admit he was a marvellous entertainer.

One of these girls, by the name of Pax Walker, was charming and very nice. She had been evacuated at the beginning of the war along with a whole load of children and teenagers being sent away to the States to be away from danger. It was her ship that was famously torpedoed with great loss of life, but she had been fortunate enough to be among those rescued from the sea, and was now helping this British organisation in New York, looking after travelling British soldiers, sailors and airmen.

She was trying to become an actress as I remember. Her great claim at this time was that she had under-studied Greer Garson in *Mrs Miniver*. Of course, Greer Garson rarely fell ill, but Pax was at least given a small walk-on part in the film as a maid or some such, so at least got herself on the silver screen, albeit briefly.

Much later Pax married an actor and returned to England. I was fortunate to meet up with her again and the last time I saw her was about 1950. Then, in 2006, I had a letter out of the blue from her, saying that she had seen me on television being interviewed in some RAF programme or other. She had telephoned the RAF Club in Piccadilly, and managed to get in touch with me. She had been living in South Africa for many years but had now returned to the UK and was residing in Dover. We spoke a couple of times on the telephone and she was hoping we would be able to meet up again. However, sadly I then got a call from her husband just before Christmas 2007, to say that she had died of leukaemia. We had been such good friends all those years earlier, purely a platonic relationship I must add, but we were not destined to meet ever again. A great pity.

One thing I do remember quite well happening in New York, although I can't recall exactly how it came about, was when my companions and I got ourselves in a situation in a downtown New York bar. We had been out for the evening and found ourselves down by the dock area and had gone into this bar for a drink. Inside there was one particular man sitting at a table, well dressed, perhaps too well dressed, certainly looking quite sharp, with a big patch over one eye that made him stand out. Seeing us enter, and it being obvious to him we were not Americans, he called us over and asked if he could buy us a drink. Never backward in coming forward, we readily agreed, not wanting to refuse this kind invitation. So we sat down and very quickly our drinks arrived and we began to chat.

I noticed he had several large mates sitting around nearby and at the table, but it was our eye-patch friend who did all the talking. I cannot recall exactly what was said at one stage but we began to argue over some innocuous point or other, nothing untoward or earth shattering, we just did not totally agree with his point of view on the matter, and were making our views known. He then said something about 'Limeys' being no good, that sort of thing, and the more the conversation went on the more agitated he became. George and I then decided we needed to visit the toilet and excused ourselves for a moment. While in the restroom in came one of these big chaps (in the movies they might be referred to as gorillas) and said to us, something like: 'Joe is a big guy round here and he don't like arguments, especially if he ain't winning. And if he gets angry he's not a very nice man. If you'll take my advice, whatever Joe says, goes!'

Well, we didn't have to be warned twice, so when we returned to the table we were all sweetness and light, and after that, whatever Joe said, went! The sequel to this was, that several years later I happened to read in a newspaper that a big gang boss in New York, named Joe something or other, well known because of a patch he had over one eye, had been shot dead in some gangland altercation. So I think overall we were very lucky we didn't continue to argue with him, and we were thankful for the 'heads-up' we got from one of his minders. I can still hear that chap's voice now – 'What Joe says, goes!'

After a week or so in New York we finally got our marching orders to report to the docks where we were assigned to sail on the *Queen Mary*, which in WW2 had been turned into a troop ship. She did not sail in convoy with other ships, using her great speed to out-run any threat by German U-boats, so we knew we would be sailing across the Atlantic on our lonesome. I would guess that apart from we three pilots, there were about 8,000 US soldiers on board too, for this being March 1944, they would be heading to join the invasion force.

Again we were pretty lucky with our accommodation on board, the three of us being given a very nice cabin that, we were told, had been used by none-other than Winston Churchill when he had once travelled to the States. I suppose the only difference was that while there was one of him, there were, in total, ten of us officers on this trip. It was a big cabin as can be imagined, but the ten of us soon filled it. Considering some of the American GIs were sleeping in corridors and on the floor of some of the lounges, we had no grounds to complain.

The reader will recall that in Sydney we had been befriended by a Mr Bisset at his home, where we were always welcome, and often played tennis at his place while enjoying afternoon tea. Well, Mr Bisset, when I was saying my final goodbyes to him, had confided in the fact that if by chance I was ever to get aboard the *Queen Mary*, be sure to ask for his brother, Commodore Bisset – he was her captain! I thought the chances of actually sailing home on this particular liner very remote so it is easy to imagine my amazement, and perhaps glee, when we found we were indeed going to sail in her. Mr Bisset's daughter Margaret, later married one of our pilots, Tony Tuckson.

We hadn't been on board very long before we made it our business to acquaint the captain that he had friends of his brother with him on board. No sooner had we dumped our gear and selected our sleeping spots, we straightaway sought out the ship's purser, asking him to bring us to the attention of the captain. The purser promised to do so, but we were mindful that this ship's captain would have his hands full with getting out of harbour, making sure all his 'guests' were stowed away, etc, so it might be some time before we heard anything further, if at all!

Then, low and behold, just a couple of hours later, over the tannoy system came the call for the three of us to report to the purser's office. Duly rolling up we were immediately taken up to meet the captain, who a year later would become Sir James Bisset.

This 60-year old had been a seaman all his life, starting as a young apprentice back in 1898 and in 1907 had started to work for the Cunard Line. In WW1 he had commanded a destroyer in the Royal Navy Reserve. Once retired from the RNR in 1933, he had been given command of both the *Queen Mary* and *Queen Elizabeth* in WW2, while commodore of the Cunard White Star Company. In 1949 the Americans would award him their Legion of Merit, to add to his British CBE that he received in 1942.

Anyway, he was kind enough to take time off to show us around the ship and later got one of his engineer officers to take us down to give us a tour of the massive engine room. Returning to his cabin, and as the ship was under American control and therefore 'dry', he showed us a cupboard full of gin, so I think we were the only people on board apart from some of his officers, who managed a drink or two as we went across the Atlantic. Not a bad little introduction. It also helped to break the monotony a bit too.

Our routine aboard ship was to have two meals a day, with a choice of breakfast time of 6, 7, 8 or 9 o'clock, with tea/dinner at either, 5, 6, 7 or 8 pm. We were lucky in choosing to eat breakfast about 9 am and dinner at 5 pm, so it helped spread our day. I have heard that airmen on some ships during the war, got the job of looking out for aircraft, on the basis we knew what to look for and then hopefully recognising the type and country of origin. I am pleased to report that nothing so onerous fell on our shoulders.

It was a pretty speedy crossing, the huge ship never seemed to slow down at all, she just ploughed on and on at full speed, although no doubt with some expert zig-zagging, keeping this up so as not to allow any lurking German submarine a chance to catch her, let alone line her up for a torpedo. In fact we did not see a single ship of any description the whole way over after leaving New York, till we arrived in Greenock, five or six days later.

From Greenock we went down to Kirkby, near Liverpool, to be cleared, and then we were allowed home on leave. I telephoned my mother, telling her I was back and she and my cousin met me at Euston station. It was quite a reunion, sad because my father was not there too. From there we caught the No.77 bus to Clapham.

I became quite popular with the local girls – and my mother

– as I had had the good foresight to bring back with me from New York a quantity of silk stockings, that were practically unobtainable in the UK, unless you had a lot of money, or knew an American GI. Fortunately my mother seemed to be coping all right without dad. She had got herself a job and was continuing to live in the family home.

After a few weeks, by which time it was becoming obvious that an invasion of France must soon be coming, I reported to Adastral House in London, to see what they had in mind for me. I was ushered in to see this P1 chap in personnel, and he said: 'Oh dear, what do we do with you I wonder?' It never ceased to amaze me that nobody ever knew what I should do. How they worked I had no idea,

The author about to go to Normandy.

but it was almost inevitable that nothing was marked on my card. If I had stayed at home, would anyone have ever noticed?

The man looked through his papers, trying to come up with some gem that might interest this fighter pilot sitting in front of him. He assumed I did not want to sit behind a desk for a while, and nor did I want to become an instructor to the latest bunch of pink-cheeked would-be aces. I concurred to both counts. Continuing with his list of vacancies, me feeling like a chap on the dole going to a job centre, he finally spotted something. 'Here's something,' he ventured, 'Air Marshal

_____ wants a PA.' He looked up smiling, until he saw the look on my face, and then his took on a defeated air. I knew the name of this air marshal, someone not particularly popular, and could find no enthusiasm at the thought of being his tea-boy. The man's finger continued down the list of jobs.

Suddenly he brightened up again and said: 'Ah, this sounds interesting, how about this?' Air Chief Marshal Sir Arthur Tedder, who at this particular time was the Deputy Supreme Allied Commander, and second in command of all Allied forces under General Dwight Eisenhower for the coming invasion, was quite insistent that the Royal Air Force should get their fair share of publicity. He had found when he was a commander in the Mediterranean, that the army always seemed to get all the kudos and publicity from the public relations men, newspaper journalists and so on, so he wanted the RAF to get a more equal amount of coverage this time, in what it did and achieved. The invasion was going to be a big event, no doubt about that – certainly the biggest invasion the world had yet seen, and he wanted to be assured that the RAF's part in it was fully covered. His idea was to have a small, separate RAF PR unit formed, which would represent and report news to national and local newspapers, Reuters, and so on, concentrating purely on RAF and flying matters.

My P1 man said they were looking for three or four chaps to take on small groups of these people, show them around, introduce them to bods in the know, and ensure they got all the good stuff on the news front to do with what the RAF were doing. Those selected would, of course, know how things got done etc, and be able to guide the press boys on what they should cover and what questions to ask. In short, they should 'know the form'.

Well, this sounded a very interesting project, with some freedom of action, so I said: 'Thank you very much'. He looked pleased to have filled the vacancy, so promised that he would get things organised and underway.

Within a few days it had all been sorted and I joined the new outfit, which was called the Air Information Unit, on 29 April, in London. I was introduced to all the war correspondents who had been recruited into this RAF unit, and wearing blue uniforms with the words 'war correspondent' on shoulder flashes, we began our task. For the next few weeks we went around in small teams to all the depots, airfields, aerodromes, bases of all description that had anything to do with air force matters. Everyone we met and everywhere we went, were busily proceeding towards invasion. My team's task was to get interesting stories to report on by interviewing pilots and aircrew and ground personnel so they could register them, via a censor, to newspapers, magazines, and so on. My job was to guide them to the chaps I felt would be the most interesting to talk to and to act as a sort of chaperone while also making certain they didn't do anything or go anywhere that would be secret or classified.

This went on throughout May and into the start of June. It was a fascinating time as can be imagined with all these preparations in full swing. Day by day it became obvious that the 'big event' was not far off. The weather in early June of course, did not give us any great hope that D-Day was in any way imminent but as we know now, it was really a case of sooner rather than later because of tides and trying to keep the lid on everything before it became obvious to the Germans that things were so well advanced.

Talking to some of the pilots involved in the pre-D-Day sorties was enlightening. The Typhoon squadrons were all engaged in trying to knock out German radar stations all along the French coast, but not favouring any particular spot, thereby continuing to keep the enemy guessing as to where actually the troops would storm ashore. I did learn that a couple of radar sites were deliberately not hit nearer the Pas de Calais area, for the planners wanted these sites to pick up on low flying aircraft – Lancasters of 617 Squadron, the famed Dambusters – on the night and morning of D-Day in order to give the impression that something was happening in this narrow part of the Channel. The Germans always expected an invasion around Calais, and it was imperative to make them believe their suspicions were correct in order to keep men and armour away from Normandy.

We also noted that all Allied aircraft were suddenly daubed with black and white stripes round wings and fuselages, a tactic to ensure people on the ground would be able to identify immediately a 'friendly' aeroplane. This would be especially needed with so many aircraft flying over what was to be a vast armada of ships, for as RAF aircrew will tell you, the navy boys were quite good at shooting first and asking questions later.

By this time I had more or less settled on a team led by myself, with Alan Tompkins, the aviation correspondent to the then *Sunday Despatch*, a chap called Scott, who, strangely enough, worked for *The Scotsman*, and Bill Turner who was a photographer for the *Sunday Pictorial*. It was a nice compact little team and we were issued with a huge Humber Estate car which enabled us to move around pretty freely. We also had special passes that got us into most places no matter how sensitive, so obviously Tedder had made it clear to all his commanders that we special press teams were to be given all the help and access we needed. It had also been explained to us, that we would be required to head over to France with the invasion forces, as soon as it was safe enough to do so. I suppose you could say that this piece of information was both exciting and not a little thought provoking. Invasions usually meant a lot of noise and gunfire, with people getting killed all over the place. The side arm of one automatic pistol I was issued with did nothing to allay these anxieties. It is one thing to be brave and 'gung-ho' sitting in a Spitfire, but quite another when faced with a fully armed blond Nazi storm-trooper coming at you.

We were in the Tangmere area on 4 June and things were obviously hotting up. Lots of aerial activity but then Tompkins was recalled to his office for some reason so we were in London on the 6th, when the news that D-Day had arrived, broke, and that Allied forces had landed in Normandy and all appeared to be going well. So we returned to the south coast to get more stories and to await our call to embark for France. We were certainly not top priority and in any event it was no use going over before airfields and airstrips had been built and established.

Our little unit set up camp in the New Forest north of Southampton to await embarkation. All was going well until the 18th when disaster struck. As is well known, a man-made harbour, codename 'Mulberry' was being constructed at Arromanches-les-Bains, by the beach, with Bayeux just inland, and to the north-west of Caen, to facilitate the landing of the tons of supplies and thousands of men needed to back-up the initial invading force. Back in August 1942 the Allies had tried to take the port of Dieppe and hold it for a day, to see if such a plan to capture a French port was feasible. That exercise had proved costly, and so the D-Day planners had decided that rather than capture a port, they would create, build and float over, the makings of a prefabricated harbour.

On the 18th, however, a storm blew up which gathered strength and raged unabated for three days. It was the worst June storm in living memory. It not only destroyed part of the harbour but drastically reduced the flow of supplies and men. From 15 to 18 June, some 35,000 Allied troops had been landed but this fell to just 9,000 on the 19th. Similarly, stores of some 25,000 tons during the same period, dropped to just 7,000 tons. This in turn led to a back-log of shipping along the south coast ports, unable to put to sea. So after waiting for another week or so, we were finally told to up-sticks and move across to Essex.

Here we were set up in another tented camp until the 29th when we eventually got the call and set off for Tilbury docks where we were put aboard a tank landing ship, (an LST), and that night we sailed off alone to make rendezvous with a lot of other ships at 'Piccadilly'. This was a codeword for a designated spot out in the English Channel where ships for France congregated before heading off to Normandy in convoy. Reaching France we were off-loaded on Gold Beach about 2 am in the morning, driving jeeps, and drove on to a small village called Creulley, which is just north of the road between Caen and Bayeux. It was here the PR set-up had made its base.

By this time, General Bernard Montgomery and his forces were supposed to have fought their way beyond the town of Caen, but strong enemy resistance had made this impossible and they were still firmly stuck outside this pivotal piece of real estate, so we were reasonably safe where we were, and just up the road was the RAF's 83 Group Headquarters, 2nd Tactical Air Force (2nd TAF). 83 Group provided the tactical support for the British Army, and was commanded by Air Vice-Marshal Harry Broadhurst DSO DFC AFC. The group had mostly Typhoon fighter-bombers, armed with either bombs or rockets. These, and all other squadrons operating behind the front lines in Normandy, were using rapidly prepared airstrips in just about any flat farmland surface they could find. Landing strips had been bull-dozed flat and runways were made out of PSP (pieced steel planking). This marvellous stuff enabled an airstrip to be operating within hours sometimes, but the only drawback in Normandy was the sandy soil. Whether anybody had realised the problem this was to cause I don't know, but it certainly gave engineering officers a headache. This sandy soil, this disturbed sandy soil, was blown all over the place from the blast caused by propeller slipstreams and the sleeve valve engines of the Typhoon's Sabre engines were particularly vulnerable. I understand that Normandy sand was used in the manufacture of sandpaper because of its wonderfully gritty nature, so little wonder engines suffered. There was another problem too. Whenever aircraft started up and prepared to take off, a huge swirl of this abrasive dust would rise over the area of the 'strip', so that the Germans could spot it from miles away given the flattish landscape. This would lead to some immediate shelling by the Germans. With the RAF's usual dexterity someone came up with a special air filter for the Typhoon within about ten days, so the engines got some protection, and as the Germans were pushed further back, the shelling lessoned appreciably.

We settled down in the grounds of a French château – which was nice – and there was a large castle on an adjoining hill. We got ourselves sorted out and began doing our job again. After checking in at 83 Group HQ, we then began to visit the various airfields and airstrips. Rather than names, these airstrips had numbers, such as B.1, B.2, etc. B.1 for instance was Bayeux. Arriving at some airstrip or other we would introduce ourselves to the officer in command, and then meet the squadron commanders and his pilots to get the latest stories about their operations. Some of these airstrips were right on top of the front lines. I recall one such place we visited, where the Typhoons were taking off in a direction away from the battle front in order to get some height before turning to dive into action, either firing their rocket projectiles (RPs) or dropping bombs from under their wings. We could stand on these airstrips, watch them attacking, and within a short space of time they were landing back to re-arm. As they taxied across the airstrips, airmen would jump up onto the wing-tips in order to guide the pilot to his dispersal area, for what with the dust, limited space, and the fact that the pilot could not see anything directly ahead of him because of the engine cowling, he would be unable to do so without hitting something.

Without any real forward movement from Caen, the RAF

were running out of places to create more airstrips, for there were plenty more squadrons ready and waiting to come into the bridgehead area. I remember there was a Canadian Spitfire wing nearby that we also visited. It was obviously pretty exciting to watch all this activity going on and my team were busily recording their stories and wiring them back to their editors, while Turner was snapping away with his cameras at everything in sight.

Later we were also able to get to 84 Group's people once they arrived and I have to say that both RAF groups were very helpful. If something big was in the offing we were informed and were able to sit in on the pilot's briefing sessions. They always let us know what was in the wind so that we could ensure good news coverage at home.

Often we were up with the advancing army units, watching from an even closer perspective our fighters and fighter-bombers hammering away at enemy troops, armour and strongpoints. One day we had set ourselves up near Carpiquet before the break-out from Caen, waiting to watch what promised to be a spectacular air strike go in. Because we were so advanced we were given an army sergeant and two of his men to keep us out of trouble, so with Alan Tompkins and Bill Turner, there were just six of us.

We had hunkered down in a ditch behind a hedgerow at the edge of a field, when, no more than 150 yards away, we spotted about 40 German soldiers, steel helmets, guns, jackboots, the lot. Tompkins got terribly excited and turned to the sergeant and said in a whisper: 'Look, Germans, why don't you open fire on them?' The sergeant, not impressed by Alan's enthusiasm and heroic outburst, remained unmoving and like his men, continued to keep their heads well down behind the bushes. Alan was still keen to engage the enemy, or should I say, for the soldiers to engage the enemy. Finally, the sergeant said, turning his head very slowly to look at Alan straight in the eyes: 'Sir, we have three rifles, three bayonets, a couple of hand grenades, while your flight lieutenant as his side arm and a few bullets. There are forty or more Jerries over there, armed to the teeth and looking for trouble. They all have guns, perhaps some with machine guns, belts into which I can see a number of grenades sticking out, long bayonets, pistols, and goodness knows what else. I don't really think we want to upset and disturb them, do you? It wouldn't really be a fair fight.'

Tompkins let this little bit of logic sink in as his eyes continued to follow this troop of enemy soldiers as they continued to trudge along on the other side of this field. You could see his mind working and good sense penetrating into his brain. Slowly he began to nod his head in agreement with the sergeant's undoubted wisdom, then said: 'No, sergeant, you're probably right.' Turner and I were glad and more than a little relieved when he said that.

Mr Scott was a lot older than either Alan or Bill, and not in the best of health so he began to be less involved in our work and rarely came out with us. He probably shouldn't have been there in the first place, but it did him credit that he did at least try and in the beginning didn't shirk his perceived duty. Bill Turner only wanted to take pictures and wasn't really fussed if it was of an aeroplane, a soldier or some bombed-out building, but Alan had been in the army in World War One and had actually learnt to fly up in Newcastle in the 1920s. He had suffered a rather nasty crash which had banged up his face somewhat but at least he knew something about aviation. He was quite an extrovert, a big man with a large beard.

In early July Montgomery was going to make a full-scale assault to take Caen and he asked 'Bomber' Harris, CinC of Bomber Command, to bomb the place. We were warned about this so we drove to a good point from where we could watch the proceedings. We had a grandstand view as all these Avro Lancasters came in at dusk and they absolutely plastered the place. I don't think it was very well thought out because the amount of debris and fallen masonry that was generated did not make for an easy assault by Allied tanks. But it was all spectacular from my team's point of view.

However, the British and Canadian troops picked their way through the rubble and by 7 July, held about half the town, the Germans still holding on to the eastern half. Monty made another effort to break out, attacking round the eastern side of Caen in Operation Goodwood. This operation was planned for 18 July and on the 17th we and lots of other people were called to a special briefing by the great man himself. I remember it as a beautiful sunny day and we were all assembled outside his caravan set up in a field near his headquarters. Once we were gathered in this open area he made an appearance and in front of a large map, indicated what was about to happen, his pointer tracing the way things were planned to go.

Basically, Bomber Command was to bomb along a line to the north-east of Caen including the large industrial area of Colombelles and to continue some miles south and west of Cagny. Following this, the American Air Force would bomb along a similar line to the north, thereby creating a corridor along which the tanks would advance more or less unopposed. Armed with this information, my team packed our bags and drove out towards a good spot that night, which was on a little hill, in a farmhouse building, and then waited for the fireworks to begin.

Bomber Command came in about 05.30 am on the 18th, followed by the Americans. The Lancasters did a remarkable job, but it was really quite frightening to sit only about a mile from this and witness all those bombs coming down. As Tompkins said, 'God help all those people down there.' Although the bombers did a good job the Germans recovered quicker than expected. The Allied tanks were delayed in getting into action and after a day or so, the attack stalled and the great break-out had not been achieved but in the end it came and the army moved forward.

The next eventful occurrence was when the retreating Germans were caught and decimated in the Falaise Gap. We helped cover this too, and some of the pictures and newsreels we saw of the slaughter were terrible. A lot of Germans died there, a perfect killing ground for Typhoons and light bombers.

And so followed weeks of attrition, the Germans defending every inch of ground, the Allies advancing slowly and at great cost, towards their final objective, the town of Falaise. The RAF, particularly the Typhoon squadrons, were constantly in action, attacking with bombs and rockets, or strafing with cannon, everything that moved in the German sector, plus actions in close support of the army. Whilst all this was happening the Americans had broken out in the west through St. Lô and Avranches, while General George Patton's 3rd Army was now rampaging through Brittany and had reached Le Mans. He now turned north, heading for Falaise in order to link up with Montgomery's forces.

We of course were observing all this from a reasonably safe distance behind the battle front, or so we thought. One day in mid-August our luck almost ran out. We had been informed that Bomber Command was to saturate the German positions ahead of an attack by Canadian and Polish troops. It was a beautiful sunny day if somewhat misty as we waited a few hundred yards behind the start line for the bombers to come in. We soon heard, then saw them thundering in, an awe-inspiring sight. It seemed to be going well, bombs exploding amongst the German positions, but suddenly all hell broke loose. Some of the bomber crews started to bomb short, and their ordnance had fallen directly on to the Poles waiting to go into action. Soon the dead and wounded were being brought back past us. It was a most unfortunate incident. However, although badly shaken, the Poles went in and achieved their objectives. Stout fellows, the Poles.

There has been a lot of controversy over the last few years about 'friendly fire' and rightly or wrongly, any commanders or even countries are unwilling to accept blame or any responsibility. Not so with the head of Bomber Command, Air Chief Marshal Sir Arthur Harris. He wrote immediately to General Henry Crerar, the commander of the 1st Canadian Army, expressing his regret and saying that action was being taken to ensure this sort of thing didn't happen again. True to his word, Harris had some of his pathfinder crews demoted and took their prized pathfinder badges away from them.

By now, however, the Allies were closing the gap and on 22 August the encirclement was complete, the Canadians and Poles meeting up with the Americans at Falaise. The Battle for Normandy was over.

I sometimes feel the scope, size and ferocity of the Battle for Normandy is underestimated. We read with horror of the carnage of the First World War, the slaughter on the first day of the Somme offensive, 1 July 1916, of losses around the towns of Ypres and Passchendaele. Equally awful were the casualties at Stalingrad in 1942-43, the loss of life during the siege of Leningrad and so on. But Normandy was a war of attrition lasting for 77 days, between the landings and Falaise. The casualties speak for themselves. The Germans lost 450,000 men, 240,000 of whom were killed and 210,000 taken prisoner. The Allies lost 240,000 of whom 36,000 were killed. It is also estimated that some 100,000 French resistance fighters and civilians were killed or wounded. The victory came at a great cost, but it destroyed the German army in the west.

Chapter Eleven

Paris and Peace

At about this time, I think it was on 23 August, we heard the Americans had been closing in on the French capital, Paris, and that French Resistance fighters in the city had risen and were making things difficult for the German occupying force, who in any event seemed about to depart.

Alan Tompkins, with his news-hound hat on, argued that now that the army and the RAF were finally moving rapidly forward, Paris was the story to follow. He tried to persuade me to go with him so I decided to broach the subject with my immediate boss to see how he felt about it. This was Squadron Leader Bell, himself a newspaper man put in charge of this Air Information Unit and he never seemed to mind much about what happened or who did what, so long as the press were being properly briefed and supplied with reports and war stories. We said to him that Paris seemed to be about to be liberated and asked him if we could shoot off there to see what was what. He gave us the all clear, so Alan, Scott and I quickly got our stuff into our car before he changed his mind and off we went. This was on the morning of 25 August 1944.

We headed off, drove through devastated Falaise and on to Argentan. We saw much evidence of the destruction of some eight German divisions that were either wiped out or taken prisoner. We had no proper road maps, just some RAF maps but reached Argentan about 09.00 and went into an *estaminet* for some coffee, finding the place crammed full of American GIs. Ordering our drinks we sat down and began chatting to some of them. A couple at our table amused us no end. One was a short, lively chap with a very individual way of talking, no doubt from the Bronx area of New York, and his pal was, in contrast, a six foot, three inch John Wayne-type Texan. The little guy prattled away, talking sixteen to the dozen, while his pal, in a slow, western drawl, made the odd comment but said very little; a man of few words it seemed.

Alan asked them how things had been for them in

Normandy and up till this moment, and the little guy explained quite forcefully that they had been through absolute hell, fighting their way out of the beach-head, through the French hedge-rows, battling German soldiers all the way to Argentan – real hell! When he looked to his companion for confirmation and support of all he had said, Tex, after a moment to think about things, and to compose himself actually to speak, finally said: 'Gee, I don't know. We fired a few rounds, ran about a bit, but we didn't have so much trouble.' This started the little guy screaming and shouting, referring to what a terrible and dangerous time they'd had, but Tex was just too laid back about it all to help support his fast-talking friend. We let them argue away about how fierce or not the fighting had been, and being unable to get Tex to agree that they had been through hell, the little guy was literally jumping up and down. We quietly finished our coffee, got up, and left them to it.

We motored on, asking the occasional civilian if we were on the right road for Paris, to be told: 'Tout droit, tout droit', but nobody seemed to have the least idea so we just travelled on. We more or less followed our noses in what we hoped was the right direction. Coming finally over the brow of a hill, at about 3 pm in the afternoon, we saw up ahead a load of tanks. Happily we spotted the Allied white star painted on their turrets, so moved forward. We knew of course that American troops had reached the River Seine at Fontainebleau on the 20th and that French tanks had reached the edge of Paris on the 23rd, at the Porte d'Orléans.

Our way was then blocked by some soldiers, and a young American officer came across and asked us in perfect French, who we were and where were we going. We explained we were British war correspondents and he immediately stopped talking French, to tell us that we had inadvertently run into units of the French 2nd Armoured Division, commanded by Général Philippe Leclerc. There was still fighting up ahead in both the outskirts and in the city itself, and everyone was waiting for an all-clear in order to enter Paris. It had, apparently, been agreed by the Allies that it was right and proper that French forces should be the first to enter the city and to take the surrender of remaining German forces there, hence the delay. Leclerc had been nominated for this historic task, moved his division up, and was just waiting for the signal to move forward.

We told the officer that we would also like to go into the city centre but he advised us to wait a while until more was known of the situation up front. He promised to come and tell us when he knew something so we sat on a grass verge in the afternoon sun to await developments. About an hour later he appeared again, said there was still no firm word from the city, but we could do him a favour. He had two French Resistance girls who wanted to be taken in if we had room in our car for them. Being gentlemen we said yes, and then, at about 6 o'clock, our American friend came back again and said they had been told they could move up. He pointed to a spot between two tanks and said that if we put our car between them, we would become part of the convoy going into Paris. So we clambered into our car, with the two girls in the back with Scott, manoeuvred in between the two tanks and moments later we were off.

Looking back, it all seems quite amazing. Here we were, a small RAF PR group, bumbling across France to see what was happening in Paris, and suddenly we were part of Général Leclerc's army column going into this great city, where, later this same day, he received the formal surrender of the German forces there, from General von Cholitz, at his headquarters at the Hotel Meurice. Was it only this morning we had had breakfast at Creulley, with absolutely no idea of how the day would end, or how far away?

The nearer the column got to the city centre the more evidence we could see that intense fighting had indeed been going on. Then came the crowds. I thought the reception on our ship's arrival in San Francisco five months earlier had been amazing but these Parisians were experiencing their first moments of liberation from four years of humiliating German occupation, and here were French soldiers returning their city to freedom once more. The populace went wild and there we were, three Britons slap bang in the middle of it all. I assume I must have been the first RAF officer to arrive in Paris, unknown, unannounced, but nevertheless, there!

One cannot adequately describe the scenes that were all about us. People screaming, yelling, singing, crying. French flags waving from the windows and balconies, and in people's hands all about us. Flowers were being thrown onto the tanks, women clambering onto vehicles, throwing their arms about the men, kissing others whose heads poked up from tank turrets. Frenchmen kissing Frenchmen, bottles of champagne and cognac being offered up to the liberators, old men wearing their First World War medals again with pride – it was just unforgettable. Men were shaking hands with the soldiers with tears of joy streaming down their faces, children were being lifted aloft to see the tanks clank by, everywhere one looked there was a scene of unimaginable joy. I wouldn't have missed being a part of it for the world. An abiding and inspiring memory.

Eventually we got to within sight of the Eiffel Tower and the two girls we had driven in, were absolutely hysterical by this time. Thanking us profusely they got out of the car and quickly disappeared into the throng. We carried on and by about 9 pm that evening we found ourselves in the Place de la Concorde. Somehow, and I don't know how, we finished up at the Grande Hotel which is just next to L'Opéra. We parked our car outside, went in and without any hassle were given a suite of rooms, in which, we were told, before the war, the King of Afghanistan had stayed. Perhaps we should have been more impressed than we were.

So, at about 10 pm there we were in this magnificent hotel room, with some tins of bully-beef we had brought with us, several bottles of champagne we had been given, living for the moment like the King of Afghanistan – well almost! Quite a momentous day; outside Caen in the morning, in the centre of Paris that night.

The next morning we got up, had some breakfast and found lots more people had arrived overnight. There is a superb hotel – the Scribe – next door to the Grande and the various press people had begun to set themselves up there. Scott had already retired from us now, no doubt overcome by all the excitement, and he remained in bed. Alan and I went over to the press room but found everything in total chaos, so as there was absolutely no point in staying around, we set off to have a look round Paris.

Alan's first suggestion was to go and explore the famous tomb of Napoleon. This to me seemed utterly surreal, but not ever having been to Paris before, I had no objection to doing so. Fortunately Alan knew exactly where it was located so we got into our car, surprisingly still where we had left it, and drove off. The tomb is in the Invalides, in the Place de la Concorde, but when we got there, it was, of course, shut. I suppose we should have guessed that it would be, but then a chap appeared who seemed to be some sort of attendant connected with the building. Quickly realising we were British, and assuming too we were part of the liberating forces, he agreed to let us in. So there we were and it was quite moving for just Alan and myself at this historical moment in the life of both Paris and France, to be standing there looking down on Napoleon's tomb on this August day. We stood there for some minutes and the attendant was very happy that the Boche had finally gone and things should very soon return to normal.

Having seen the tomb, Alan was bitten by the bug and was keen to take the opportunity to visit other places of interest. Anyone would think we were on holiday. He suggested we go up to the Sacré Coeur, that wonderfully placed basilica on high ground to the north, overlooking the city. Surprisingly we again had no great difficulty in driving about. There were lots of people around of course but not that much traffic on the roads, just army vehicles, jeeps and trucks.

Arriving at the famous artists' square at Montmartre, we parked and walked round to the basilica, strolled inside and took in the magnificent interior. The place was full of people, many at prayer, no doubt rejoicing and giving thanks for the city's deliverance and liberation from oppression. Again we stood there for quite some while taking in these historic scenes. It still seemed totally unreal to us that were could even be here in the first place.

Coming out and starting to walk to our car, a Frenchman came up to us and in reasonable English, asked who we were, etc, and Alan explained that he was a war correspondent and that I was an RAF officer. He could obviously see that from my uniform but he was pleased to welcome us both and shook our hands warmly. He was, he stated, a member of the city's resistance movement and asked if we would care to see their headquarters? We agreed that this would be interesting, so he led us towards the basilica building, saying that the headquarters was actually situated in the waterworks beneath the Sacré Coeur. Arriving at the spot he was making for, he bent down, lifted up a manhole cover and led us down some steps. Right at the bottom was the Montmartre section of the French Resistance. It was set up like a control room with radios, transmitters and receivers, a radio log book, etc., and he began to show us around the place. He said they had been working and hiding down here all through the occupation but that the Germans had never suspected its location and so had never discovered where they had been.

He then invited us to write something in the radio log book to mark the occasion, which he no doubt felt could now double as a visitor's book, and we both did so and appended our signatures. Some 18 years later, Alan's son visited Paris and Alan told him about this place and to see if it was still there, as he would find it very interesting. Well, the son did just that, for by then it had become something of a museum. The log book was also there too and the lad had flipped back the pages to August 1944 and there he found the entries made by his father and I. He later wrote to me, reminding me of what I had written:

Flight Lieutenant R W Foster DFC RAF, offers his sincere congratulations to Paris. He has fought the Boche for 4¹/₂ years and is delighted to now watch his downfall, towards which the brave Paris people have contributed. Vive la France.

Our resistance man now thought it time for some refreshment, so we went back up top and met up with a couple of his friends, and piling into our Humber, directed us all to a nearby café. Apparently they had used this place regularly during the war for a letter drop location and so on, which was run by a good friend of theirs.

We went into the café, cum bar, and the owner offered us all beer. Well, we started drinking and then somebody started singing the *Marseillaise*, and we felt we needed to respond with 'God Save the King', and thus began a number of patriotic tunes, such as 'It's a Long Way to Tipperary' which, although it came from another war, seemed appropriate. By then the noise and the news of what was happening had brought quite a number of people to join in our impromptu celebrations. Several people from the Montmartre area thronged into the small bar, and it got noisier and boozier as time progressed.

The proprietor really got carried away in all the excitement and actually ran out of beer so began to offer drinks from any bottles that could be seen on the shelves. As fast as he opened them they were emptied. I said to one chap who could speak some broken English about this guy's generosity and he replied, well, he had known him for over 30 years and he had rarely given anything away for free before. In the end we literally drank the place dry. His final act was to raise his arms, and with his head to one side in typical French fashion, declared: 'C'est finis!'

By the time we got back to the hotel, staggered more like, although somehow I drove, we found that the people in the nearby press centre in the Scribe Hotel were finally up and running. Alan thought that we should actually start to do some work and send off a report or two to tell our people back near Caen what had been happening. Then we learnt that Général de Gaulle was going to make a triumphal march down the Champs Elysées from the Arc de Triomphe. This seemed too good to miss, so with nothing better to do I decided I would go along and watch the proceedings, while Alan remained working on his reports.

It was an amazing sight really, for nobody seemed to mind what we did or where we went, absolutely no restrictions at all. So I drove out of the Place de la Concorde, went up the Champs Elysées a short way and pulled in by the side of the road, to await developments. The whole place was full of people all waiting for the show, and those I had parked in front of pulled a bit of a face but assumed I was someone of immense importance so said nothing. Then a couple of them asked if they could get in and sit in the car, which would give them a bit of comfort and a better view. I didn't mind and then, very quickly, a number of people piled in and several others clambered onto the roof.

In due course, from behind us, we could see some movement and finally a procession began to move forward. In the front was de Gaulle, with Général Leclerc, and a huge entourage, with flags flying, all moving slowly, even majestically, along the avenue, de Gaulle, his hands stretched out to each side in supplication, acknowledging the rapturous applause from the populace. Behind them came a convoy of vehicles, all heading slowly down from the Arc de Triomphe with its flame to the unknown warrior of World War One.

As de Gaulle passed me, amidst all this cheering and singing, there was a slight gap in the procession between the first couple of cars and those following. Someone in the car nudged me and suggested that I pull across and join in. By now I was game for anything so started the engine and quickly swung out and into this gap. No one seemed to object, so suddenly we were part of the Général's parade.

Since that day I have seen any number of pictures of the parade and some newsreels of it, but unfortunately none ever managed to pan back far enough to take in anything beyond the walking group and the first two cars, so I have never seen my Humber with its Parisians waving from its windows, and waving flags from the roof as we headed slowly towards the Place de la Concorde.

At one stage some firing broke out from some ministry building or other but whether it was hostile or part of the jubilant celebrations I never discovered, but nobody seemed to be firing at de Gaulle directly, yet there was a moment's hesitation. The people on my car roof rapidly disappeared while those inside with me were all cowering down. I just sat there without flinching, but in case the reader thinks this very brave of me, I should point out that with so many in the car, we were four on the front seats, I was totally jammed in behind the wheel and up against the door handle so couldn't have opened the door to escape even had I wanted to! I couldn't even get a hand to my holstered pistol.

As the seeming danger quickly passed, one of my passengers remarked how brave I was just sitting there as if nothing untoward was happening. With due humility I shrugged off the suggestion of my bravery, so at least I had managed to keep the honour of the RAF intact. After all, I am certain there were no other RAF people present in that parade, and if they were, they were not as close to the front of it as I was.

Within moments the parade continued on but I decided not to proceed further once the bottom of the Champs was reached, so letting my passengers out, I peeled off to the left and returned to the hotel to pick up Tompkins. By then he had met up with an elderly Frenchman, who turned out to be a professor at the Sorbonne and had got talking. The man said he would be delighted if we would both join him and his family for dinner at his home that evening and it seemed rude to refuse such an offer, so after all the excitement of the day, we later drove to his house where his wife had prepared a very welcome meal. Food, of course, was not plentiful in Paris, but it was a delicious and well appreciated casserole of some description, washed down with some good wine. So we ended the day with this family, replete and in soft chairs, finishing off with a glass of very fine cognac – all very different from what we had been used to in recent times.

On the Sunday we mooched about and did so for the next couple of days, soaking up the extraordinary atmosphere and any drink that someone might deem to offer the conquering heroes. I remember one day another Frenchman came hobbling up to us on two crutches, much like my late father would have done. He wanted to buy us a beer which we felt obliged to accept, but we then returned the favour. Tompkins nodded to the missing leg and asked: 'Les Boches?' The man smiled and replied: 'Non, RAF!' He had apparently worked in either the Renault or Peugeot factory when the RAF bombed it and he had not managed to get out to the shelters in time. Thankfully he didn't seem to harbour any animosity, especially towards me.

Although liberated, Paris was not totally out of danger from the enemy and on both the 26th and 27th German bombers caused casualties amongst the celebrating Parisians, but it was little more than a defiant gesture by the Luftwaffe.

By about Tuesday we had more or less run out of things to do and see, and then we received an irate message from our people in Creulley asking what we were still doing in Paris, and requesting that we return to cover the activities of the RAF. We agreed we had had a good run for our money, so packed our bags and made our way back to our headquarters.

On getting there, it was noticeable that it was more or less deserted. The Allied armies were streaming north and east, the RAF were rapidly moving forward, so we too were off, which ended my little tour of Normandy with its interesting diversion to Paris.

We followed the army and air force, continuing our reporting, until we finished up in Brussels, the Belgian capital, two days after it too had been liberated. We set up an office there but with the invasion long over, and the war settling down to something less extraordinary, the reason behind our section's activities was now no longer viable.

There was some excitement during the Arnhem show, Tompkins reporting back on what we could glean about the troops parachuting in and the subsequent attempts to drop supplies to the men around the famous bridge, etc, but sadly the whole thing was pretty depressing. By late September it looked like our PR unit would soon come to the end of its usefulness. Then I caught tonsillitis, and found myself in hospital for a week or so. When I was finally discharged I was told to report to Fighter Command HQ at Stanmore, which I did, and my role as a PR 'minder' thus came to its conclusion.

I arrived back in the UK in October and received the by now familiar blank faces when it came to getting some sort of posting from Fighter Command. I was told to go on leave. This I did, and awaited developments, but at least I was able to spend Christmas at home. I waited and waited, occasionally making the journey back to Stanmore to jog some elbows, and to try to beard someone face to face on what my future might be, but every time I was told to go home and wait some more.

This went on well into the New Year and I thought this was getting crazy and if I wasn't careful I would find myself arrested for being AWOL. Then suddenly the war was over. I had started the war at home and now it ended while I was home. I had come full circle. On 3 September 1939 I had sat and listened to Neville Chamberlain saying the Britain and her Empire were again at war with Germany and now, in May 1945 I was again listening to a prime minister, this time Winston Churchill, telling us that the war with Germany was over.

My mother, my cousin and myself quickly took a train from Clapham Junction station up to Victoria, where we walked over to Buckingham Palace and joined a massive throng of joyful humanity all singing, dancing, hugging, kissing and climbing on anything that could be climbed upon, in order to watch the King and Queen, the two princesses, together with Churchill and other dignitaries waving to the huge crowd that had spontaneously gathered in front of them. I had a bottle of gin, half of which was gin and the other half I'd filled with tonic water, and this went down very well. This may not seem, what we may nowadays call PC, being an officer and a gentleman, swigging not only a bottle of spirit, but with it, to all intents and purposes, looking like neat gin, but it was a very special day and nobody worried about such niceties. The war was over and we had won.

By the time things began to calm down, all public transport

was gone so we had to walk home. It was no hardship and probably I was by then feeling no pain. We stopped at various pubs en-route to add to our liquid intake and partake of more hugging and kissing, and finally got home about midnight. There our next door neighbours were having a party which we joined and I have to say that the next day was all a bit of a blank.

After another period of uncertainty, not knowing if I would be needed in the RAF or whether I would be demobbed, I once again decided to try Stanmore's personnel people. This time, low and behold, someone had actually found my file in a corner somewhere, or in someone's out-tray, but with things very much winding down and with the RAF pretty full of new pilots still rolling of the production line, I was sent up to RAF Bentwaters in Suffolk, located just north-east of Woodbridge.

Bentwaters was a largish aerodrome that had been built in 1942-43 and opened in April 1944. Bomber Command had a care and maintenance unit here, although it had been originally intended for the American Air Force. It was mainly used as an emergency landing airfield, being just inland from the North Sea coast. Then ADGB (Air Defence Great Britain, a force born once Fighter Command was split into Home Defence and 2nd Tactical Air Force) had taken occupation and had Mustang fighters based there. By the time I arrived most of the aircraft were Spitfires.

I became a sort of supernumerary administration officer with a whole variety of jobs and responsibilities. In due course the station admin. officer left and I was promoted to squadron leader and took over his job. In this capacity I stayed on at Bentwaters for the next eighteen months.

It was a very peculiar time. Several squadrons of Spitfires seemed to be around, all coming and going, and rarely stopping for any length of time. People were being posted in, then posted out again, many arriving from the Continent, being merely dumped here to be sorted prior to leaving the service. As one can easily imagine the vast majority wanted little else than to finish with the RAF and return to homes and families. All they were waiting for was their demob number to come up. Some people opted to stay on for short periods because that was the way the system had to work.

Part of the conditions when one joined up at the start of the war, was that if you were employed, the employers were committed by law to take you back once peace returned. However, because of the rush that would have occurred if this had been allowed to happen without any phased return to civilian status, it would prove an administrative nightmare. Therefore, if your employer was in agreement, one could, if happy to do so, remain in the service for up to eighteen months, after which your former employer was still committed to welcome you back to your old job and position.

Shell-Mex and BP was by then, of course, part of the Petroleum Board, so that the old firm I had known pre-war was effectively no more. So I saw the staff manager at Shell-Mex House and he said I may as well continue to enjoy myself in the RAF and later might be a better time to return to the fold, once it became clearer how things would shape up. I had already decided that the RAF, especially the peacetime RAF, was not for me but I was happy enough to take his advice and carry on for this short post-war stint. So I remained at Bentwaters, watching this steady stream of men disappear back into civvie street. In August the war with Japan came to an end, and we had the inevitable party, but again, I don't recall too much about it after the first few hours.

Gradually squadrons began to disappear or were disbanded, and I soldiered on with the paper work. I had three station commanders during my stay there. The first was Wing Commander Jarman who had been shot down in 1940 and been a prisoner of war. After he left I had Wing Commander P B 'Laddie' Lucas DSO DFC, until he left the service in 1946. He was a great chap, and brother-in-law to Douglas Bader. Finally Wing Commander John Ellis DFC, a Battle of Britain pilot who had flown with 610 Squadron. John arrived with the Meteor jets of 226 Operational Training Unit in 1946. So I was really fortunate in having three first class men in charge of the station while I was there.

I became adept at pushing vast quantities of paper around, in and out trays being used extensively and with aplomb. With most people anxious to get their demobilisation papers and be off, it wasn't very easy to get any sort of motivation from those passing through, or to get essential work done. We organised sports days to help pass the time, football and cricket matches, concerts and concert parties – all very essential, for at one time or other we could have up to a thousand bods all milling about, and all needing something to help occupy their time.

Most of them were housed in Nissen huts so when that awful winter of 1946-47 struck with deep snow and freezing conditions it was essential to keep people occupied. There was no way we could get the airfield cleared for flying either, even if we had wanted to. However, we survived. Survived better than civilians actually because the armed forces could always get their supplies of coal to heat buildings and so on.

We had a lot of WAAFs on the station too so that was something else I had to keep tabs on with all these blokes wandering around more or less at a loose end. Then we gradually lost all the WAAF officers who had, till then, been able to keep everything in check. I remember one WAAF officer coming down from Fighter Command HQ to tell me in no uncertain terms that I was morally and spiritually responsible for all these WAAF other ranks, now they were without officers, which some of my colleagues thought highly amusing. I did of course, take it all to heart!

Gradually Bentwaters began to run down and I got my papers through in March 1947. We had a bit of a farewell do but it was a little muted as by then most people had gone, certainly anyone I had become friends with. So, leaving my WAAFs in someone else's tender care I went up to Lytham or some such place, collected my civilian suit and came home.

My only really outstanding memory of my time at Bentwaters, and I suppose I am way past any chance of being put on a charge for wilful damage to RAF property, or at least, being a part of such an activity, concerned my office safe. As admin officer I was in charge of all sorts of station papers, including all important documents and demob stuff, which obviously I kept securely in this safe. Then came the day I discovered, to my horror, that I could not find the key. This was a very serious offence and one that might very easily have got me into deep trouble.

We had working with us, an admin civilian who had in fact been in the Royal Flying Corps in WW1. He lived locally in Woodbridge and although too old to be in the RAF had volunteered his services in a civilian capacity and the RAF were pleased to have him. He was a wise old bird – probably in his 50s, which was old to me at 27. We were talking over a pint of beer the evening I had lost this key and I mentioned it to him in case he had seen it lying about somewhere. Well, he hadn't, but knew enough about the RAF to understand the seriousness of my predicament. He went off saying he would give the matter some thought, although I wasn't too hopeful of a quick and satisfactory solution to my problem.

The next morning he came to see me and said he had gone through the station's inventory and had discovered that we had one more safe than listed. Living in Woodbridge, he had become friendly with a bunch of soldiers, recently back from Germany, serving with the REME, whose job it had been to blow open all the German safes that had been found or captured, for senior officers and intelligence bods.

So on the Saturday afternoon, which would be a quieter day, he brought said group of soldiers in aboard a truck and we man-handled the safe onto the back of it, then drove to the far side of the aerodrome where there was a blast hangar. They dug a large hole, dropped the safe into it, then told me to go and keep my head down behind something solid and wait.

In due time there was an almighty bang and when I came back to the hole, there was the safe with its door hanging off its hinges. Thanking these blokes profusely and giving them some beer money for their trouble, I took all the stuff out, nothing having been damaged. They left the safe in the hole, refilled the hole with earth, effectively hiding the thing. For all I know it is still there. We then went back to my office, brought in the spare safe and my life was saved.

I have to say I never lost or mislaid a safe key again and funnily enough, the missing one did eventually turn up. It must have been 20-odd years later that I suddenly discovered it down the lining of one of my suitcases. I knew instantly what key it was and where it had come from.

Chapter Twelve

Après la Guerre

I returned to Shell-Mex & BP in 1947 and to the job I had left in 1939, in the buying department, although the actual department had been evacuated from London during the war and was now situated in Oxford. I was only there for a few months but got thoroughly fed up and it wasn't a particularly interesting job, so I managed to get a position in the company's Manchester set-up as, for the want of a better description, a salesman.

I hadn't entirely finished with the RAF though, for while working in Manchester, I joined the Royal Auxiliary Air Force with a flying control unit. I knew nothing about fighter control itself, always being on the receiving end of a controller's chatter, but I learnt how to do it. My unit was 3613 Squadron, based at Ringway, which was, as this number indicates, closely associated with 613 (City of Manchester) Squadron RAuxAF. It was commanded by Squadron Leader J S Morton DFC and operated with Spitfire XIVs and then Spitfire F.22 fighters. During the war it had been with Army Co-operation Command flying Tomahawk and Mustang fighters, and later with Mosquito VIs became part of 2 Group, Bomber Command. 'Black' Morton had been with 603 Squadron pre-war, and had flown with this unit during the Battle of Britain, and later operated Beaufighters at night with 219 Squadron.

Its next CO was Squadron Leader J B Wales OBE DFC TD, and he was there when the squadron began to convert to de Havilland Vampire jets. Jack Wales had won his DFC in Burma in 1943 flying Hurri-bombers. He was also a test pilot for Avros. He was killed in December 1956 taking an Avro Shackleton MR3 through some stalling tests with A&AEE over Derbyshire. It crashed and Jack, with three civilian test engineers and observers, all died.

The RAuxAF disbanded in 1957, the squadrons going first and then the control units later. It was then that I went back down to London where I joined the Aviation Department with

Shell, and I was to remain there until I retired in 1975.

I lived in a flat in Sutton, Surrey until I met Kaethe, my future wife. It was an interesting time with Shell-Mex & BP, meeting many people I had dealt with before and lots of new people too. Some from the aero club and so on. Being then sales manager for the UK I travelled about the country on occasion.

In Sutton I had my mother living with me, and I had so far avoided marriage. We had a neighbour called Freddie Stroud and his wife. Freddie had been a tea planter in India but during the war had served with the lst Punjabi Regiment, then returned to tea planting afterwards. During their summer leaves he and his wife decided to establish a base in England where they could stay during leave periods. Every time they came home we all spent time together, Freddie and I getting on famously. He had a couple of friends who had also served with the Punjabi regiment, and much later we started having the odd lunch together.

One day in 1972 Freddie rang me and said to come over and have a gin, and that he had also invited another, new, neighbour, a nice looking lady he added. So I did and was introduced to Kaethe, who had been working and living in Geneva, and we spent the evening chatting over drinks and nibbles. She was working in London too so every once in a while we would meet up for a drink, and this continued over the next couple of years. We would also meet on the railway station on the way to town, that sort of thing. It was purely platonic at first.

After I retired in 1975, I took my mother on a holiday trip to Australia in order to have her visit some family members out there as well as me having the opportunity of meeting up with old friends in Sydney, including Margaret Gilligan. We had a great time.

It was my mother's brother who lived in Australia. He had been in the Royal Horse Artillery in the First War and emigrated out there in about 1924 with his wife and kids, to work in Western Australia. It proved a hard life at first, being given a piece of bush land which had to be cleared of trees and scrub. His background had been farming and he'd been used to horses in the army but it was still hard. They went into business at Pemberton, some 200 miles south of Perth. I seem to remember him saying they had initially been given just a cow and a chain-saw and told to get on with it!

They had very little help and with three kids, the eldest, Jack, being about my age, so around five, found they had quite a task on their hands. My uncle's name was Dennis but everyone called him 'Dean'. He was a pretty tough character and stuck to the task. Several of his neighbours in similar circumstances gave up the struggle and he was able to buy their land, so finished up quite well off. He died in about 1960 but my mother was keen to meet his wife Winnie again, and the kids who had all grown up now, so our visit was a sort of retirement trip for me and a family reunion for her.

Then in 1979 Kaethe retired from her job and so we began to see more of each other, and in the end we decided to get married. We set up in a bigger place in Sutton, and when my mother passed away the following June, we carried on there until the time came to move on. My mother, of course, was a Sussex lass, having been born in Crowborough, so we finished up in 1987, in St Leonards-on-Sea, in East Sussex. Kaethe wasn't worried where we lived so long as she could get into London without too much difficulty.

I am reminded of the occasion Kaethe and I went to see her mother who lived in Berlin, on the eastern side of the wall which had not yet been taken down. While we were there she said her mother had told a neighbour of her's about our coming over and that I had been a fighter pilot during the war, and he wanted to meet me. He was a very nice chap, a little older than me I would guess and as I sat with him talking – he spoke very good English – he suddenly said: 'I think I may have met you somewhere before.' I replied that I didn't think so, and I had certainly never been to Berlin before. 'No, I don't mean here,' he continued, 'it's just that I happened to be a rear gunner flying in Heinkel 111s in the war, so I might well have seen you over England, as I shot at a lot of Spitfires.' I smiled but didn't enlighten him about the fact that over England I had been in a Hurricane, understanding as I do, that most German airmen believe they only fought Spitfires. I did comment to the effect that in any event, we had survived and we were both still here. 'Yes,' he said, 'probably neither of us were very good shots.'

I also became involved in the Royal Air Force Association in Sutton, being a member and at one time chairman of the local

RAFA Club, and I also helped out with a local Air Training Corps squadron in Morden, Surrey. Once we had moved to the south coast I also joined the Bexhill RAFA Club and Aircrew Association. I keep up my interest in Battle of Britain reunions and associated functions, Westminster Abbey each year, and the reunions at Capel le Ferne, near Folkestone, where Geoffrey Page had been the guiding light to a very special Battle of Britain Memorial that has been set up there, overlooking the English Channel.

We enjoy our retirement, have lots of friends, and as well as taking holidays, I keep busy attending RAF functions when invited, signing lots of books and prints for the latest generation of air enthusiasts and historians. It is nice to know we are remembered, particularly my many friends and former comrades who are no longer with us. Life goes on.

Epilogue

I had no plans to return to Australia after my 1975 trip but it is strange how things happen in life. In 1980 Kaethe and I travelled to Hong Kong were we stayed with my cousin and his wife, who lived and worked there. They arranged for us to tour parts of China which was very nice, going to all the usual tourist attractions such as Beijing, the Great Wall, the Terracotta Warriors, and so on.

Returning to the island, and being so close to Australia, I suggested to Kaethe that we visit Sydney. She wasn't over-keen to do so but agreed. So, leaving Hong Kong we flew down to Sydney, hired a car and motored through the Blue Mountains etc. Funnily enough, she fell in love with Australia and at the end of a fortnight there, even suggested that we might move there permanently!

I had never made any attempt to get in touch with any of the old comrades and friends I had met out there during the war apart from Margaret Gilligan, who I did contact on the previous trip five years earlier. She had married by then and had five grown-up children, but we did in fact meet them on this second trip. Returning to England I thought that this would no doubt be the last time I would go to Australia, but then, quite out of the blue three years later, I received a letter from a Doctor Alan Powell who had been asked to write a definitive book about Darwin during the war. He asked if he could meet me when he next came to England in order to talk about my time in Darwin and hopefully I would provide him with some background to the Australian wing's time and activities there.

It so happened that Kaethe and I had decided to take a trip round the world in 1984 and after meeting up with several friends across the USA, we planned to fly across to Sydney. So I wrote back to Doctor Powell, telling him of our plans the following year and suggested we met in Darwin. So, in 1984 there I was again, after a lapse of forty years.

In my ignorance I said to Kaethe that I would show her where we had lived in the bush. Once we drove out of Darwin to where I remembered our camp at Nightcliff to have been, rather than scrub and bush, we found it was now a lovely suburb of the town, with lots of pretty houses, planted green gardens, manicured lawns, flowers, etc. It was very pleasant on the eye but something of a personal disappointment. This was present day Nightcliff. Darwin airport was still there, however, and the really outlying areas hadn't changed at all.

Again I returned home, thinking that this surely must be the last trip down-under. However, in 1990, with the 50th Anniversary of the Battle of Britain, many veterans had been to Buckingham Palace and there had been a big march-past, and then on the Sunday there was to be a service in Westminster Abbey. When we arrived there we found a long queue of people waiting to get through the security gate and as we shuffled along, a voice said: 'Hi – Bob Foster?' I turned round and this fellow asked: 'Do you remember me? I'm Pete Watson, 457 Squadron.'

Well, of course I did. He had come over from Australia for the celebration and had spotted me in the queue. After the service we met up again and had a good old chat and he told me about the Spitfire Association of Australia, which I had never heard of. He said that they had an AGM every October, so that if ever I found myself out there, I should make sure I attended. I thought little about it until the following year when I suddenly decided to go.

RWF back in a restored R4118. *(John Dunbar)*

All this got me thinking about Darwin again when we returned home that Sunday, and then in 1995, with the 50th Anniversary of the war ending, we decided to go back to Darwin yet again, being still in touch with people there, for the VJ Day anniversary.

Sadly, I was the only person from No.1 Fighter Wing to attend, no Australian veterans turned up at all, so I was the sole representative. Nevertheless Kaethe and I had a good time, attending a number of special events, some more liquid than others.

At this time it was discovered that there was no memorial to No. 1 Wing in Darwin, so it was decided to petition the government to rectify this omission and in the end they agreed. In 1996 this little memorial was to be put up, so we went back to Darwin again for the ceremony. There is a war memorial on the esplanade and our plaque was placed next to a number of other small regimental tablets, each commemorating the various army units stationed in and around Darwin during the war.

This time a couple of chaps came up from Sydney to represent, with me, the wing. One was Roy Boles, the other Bewick Hack. Hack had been in 54 Squadron too, but after I had left it. So that has been my last visit to Darwin with all its memories.

We went back to Sydney a couple of years ago, courtesy of the British government scheme whereby they paid for veterans who wished to revisit places special to them and where they had served during the war. So Kaethe and I took advantage of this generous offer and I arranged for it to coincide with the AGM of the Australian branch of the Spitfire Association that October.

By now virtually all my old mates and associates had gone, just a few of the old Australian ground crew blokes were still around. Most of the association members were really little more than people interested in the aircraft itself, and its role in the war. In other words they support it.

There were quite a number of people at this AGM and towards the end of it I decided a few words might be nice, so stood up and commented that it was wonderful to be back in Sydney again and was pleased that the association was flourishing, then talked about Darwin for a few moments, then about 54 Squadron's time there fighting the Japanese, and how the squadron was still in existence and flying Jaguars, although they were about to lose them, etc, etc.

At the end I sat down and a little later I heard some chap sitting in front of me ask his companion: 'What was that bloke talking about? Who was he?' The other chap shrugged his shoulders and replied: 'Oh, I don't know, something about some RAF squadron up at Darwin some time or other.'

I thought that just about sums it up! *C'est la Guerre.* They just hadn't a clue what I'd been talking about, what we had done, and obviously to some people we just didn't exist. Sad, but that's the way it goes.

Fortunately the men of the RAF are not totally forgotten, especially by the generations who followed us. Most of what we did is remembered and most of the few of us who are left are encouraged by the enthusiasm of these people, many being amateur historians. I, and others, meet them at air shows, reunions, book and print-signing days. Letters drop regularly through my mail-box from these youngsters, asking often very good questions about what we did and how we did it. I never tire of it and feel it incumbent upon me on behalf of those no longer with us to help keep the memories of those days alive.

Many of my good friends and comrades gave their lives in the struggle for victory and peace and must not be forgotten. It is no glib expression, and it is perfectly true, that for our tomorrows, they gave their todays.

Record of Service

EFTS, Anstey	1 May 1939 – 26 Jun 1939
No.1 ITW, Cambridge	10 Nov 1939 – 30 Dec 1939
No.12 FTS, Grantham	30 Dec 1939 – 3 Jun 1940
No. 6 OTU, Sutton Bridge	3 Jun 1940 – 8 Jul 1940
No.605 Squadron, Drem	8 Jul 1940 – 6 Sep 1940
No.605 Squadron, Croydon	7 Sep 1940 – 25 Feb 1941
No.605 Squadron, Martlesham	25 Feb 1941 – 31 Mar 1941
No.605 Squadron, Ternhill	31 Mar 1941 – 31 May 1941
No.605 Squadron, Baginton	31 May 1941 – 25 Sep 1941
No.55 OTU, Usworth	29 Sep 1941 – 11 Apr 1942
No.54 Squadron, Castletown	14 Apr 1941 – 1 Jun 1942
HMT F6 (at sea)	18 Jun 1942 – 14 Aug 1942
RAAF Richmond, Australia	24 Aug 1942 – 14 Jan 1943
RAAF Darwin	17 Jan 1943 – 28 Oct 1943
Sydney on leave	1 Nov 1943 – 29 Nov 1943
No.2 OTU, Mildura	30 Nov 1943 – 17 Dec 1943
No.1 Combined Defence Wing	18 Dec 1943 – 3 Feb 1944
No.1 Embarkation Depot	4 Feb 1944 – 14 Feb 1944
USS *Matsonia* (at sea)	14 Feb 1944 – 1 Mar 1944
San Francisco, USA	1 Mar 1944 – 6 Mar 1944
New York, USA	6 Mar 1944 – 19 Mar 1944
SS *Queen Mary* (at sea)	20 Mar 1944 – 26 Mar 1944
Leave	26 Mar 1944 – 25 Apr 1944
Air Information Unit, UK	29 Apr 1944 – 29 Jun 1944
Air Information Unit, BLA, France	1 Jul 1944 – 6 Oct 1944
Fighter Command HQ	6 Oct 1944 – 11 Jun 1945
RAF Bentwaters, Suffolk	11 Jun 1945 – 4 Sep 1945
School of Admin	5 Sep 1945 – 3 Oct 1945
RAF Bentwaters	4 Oct 1945 – 1 Mar 1947
No.3613 Sqn RAuxAF	1949 – 1957

Bibliography

Lion and Swans, by Fred Woodgate, (1996). *Hurricane R4118* by Peter Vacher, (Grub Street, 2005). *Spitfires over Darwin 1943*, by Jim Grant (R J Moore, 1995). *We Never Slept* by Ian Piper (1996). *Men of the Battle of Britain* Ken Wynn, (CCB Associates, 1999). *Croydon Airport and the Battle for Britain 1939-1940*, by Douglas Cluett, Joanna Bogle and Bob Learmouth, (London Borough of Sutton, 1984). *Air War Against Japan 1943-1945*, Australian War Memorial, by George Odgers, Canberra, 1957.

Index